Special issues in child care

To Janice
With all Best
Wishes
Maureen O'Hagan

Special issues in child care

Maureen O'Hagan BEd, MSc, MIHE, RGN, NNEB

Director, Council for Early Years Awards,
London

and

Maureen Smith BEd(Hons), CQSW, RGN

Senior Assistant Director, National Nursery Examination Board,
St Albans, Hertfordshire

Baillière Tindall

LONDON   PHILADELPHIA   TORONTO   SYDNEY   TOKYO

Baillière Tindall
W. B. Saunders
24–28 Oval Road, London NW1 7DX

The Curtis Center
Independence Square West
Philidelphia, PA 19106–3399, USA

55 Horner Avenue
Toronto, Ontario M8Z 4X6, Canada

Harcourt Brace & Company, Australia
30–52 Smidmore Street
Marrickville, NSW 2204, Australia

Harcourt Brace & Company, Japan
Ichibancho Central Building, 22–1
Ichibancho
Chiyoda-ku, Tokyo 102, Japan

First published 1993
Sixth printing 1997

British Library Cataloguing in Publication Data is available
ISBN 0–7020–1604–7

Typeset by Columns Design & Production Services Ltd, Reading
Printed in Great Britain by Butler & Tanner Ltd, Frome and London

Acknowledgements

Publisher's acknowledgements

The publishers would like to thank the following for their kind permission to reproduce material in this text: W B Saunders for Figure 1:11, in Foster *et al*.: *Family-Centered Nursing Care of Children*, 1989; Figure 1:12 from *The Origin of Form Perception* by Robert L. Fantz, Copyright © 1992 by Scientific American, Inc. (all rights reserved); Figure 1.2 of baby looking into mirror, supplied by Doreen Smith, Smith and Paul Associates for *Child Development* by Hutchinson & Oliver (Eds); BBC Books for Figures 1.1 and 3.1, in *'Look What I can Do' Creative Action Ideas for Under Sevens*, by Kate Harrison, Edited by Brian Scott-Hughes; BBC Education for Figures 1.14 and 8.1, in Brown: *All Our Children*, 1990, courtesy of Luke Finn; Figure 3.5 in Baker: *Reading Through Play*, 1980, reproduced by permission of Simon & Schuster, Hemel Hempstead, UK: Centre for Language in Primary Education, for Figure 3.6 in *'Language Matters'*, 1988: Numbers 2 and 3, ILEA: Sheffield Education Department for Figure 3.8(a–d), from *Guidelines on the Organization, Curriculum and Assessment for 4 Year Olds in Reception Class*; County of Avon Local Education Authority for Figure 3.9(a,b) in *Primary Science Working Paper 2, Examples of Curriculum Planning 1985*; Trentham Books Ltd for Figure 3.10, in *Early Childhood Education: The Early Years Curriculum and the National Curriculum 1989*; Stanley Thornes (Publishers) Ltd for Figure 5.1, in Reynolds: *Finding Out About Child Development*, 1984; Figure 5.3 an extract from the *Self-Help Section of the Portage Checklist*, reproduced by permission of NFER-Nelson; Central Office of Information for Figure 6.2, in Weller: *Helping Sick Children Play*, Baillière Tindall, 1980; and to Kathleen Preston for Figure 6.3, in Weller: *Helping Sick Children Play*, Baillière Tindall, 1980.

Thanks also to Louise Burston, with the co-operation of North Mundham School, Chichester, for Figures 1.13, 2.2, 2.3, 2.8, 3.3, 3.4, 3.7, 4.2, 4.4, 4.5, 6.1, 8.2 and 8.3; to Barnaby's Picture Library for Figures 4.3, 9.1, 9.4, 9.5, 9.6 and 9.7; Sally and Richard Greenhill (Photographers: Photo Library) for Figure 2.1 (in *Under Five and Under Funded* booklet), Figure 5.2 (in Brown: *All Our Children*, 1990), and Figures 4.1 and 9.3; to Nik Screen (Photographer) for Figure 10.1; and to Sian Burston for the illustrations on the chapter opening pages.

Finally, we are also grateful to Patricia Geraghty for Figures 1.5, 1.15, 2.4, 2.5, 2.6, 2.7 (from Geraghty: *Caring for Children: A Textbook for Nursery Nurses*, Revised 2nd edn, 1990, Baillière Tindall.

Every effort has been made to contact copyright holders of material reproduced in this textbook. In the few instances where this has not been possible, the publishers invite such copyright holders to contact them.

Authors' acknowledgement

Thanks are due to all our students and colleagues with whom we have worked over the years.

Disclaimer

Please note that the views expressed in this book are those of the authors and are not necessarily the views of their employers.

"This book is dedicated with love and thanks to Rodan, Mike and Cass."

Maureen O'Hagan

"To my father Harry Hamill and mother Emmie Hamill who loved children and understood the 'magic' of childhood, and to my husband Richard and sons Ian, Andrew, James and Daniel."

Maureen Smith

Contents

10 **Management skills** **203**

Introduction

As any reader who has taken a course of study in child care and education will know, there is not one textbook which is able to provide a broad spectrum of the knowledge that is required for the course. The authors have tried to overcome this by producing a text book which is able to offer a broad knowledge base. When the National Occupational Standards in Child Care and Education were developed they provided a totally new format for looking at the way qualifications are developed. Both authors were involved in these new developments and this provided the impetus for them to write a textbook which would meet the needs of future candidates and students.

In 1991 the National Occupational Standards in Child Care and Education (known as 'the Standards') were published. The Standards have been developed through a process of functional analysis which involved consulting hundreds of expert practitioners in the field in order to identify the skills and competences needed by practitioners to work effectively. A separate project took place to compare different methods of specifying underpinning knowledge and understanding (UKU). This project also drew upon the knowledge and experience of expert practitioners in the occupational field and assisted in the knowledge specifications within the Standards. The breadth of competence needed to work in this field and the associated UKU draws from all disciplines involved in child care and education and for the first time it is possible to see within the Standards a comprehensive and truly integrated approach to work with young children and their families.

This textbook is closely aligned to the Standards and aims to provide the UKU for many of the units at levels 2 and 3. However, the depth and breadth of our material is generally greater than has been covered in may previous textbooks which have aimed to cover the whole of the knowledge base for this field. As a result of this there are areas such as physical development and care, which after careful consideration, we have not included believing that there are other texts which adequately cover this area of UKU. The content of this book is designed to give practitioners and candidates a sound basis of knowledge and understanding linked to competent performance, to enable reflective practice and facilitate evaluation of their own practice and that of their workplace or work placement. Our view as authors is that practitioners in this field constantly undervalue themselves and their expertise and this text aims to give them support in defining the skills and knowledge already inherent in their practice but often unrecognized.

When Dr Denise Hevey and her team were compiling the Standards they recommended that there were a set of underlying principles and assumptions which are 'integral and indivisible in work with young children'. These are the values which effect good practice and include statements such as, treating and valuing children as individuals, promoting equality of opportunity, celebrating and respecting cultural diversity, working with parents in partnership, and meeting children's developmental needs. The Standards integrate these aspects of good practice within the units and elements. The authors have used the same methodology as the Standards by ensuring that all chapters have taken the integrated approach. However, Chapter 8 examines the legislation that underpins good practice and the impact that this legislation has had on the delivery of good quality child care and education.

Each chapter in the book has links with one or more units within the Standards and this is made explicit in the chapter objectives. Some units mentioned are not yet part of existing qualifications but will be in the future.

All the chapters in this book, with the exception of one chapter, contain a series of 'scenarios' designed to illustrate the points being made within the text and to encourage further thinking. Chapter 1 looks at child development and contains a section at the end with some ideas for observing and assessing the developing child. Each chapter contains a reading list. There is an address and resource section at the end of the book.

At the end of each chapter are suggestions for assignments which will be useful in various ways. For instance, candidates for NVQs may undertake these as part of their evidence collection. This is likely to be most effective when undertaken in collaboration with the assessor who will offer help and guidance. In some instances assignments will form part of performance evidence as they will relate directly to the work situation, in other cases they will form part of the UKU.

Tutors for a wide range of different programmes in the field of social care or child care and education will find the material within scenarios helpful to stimulate discussion and the ideas for assignments useful in the design of learning programmes based on the material within the text.

Chapter 1
The developing child

Chapter objectives _____

Importance of child development   Emotional development
Critical periods   Attachment theory
Cognitive development   Self-esteem
Perceptual development   Fears and anxieties
How children learn   Social development
Piagetian theory   Socialization
Critique of Piaget's work   Moral development
Language development   Observation and assessment of children
Symbolic representation   **Links with units C5, C10, C11, C14, C16**

Introduction

The study of child development is relatively new and much of it is derived from aspects of different disciplines, such as psychology, or biology, which have been drawn together to provide a multi-disciplinary, holistic view of the child. As with all ideas about the way things are or should be, it is important to acknowledge that research takes place within a particular culture or society and within a certain time frame. Much modern research has taken place within the western, industrialized nations and the results cannot always be applied to other cultures and societies, particularly those which are profoundly different in ideology, family patterns and child-rearing practices.

How children grow and develop underpins all work with young children, and it is essential that all who work in this field have a basic understanding of child development. Although this chapter does not consider research methods and their relative validity, it is important to understand that research does not necessarily provide 'the truth' but will reflect the design of the research and the theoretical perspectives behind the work. There are different theories of development which can be confusing, but certain commonly accepted principles need to be known and understood in order to work effectively. It is therefore necessary to draw out from the competing perspectives those elements which early years workers use and find useful in their everyday work, recognizing that this will of necessity be selective rather than exhaustive. The chapter aims to cover aspects of children's social, emotional, cognitive, moral and language development, but does not consider physical care and development. As child development studies form a large and important area for early years workers it is recommended that particular areas of interest are followed up using the references at the end of the chapter.

Figure 1.1 Look what I can do!

Normative measurement

Although development is often assessed using normative measures (how a child performs compared with the 'norm') it is important to recognize that this method has pitfalls and can be judgemental resulting in children being labelled 'backward' or 'deficient' in some way. It is important to emphasize that all children develop at different rates and there are no hard-and-fast measures against which a child can be judged. It is essential to take into account the social and cultural context within which the child receives care and education and the child's special needs. The use of these types of measure do, however, provide a broad framework which is helpful to workers in making assessments of children's progress. In view of this, the chapter considers 'norms' of development linked broadly to the age/stage of the child.

Integrated development

Although the chapter looks at aspects of development separately, it is important to stress that children develop in an integrated and holistic manner. If a child's physical development is impeded, then their capacity to explore the world will be affected. If a child has poor self-esteem and is under emotional stress, then their capacity to learn and to relate to others will be affected. All these developmental threads are closely linked and interdependent. Workers with pre-school children usually aim to promote the all-round development of the child.

Stages and sequences in child development

Although there are a variety of viewpoints concerning the developing child, there is a good deal of evidence that children's developmental patterns follow the same sequences but at different rates. For example, nearly all hearing children pass through a 'pre-linguistic' stage which includes babbling, imitating and practising sounds which form the basis of their first words. However, babies vary considerably in the time they take to reach the stage of word production. Most will reach this stage at around their first birthday, but some will talk earlier and others later. All will have gone through the pre-linguistic stage.

Critical periods and emergent skills

One of the most exciting and rewarding aspects of caring for young children is to see them grow and develop. As children mature and pass through the various stages of development many researchers think there is a 'critical' time when a child is most ready to develop particular skills or concepts. A 'critical' time is thought to be when a child has physically or mentally matured to the point they can move on in learning and development. In order to do this they will need an environment which allows them to do so and opportunity to practise. For example, children may be ready to walk at around fifteen months: their nervous systems, muscles, balance and co-ordination have developed sufficiently and they are confident in movement. If they are then kept indoors, sat in a buggy all day they are unlikely to walk. This is an obvious example but there are other aspects of development which are much more subtle. As a result, carers must be aware of what stage children have reached in their development, take note of their emerging skills, and provide support for them which will encourage the next phase of learning. This requires sensitivity by the adult and an awareness that it is possible to hold back children who are ready for further learning. This is most likely to occur when adults measure a child's progress against developmental scales linked to age and do not allow for individual differences or assume that a child cannot learn a new skill or concept because research shows that the 'average' age of doing so is different from the child's. In viewing development, it is essential to be aware that children's progress is not always clear-cut and there will always be overlap between stages. You will notice that children practise emergent skills over and over again, and the secret of effective work is to identify these and to plan activities, experiences and routines which stimulate and encourage these aspects of development. The adult's role in promoting development is very important and is considered further in this chapter.

Cognitive or intellectual development

Cognitive or intellectual development covers thinking, reasoning, problem-solving, memory, aspects of perception through the senses, concept formation, concentration, attention, and many other mental functions not all of which can be dealt with here. All aspects of development are linked, but there is a particularly strong link between cognitive and language development as each is thought to influence the other directly. When the various components of cognitive development are put together they constitute what is usually called 'intelligence'.

Intelligence testing

Earlier this century there was a great emphasis on intelligence and intelligence testing, for example the work of Alfred Binet leading to Stanford–Binet tests. These tests were supposed to measure how intelligent a person was and to predict future achievement. The 11+ examination which decided if children should go to grammar schools was widespread in Britain until the 1960s. Research at that time revealed that this exam was not so much a fair assessment of 'intelligence' as a selection based on culture and social class. Children from working-class homes, regardless of their potential ability, did not do so well at these tests because the language and concepts tested were often middle-class and beyond their experience. Testing children in this way led to 'labelling' them either bright and intelligent or otherwise. Further research (Rosenthal and Jacobsen, 1968) showed that such labelling leads to adults having lower expectations of the children and the 'self-fulfilling prophecy', i.e. children fulfil those low expectations and do not reach their full potential.

Later work has challenged the idea that it is possible to test intelligence fully, and that the best that can be done is to test certain components such as memory span or number ability. This can only test a sample of any individual's abilities and major decisions should not be taken on such limited evidence. Many workers or researchers do not agree with tests on the grounds that 'intelligence' as a separate concept is not open to definition, and testing is socially biased. Some educationalists and psychologists consider there are advantages to using tests that are especially designed to be bias-free as they can be used to assess a child's particular abilities and where extra help is required. It is worth noting that there are difficulties in producing bias-free tests and it is arguable whether they are possible at all.

Nature/nurture debate

There is considerable discussion concerning whether intelligence is determined by genetic inheritance or by the environment in which a child is brought up. Binet, for example, thought that intelligence as such was fixed at birth and depended on inheritance. Other educationalists and psychologists feel that the environment and educational experiences to which a child is exposed are more important than genetic inheritance.

Research on identical twins who are brought up separately has been used to study which of the above factors is most important. These studies generally support the idea that a good deal of intelligence is innate, but some have been criticized as being biased and unscientific. There have been many other studies which stressed the importance of the environment in determining intelligence. Partly as a result of these, workers in the 1960s onwards introduced compensatory education programmes designed to benefit the poor and socially disadvantaged. For example, Headstart in the United States worked with parents and children and has led on to the High/Scope Curriculum (see chapter 3).

The evidence for either side is not clear-cut, and on balance it seems that both factors play a part. However, it is unlikely that any child's potential will be reached in an environment which is uncaring or unstimulating. In general, it is more important in early childhood to create an environment which maximizes opportunity and development for all, rather than attempting to create an elite group and concentrating on the academic prowess of its members.

Creativity

Creativity is often linked with 'intelligence', but research has shown that creative people are not always those who score highly in intelligence tests. These tests usually measure the ability of a subject to solve problems and give 'correct' answers in a particular manner which eliminates alternatives, this is known as convergent thought. Creativity might take many forms such as art, music or sculpture or the ability to solve problems in unusual and different ways. This latter type of ability is linked with the ability to think divergently and consider new options. Our scientists, engineers and mathematicians, as well as our artists and writers, need to be capable of divergent thought.

Workers with young children need to encourage children's creativity. This is done in many ways, but giving children open-ended problems, for example, will encourage them to think in a variety of ways, as will allowing them to explore and play with materials and activities with no right or wrong answers and where all results are acceptable. If children are often given adult-centred tasks such as painting within the lines (not the child's lines), using a template, or sticking a pre-cut piece of paper on a card to take home, they will find difficulty in achieving high levels of representational ability. Eventually they may not be able to trust their ability to draw or make things and could develop negative attitudes about themselves. Although this applies to all children, highly creative children can find themselves particularly frustrated and unhappy in a restricted environment, and as a result will under-achieve and not develop to their full potential.

Attention and concentration

If children are to learn effectively, it is important that they can concentrate and attend. Most children can do this to a greater or lesser extent and can be helped through age/stage-appropriate tasks and other techniques such as behaviour modification in order to improve. Some children find persistent difficulty in attending and may be labelled 'hyperactive'. There is increasing evidence that hyperactivity and food allergies are linked but some children are hyperactive for no known reason and may or may not improve as they get older.

Perceptual development

Perception is how persons extract information from the world around them. Studying how babies perceive the world around has led to some important findings, especially with regard to their emerging abilities. Studying how babies perceive the world allows us to understand how we might best provide for their needs. Recent research has revealed that babies are far more active and sophisticated in their interpretation of events and more able to make use of the world around them than had ever before been realized. In view of this it is important that workers provide not only a loving and caring but also a stimulating environment. This involves meeting the babies' physical needs, giving consistent care, developing firm attachments between baby and carers and surrounding them with appropriate levels of sensory stimulation in the form of light, colour, sounds, smells, tactile experiences such as massage, textures to feel and explore and adults to talk to them and with whom they can respond.

Perceptual development of young babies

1. All senses are working at birth.
2. Face, hands, abdomen and soles of feet are more sensitive to touch.
3. Newborns can feel pain.
4. Babies of a few hours old will orient to direction of sound. At two weeks they will stop crying and attend to human voice. Babies quieten to low sounds such as whispers and alert to higher frequency sounds. At one month, they will recognize different speech sounds. At three months, they will imitate low or high pitched sounds. At four months, babies can link familiar sounds with objects, for example mother's face with voice. From around five months, babies begin to respond to their own name.
5. Babies can distinguish mother's smell from others.
6. Babies prefer sweet tastes especially breast milk.
7. It is thought that newborns do not at first see in colour. Their focus is poorly developed but they can focus best at objects about eight inches away. They will track movements of objects and people. They are light-sensitive and seem to prefer the human face. Babies scan with their eyes and focus on the edges of objects. They appear to copy facial expressions. From two months on there is evidence of depth perception which is related to size constancy. If this does not occur, babies would not be able to perform simple acts such as reaching out for objects as they would not be able to judge distance in relation to size. At about four months babies can discriminate between two- and three-dimensional objects, and they can focus on their hand whilst sitting or lying and on an image of self in mirror.

At five to six months, they prefer complex things to look at and enjoy bright colours. From six months on, babies can focus on small objects and are more able to follow rapid movements.

8. Object constancy or the recognition that things exist when out of sight occurs from eight to twelve months.

Figure 1.2 Baby looking in a mirror

How children learn

Learning is a controversial area of development and there are a variety of different perspectives. Two of the most important are outlined below and the relevant points for early years workers are identified. The importance of play in children's learning is covered in chapter 2, but it is widely understood that one of the principal means by which young children learn is through talk and play.

Learning theory

One view of human development and learning is based on the idea that learning as such cannot be measured, only the resulting behaviour. Psychologists such as Skinner who take this line are called 'behaviourists' and they believe that learning takes place through conditioning or through observation of role models. Although there are variations within learning theory, the main points are as follows.

Classical conditioning (Pavlov)

The work of Pavlov on the behaviour of dogs is a famous example of classical conditioning. Pavlov discovered that if a light was flashed before a dog was fed, the dog would learn to associate the light with food and eventually would salivate in anticipation of being fed in response to the light alone. This learning was based on association of an event with a particular result often linked with a reflex action.

Operant conditioning (Skinner)

Research with babies is more difficult than with dogs and the concept of operant conditioning is more relevant. This is also learning by association, but it is the association of a behaviour with the consequence of that behaviour. Operant conditioning suggests that learning takes place as subjects' responses to various stimuli are either rewarded or punished. This is called either positive or negative reinforcement. Behaviour can be changed over time by rewarding a person via a variety of reinforcers such as praise, food, toys, a hug. Unacceptable behaviour may be modified or changed by offering rewards for change, withholding rewards, avoiding unpleasant happenings and so forth. For example, a child who persistently demands attention at the expense of other children might find this behaviour is largely ignored whilst any positive behaviour is rewarded. As the main purpose is to gain adult attention this acts as a negative reinforcer for the demanding behaviour, but as positive reinforcement to encourage good behaviour. Active punishment such as smacking is not considered an effective means of changing behaviour as it does not promote something positive in place of the negative.

Social learning

Social learning theorists (e.g. Bandura, 1973, and see 'Social Learning' below) emphasize the effects of social forces and believe that children can learn through imitation and modelling their behaviour on important people in their lives. This theory stresses the importance of role models for children's learning.

Learning theory offers a clear idea of learning but does not adequately explain the complex beings that children are. Children often experiment and play in new ways not because they will get an external reward but because they enjoy what they are doing. This theory does not explain where new behaviour which has not been observed, imitated or reinforced comes from. However, the concept of modifying behaviour through reinforcement, modelling and so forth is often used by different professional groups involved in child care and education. This is discussed further in chapter 9 on children's behaviour.

Piaget's theory of cognitive development

Jean Piaget (1896–1980) has been a powerful influence on our understanding of children's development, and his work has been widely used by educationalists and many who work with children. His theory of cognitive development is complex and is discussed here in outline only. Although there has been criticism of the theory, much of it remains as important guiding principles for workers with young children.

Piaget believed that children were active agents of their own learning and that a major task for them was to develop an ability to organize experiences and learn from them in a way which enables them to make sense of the world. He believed that intelligence consisted of the ability to make adaptations to the environment by taking in information, processing it, and then using it appropriately (assimilation). Some children would be able to do this more efficiently than others. The early phases of this process occurred through reflex activity such as searching for the nipple, combined with the child's inborn strategies for exploring the world (seeing, hearing, touching, smelling, grasping, sucking and so on). Piaget felt that new information taken in by the young child would then require change or modification of their existing mental concepts or categories/maps (schemas) through a process of 'accommodation'. For example, a toddler may have been used to drinking out of a red cup and has a schema that says 'all cups are red'. When presented with a yellow cup the child has to learn through assimilating the new information and changing the existing schema to accommodate the new information which says they may be yellow. Each child has to achieve a balance or equilibrium in learning through this process. If there is too much new information assimilated, and the child does not have time to deal with it, i.e. to experiment, explore, practise and become familiar with it, they will become confused and over-stimulated. When this happens the process of accommodation cannot occur efficiently and the child's learning is impaired.

As well as schemas, Piaget describes other mental structures called 'operations'. These enable us to combine schemas in a logical manner and make links between different areas of experience. Using the above example, a child may have a schema for drinking cups which involves them being red; the schema will change to cover yellow cups at this level. As the child grows and develops it will realize that cups may be different colours, shapes, sizes and materials and used at different times for different purposes. This involves combining schemas for shape, size, and so forth, and imagining different varieties of use through the use of mental 'operations'.

Concept formation

A major task for the development of thought is the formation of concepts, these are cognitive categories that help organize experience and acquire new areas of knowledge and understanding. The way young children form basic concepts is linked to their perception of the world and other cognitive tasks such as the ability to conserve or classify. Children who can conserve are able to develop accurate concepts in such areas as those mentioned below. Children have to learn to concentrate and to discriminate which features of a situation are important, and this demands developmental 'readiness'. They must also have real experience of as wide a variety of materials and objects as possible to consolidate and extend their learning. This is one of the reasons that the early years curriculum stresses active learning using concrete experiences and encourages children to handle objects and materials. In doing this they explore the properties of new or unfamiliar items and modify their existing schemas.

Basic concrete concepts such as eggs, chairs or dog are understood by very young children through the adult labelling the object consistently and the child understanding as much about the object or event as possible. It is much later, at around seven years onwards, that the child can then place eggs into the inclusive category of 'food', or dogs under the classification 'pets' and then the wider classification of 'animal'.

Children under age six or seven years do not usually have a firm grasp of simple counting and number: this means understanding what numbers really mean, not just rote counting, e.g. six will remain six in every situation. This is learned through trial and error and experience in different situations with a variety of materials. More difficult concepts such as 'time' or aspects of number take longer to grasp firmly and reliably. Often, children seem to understand the idea of 'soon' or 'next', but they are not able fully to appreciate all that this means in terms of the passage of time. Children are around eight years of age before they really understand the passage of time, and even then it is at a simple level, and are around twelve years before they understand time, speed, distance, age and their interrelationships.

Abstract concepts such as honesty, peace or justice and complex physical concepts are likely to take much longer to establish, and many children are into adolescence or adulthood before they are understood. Evidence from various sources indicates that some adults never reach this level of higher-order thinking.

It is important, as always, that workers with young children are aware of where the child has reached in terms of concept formation. Once this is identified appropriate experiences and activities to support concept learning can take place. Modern research stresses the role of the adult in supporting children's conceptual development far more than Piaget recognized. Adults must support concept formation through their talk and interaction with children. Children need adults to help them to understand concepts and require many opportunities to handle materials, to practise using objects and to talk and discuss.

Conservation

According to Piaget children initially judge the world around in terms of what they see, and do not understand the underlying principles that are apparent to older children and adults. At around the age of seven they gradually begin to understand that objects and events are not always exactly what they seem. One aspect of their ability to do this is called 'conservation' which is mentioned in the table below. It is a difficult concept and the following practical examples are those that it is possible to try and experiment with children.

Conservation of mass. This can be demonstrated by using two balls of clay or Plasticine which the child agrees are the same. One of these balls is taken and rolled into a sausage shape in front of the child who is then asked if they both have the same amount of clay. Most children under six or seven years will say that the sausage shape is larger: the children are not able to 'conserve' mass.

Conservation of number. The child is shown two rows of buttons and agrees they have the same number. One is spread out to make a longer row and the child is asked which row contains most buttons. According to Piaget, children under seven are likely to say that the spread out row has more buttons.

Conservation of length, area, quantity, weight, volume, and so forth, develop and can be tested in similar ways.

Reversibility. Reversibility is a key concept linked with the ability to conserve. Children learn that when materials have been changed they can be changed back again.

Piaget's stages of cognitive development

A key aspect of Piaget's theory are the four stages of development through which all children pass. Children in each stage have particular capabilities beyond which they should not be expected to function. The following sections are based on Piaget's stages but include other relevant aspects of development.

Figure 1.3 Conservation of mass

Figure 1.4 Conservation of number

Sensori-motor stage (birth–2 years)
Key features of this stage are:

- Learning through the senses and own activity in exploration and discovery.
- Child is egocentric and sees the world only from its own viewpoint.
- At 8–12 months the child achieves 'object permanence', i.e. it realizes that objects exist even when they are out of sight.
- Learning, in part through trial and error, that things can be made to happen.
- By two years the child is making things stand for other things through words, images or simple role play. This indicates start of internal 'thought'.

Pre-operational stage (2–6 or 7 years)

- Child can now use symbols such as language to stand for other things, e.g. in pretend play.
- Thinking is still tied to concrete objects and events and what is seen. Child cannot comprehend abstract concepts.
- Child is egocentric, i.e. sees everything from its own point of view.
- Child cannot yet 'conserve' (see earlier). Child focuses on one aspect of situation and ignores others.
- Child cannot classify by more than one feature until around four years, i.e. can group all red objects but not round red objects.
- Concept formation is an important task for young children. At this age they cannot grasp class inclusion, e.g. cows are part of a larger class of animals or daddies are part of a larger class of men.
- Pre-operational thought is rigid: things are seen in black and white. 'Moral realism' means

children expect everyone to share their view of right and wrong which is itself based on what actually happens rather than motives for behaviour.

- Reasoning is often illogical, e.g. children hurt themselves against a toy and proceed to smack the 'bad' toy. This assumption that objects have consciousness is called animism and can be the root of many fears.

Concrete operations stage (7–11 or 12 years)

Key features of this stage are:

- Thinking is becoming more rational but child still needs to be able to see and manipulate objects to help check what it is doing and thinking. The child finds it difficult to think in the abstract.
- Child can see things from others' points of view, but egocentricity persists as the child tries to make difficult facts fit into its own ideas rather than changing its own viewpoint to accommodate the facts.
- Child can take into account several features of objects and events at the same time and group objects by several common features.
- Child can solve several conservation tasks and understands reversibility and transformations.
- Child recognizes there is more than one solution to a problem.
- Child understands quantity and one to one correspondence.
- Child has better understanding of some abstract concepts.
- Child's memory and concentration span are improving.

Formal operations

This is the stage defined by Piaget which starts at around twelve years of age and extends and develops throughout adulthood. Formal operations stage is characterized by the ability to think logically and in the abstract. The period of change from concrete to formal operations takes some years, and it is not clear whether all adults complete the transition. Research indicates that some adult's thought processes remain dependent on concrete objects and find difficulty in thinking in the abstract. It is important to recognize that Piaget's stages were derived from observing children in a white, middle-class, Eurocentric culture, and defining higher-order thinking in this way is a product of that culture. Although few in the industrialized West would disagree with the premise, there are cultures and societies where children are not brought up to use or to value formal logic skills in the way we are, but this does not necessarily mean these children are 'backward' or deficient in any way.

Critique of Piaget's work

Piaget's work was a major breakthrough in our understanding of the developing child, and this must not be under-estimated. However, work by a variety of researchers has challenged or built on some of his methods and conclusions (for example, the work of Vygotsky, Bruner or Donaldson).

Some criticism's of Piaget's work are as follows:

- Piaget took as his starting point what children could *not* do, rather than what whey could do.
- Piaget emphasized the role of the intellect but did not adequately consider the impact on it of other areas of development such as language or emotional development.
- Piaget under-estimated the social and cultural context in learning and cognitive development. Modern research has stressed that learning occurs within the context of everyday social interactions.
- Individual differences between children are not adequately considered and there is no clarity on the overlap between stages.
- Children much younger than Piaget indicated can decentre (take into account several aspects of an object or event at the same time), conserve and understand reversibility and also demonstrate other cognitive skills. This is thought to be due to the manner in which the original experiments were done and the language used. It is thought that children did not understand the tasks, not that they could not do them.
- Children under seven are capable of some logical thought when they fully understood what is being asked.
- Very young children are capable of seeing some things from other points of view.
- Piaget's idea of fixed stages of development has been largely superseded by the idea of sequences. This means that children's learning in any particular area will follow the same basic order, and use the same rules and strategies for learning. Workers with young children need to 'tune in' to these sequences in order to provide individual children with correct educational experiences not those based on the assumption that children cannot move on in their learning because they are tied to a particular age or stage.
- Restricting the view of the young child as a learner not capable of logical thought or understanding complex issues could artificially restrict the curriculum offered and lead to lower expectations.
- The role of experience and adult support in learning is much more important in an individual child's progress than Piaget had allowed for when discussing stages of development.
- Piaget's work indicated that the child would learn from its own inner motivation, and stressed that the role of discovery learning which involves a child finding out for itself. This idea of the 'solitary' learner has been challenged by recent work which stresses the importance of the adult or other children in supporting learning.

Development of language and representation

The development of language is an important milestone for the growing child and a major achievement. Language and the use of symbols helps children to communicate their wants and needs to the outside world. It helps to extend their experience beyond their immediate environment, and to express their feelings. Play and the ability to talk and interact verbally with others offers the child a powerful means of learning. The development of language is closely linked to children's thinking and conceptual development.

There are four main ways in which language is used:

1. Listening and understanding (receptive speech). Children always listen and understand language before they use it.
2. Talking (expressive speech).
3. Reading.
4. Writing.

These four are closely linked, and the latter two depend on success in listening and talking. In the case of sensory impairment, different strategies are used to facilitate reading and writing. This section will consider only receptive and expressive speech; chapter 3 looks at reading and writing and contains references for further research.

Origins of speech

Linguists and psychologists have studied the origins of speech and language in children and have very different views on how it is acquired. Learning theorists think it is learned through imitation, and in part this is true, but this does not explain the child's capacity to create and invent entirely new sentences they could never have heard. Chomsky (1968) and other theorists state that children have an inborn capacity to acquire language, and that part of the process of successful acquisition is associated with hearing language used. Their 'language acquisition device' sorts out the appropriate set of rules for the language they hear.

Backing up this argument, there seems no doubt that when children begin to speak they use grammatical 'rules' to create an infinite variety of new sentences and phrases. Proof of this also lies to some extent in their usage of 'virtuous errors'. For example, they may have learned that plurals often end with an 's', therefore the child will apply the rule to make sheep into sheeps. This shows that they are not merely repeating what they have heard but are attempting to apply rules in their speech.

Language and thought

Piaget's view was that children's language development was constrained by their stage of cognitive development. In other words, language would not proceed ahead of the child's basic thought processes as the two are closely linked. Others, such as Vygotsky and Bruner, suggest that it is as children talk and interact with others that they progress in language and thinking.

Baby talk

Babies and children respond to the use of 'motherese' or baby talk. This describes the short sentences and simple language structures used by adults in communication with them. Motherese is slow speech, using a higher pitch than normal, and is used in a repetitive manner to refer to objects and people around. A key feature is the expectant pause when adults wait for the child to communicate and vocalize back to them. Babies and young children are thought to attend more closely to this type of speech and learn from the repeating grammatical patterns. Adults often imagine what they think the child is saying or interpret facial expressions or slightly modify and expand a child's own speech and repeat it back to them and this helps to further language development. For example:

Baby   Looks at teddy and says 'ta ta'.
Mother   Pause, then 'Yes...here's your teddy'.
Baby   Pauses and looks again at teddy. Points 'ta ta ta'.
Mother   Responds to imagined or implied request from baby, 'Yes...
          Mama wants to kiss Teddy.'

This kind of turn-taking response using slow, high-pitched repetitive speech encourages children to talk and enjoy interactions with adults.

Language and social context

During the 1960s and 1970s there was a linking of failure at school with the way in which children used language. It was thought that working-class children used a restricted language code with prevented them understanding and taking advantages of school opportunities (Bernstein, 1961). School staff, who were likely to be middle-class, were thought to use an elaborated code of language which gave middle-class children an advantage in educational terms. As a result of this type of research, compensatory education attempted to provide a linguistically enriched environment for working-class children without always recognizing that the children's own language and culture was important and valid in its own right. Associated with this was an assumption that the reasons for educational disadvantage were rooted in the home. Modern research has found that children's language develops in the much the same way regardless of home background, and that listening to stories and participating in everyday conversations were crucial factors in the development of language and literacy (Wells, 1985, 1987).

Bilingualism

Many children in Britain today speak more than one language. Such children may use English at school and a home language with their family. Although there is debate about the effect on the child of learning two languages, and concern when a child does not develop fluency in either, there is an emphasis now on the cognitive advantages of being able to use two systems and move from one to the other. Being bilingual does not seem to affect literacy skills and seems to increase creativity and divergent thinking. It is important that the home language of bilingual children is seen by them to be valued and respected.

Egocentric speech

This is the 'talking away to themselves' that those who care for young children are so familiar with. Psychologists and linguists have different views on the purpose of egocentric speech, which can be short sentences or 'telegraphese' which accompanies play or a long and complex egocentric monologue. To assess whether true egocentric speech is being heard, it is useful to listen and to ask oneself at what or whom is the language aimed? Egocentric speech is usually aimed at the child itself.

It can be very enlightening to 'listen in' on children's egocentric conversations, as often deep or hidden feelings may manifest themselves. Talking to themselves is a form of externalized thinking through which children regulate and plan their own behaviour. It usually accompanies play, but can occur when a child feels frustrated. Egocentric speech is often stimulated by the need to solve problems which are difficult to 'think through'. As the child's thinking becomes internalized there is less need for egocentric speech and it eventually disappears.

Promoting language development

Children need a language-rich environment from their earliest days. This can be through songs, rhymes, stories, actions, talk in everyday activities. When children experience this they are able to use language freely and to enjoy it. In addition, the carer should:

- Regularly share stories, both read and told from the earliest months of life.
- Be able to change and adapt stories, rhymes and songs to avoid stereotyping and encourage participation by all.
- Use or encourage the use of books and language activities from a variety of languages and cultures.
- Use or encourage the use of mother-tongue stories, rhymes and conversations for children whose first language is not that of the setting, and allow other children to participate.
- Use simple, clear language with lots of repetition (see 'Motherese' above).
- Adapt or design stories and other language activities for use with children who have sensory impairment.
- Provide a stress-free environment where children do not feel pressurized to talk or 'perform', and are not criticized when they make mistakes.
- Use open-ended sentences which do not require 'correct' answers, and give time for children to reply.
- Give time and opportunity to verbalize feelings, and where necessary provide appropriate vocabulary in a sensitive way.
- Provide practical situations where it is expected that children communicate.
- Listen carefully and responsively to children and feed back corrections to their language in natural conversations.
- Understand when children might need help from speech therapists and so forth.
- Check that the child has no hearing difficulties.
- Encourage child–child conversations as well as child–adult.
- Use a range of songs, rhymes and finger plays to extend language.

The development of language

Pre-linguistic stage

Age	Key features
1–3 months	Cries when hungry or has discomfort. Orients to sounds and is startled by sudden noises. Appears soothed by human voice especially mothers. Coos when contented (occurs in deaf babies).
3–6 months	Babbles and coos. Vocalizes vowels and consonants and syllables: 'ba ba ma ma'. Laughs out loud. Cries when upset or hungry. Searches for source of sound. Responds to tone of voice.
6–9 months	Continues to babble and imitate speech sounds. Uses long repetitive strings of sounds: 'mememe adadad' (deaf children usually do not use repetitive, tuneful babble). Babbling more linked to the language of the parents rather than 'universal' sounds. Will shout and vocalize in order to communicate.
9–12 months	Continues to imitate speech sounds. Uses 'jargon' which is strings of sounds which go up and down like conversation. Shows understanding of 'bye bye', simple instructions such as 'give it to me'. Also understands simple words in context: 'cup' or 'teddy'. Uses most vowels and consonants. Understands, and maybe names, 'mama' or 'dada'. Points to objects.

Linguistic stage

Age	Key features
12–15 months	More 'jargon'. Uses gestures and understands 'no'. Less likely to cry for attention and more likely to vocalize. Has 2–6 word speech vocabulary and understands many more.
15–18 months	Uses 6–20 words. Points to parts of body. Points at pictures and may label. Uses gestures widely and 'jargon'. 'Echolalia' which is echoing prominent word or last syllable. Enjoys rhymes and tries to sing. Uses holophrases which are single words with different expression to mean different things.
18 months–2 years	Uses around 50 words and understands many more. Beginning to put words together, e.g. 'dada come'. This is known as 'telegraphese'. Refers to self by name. Asking for names of objects. Joins in songs, rhymes, finger plays. Obeys simple instructions such as 'close the door'. Echolalia remains.
2–3 years	Develops large vocabulary and understands more. Beginning to use plurals and pronouns but makes 'virtuous errors', e.g. mouses instead of mice. Egocentric speech during play. Holds simple conversations. Ask questions using what, where and who. Loves stories, especially when repeated over and over again. Can use short sentences including adjectives. May stutter when excited.

3–4 years	Speech inflections are more adult. Large vocabulary and uses grammar correctly in most cases. Still has problems with sentence structure and pronunciation and uses infantile form. Can have quite complex conversations, especially about past events. Asks many questions using why, when and how. Still enjoys and repeats songs and rhymes. Enjoys jokes and nonsense talk. Confuses fact and fantasy in stories. At four years gives own name, age and address.
4–5 years	Speech usually correct and becoming more sophisticated. Asks meanings of abstract words and uses them and other interesting words but not always correctly. Understands and then uses adverbs and prepositions. Talks freely and uses imagination. Answers questions in detail and can elaborate.

Symbolic representation

Although language itself is a form of symbolic representation, there are many other ways in which children make one thing stand for another. Children also communicate symbolically through dramatic play, music and movement, construction, and so forth, and adults have an important role in encouraging this.

Figure 1.5 Child drawing with large crayons

The development of children's drawing follows broadly the same universal sequence from scribble to line to drawing, and is an important indicator of the child's internal world, a kind of 'visible thinking'. Drawing can also help a child to express feelings and happenings that are too difficult to put into words.

It is likely that a child will be able to 'scribble' from one year onwards and reach the 'realism' stage of clearly representing what is seen at about the time they are in the first years of formal school. Only at the latter stages of this sequence can we be certain that children have a clear internal picture of a person in relatively correct proportion. This also indicates a developing sense of self and an ability to observe the world. The stages are as follows:

1. *Scribble stage.* At first the child will hold a crayon or pencil and move it backwards and forwards. These will develop into multiple and circular scribbles where, as well as backwards and forwards, the crayon is lifted from the paper and moved in different directions.

Figure 1.6 'Scribble' stage

2. *Schematic stage.* Marks inside circle and circle crossed with lines. Sun designs.

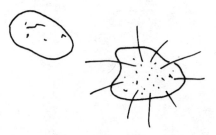

Figure 1.7 Schematic stage. marks inside a circle and sun designs.

3. *First representation.* This is usually a face.

Figure 1.8 First representation. "My Mum and me", by Kelly, aged 4 years.

4. *Heads and bodies.*

Figure 1.9 Heads and bodies, by Daniel, aged 5 years.

5. *Realism stage.*

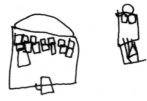

Figure 1.10 Realism stage. "My flats", by Liam, aged 5 years.

Social and emotional development

The basis of healthy social and emotional development is a positive self-image and good self-esteem. For these to develop satisfactorily children need a basis of love, encouragement and acceptance through which to face the outside world and to make positive and fulfilling relationships. How well a child relates to others depends to some extent on the development of trust which comes through having early basic needs for food and comfort met in an atmosphere of unconditional love and care. This is the kind of loving acceptance which does not depend, for example, on a child's appearance or behaviour, and where carers value individual children for what they are. This is particularly important during the first year of life, as the quality of a child's first relationships will affect all subsequent relationships. Although these needs are often met within the traditional nuclear or extended family, these are not the only effective structures that can provide emotional and physical security for our children. Today there are a whole range of different relationships and family structures within which children thrive. It is clear, however, that children do best in a small family-type group rather than a large institution where close and intimate bonds cannot be formed. This is discussed further in the section on attachment.

Stages of social and emotional development

Age	Key features
1–3 months	Babies respond to human contact particularly that of primary carer through smiling, quietening and body responses. Gazes at human faces.
3–6 months	Responses are more sustained. Preference for the primary carer is growing. Smiles at most people. Vocalizes and enjoys turn-taking communication.
6–9 months	Fear of strangers appears, and distress at separation from primary carer or carers. Interacts in different ways with family members.
9–12 months	Fear of strangers appears to increase although this depends on the setting, whether known carers are present, and so forth. Will use a 'comfort object' such as a piece of blanket, familiar toy or dummy, or thumb to suck. Capable of different emotions, e.g. rage. Seeks attention.
12–15 months	Emotionally unstable and needing reassurance. More demanding, assertive and independent. Temper tantrums may start. Early toilet-training may set up anxiety.
15–18 months	Resists changes in known routines. Can be defiant. Does not see others as individuals. Still careful with strangers but showing some interest also. Beginning to distinguish 'you' and 'me'.
18–24 months	Increasing independence brings with it strong emotional feelings. Anger, and frustration lead to more tantrums. The increase in language and symbolic thought allows some feelings to be expressed through imaginative play. Does not like to be told 'no' and will express rage at being thwarted. Shows pleasure in own possessions. Can distinguish between self and others but remains self-centred. Follows carers around and is more social.
2–3 years	Becoming more stable, equable and confident but still mood swings from positive to negative and will vary between being dependent and clinging, to being rebellious and uncooperative. Can experience sibling rivalry. Needs support and reassurance in transition to nursery but is learning to separate from carers. Has sense of own identity, knows name, place in family, gender. Has irrational fears.
3–5 years	More stable and emotionally secure. Enjoys helping at home or in the nursery and enjoys adult approval although sometimes difficult and cheeky. Can be friendly and caring to younger children and animals with occasional aggressive lapses. Although much more independent, the child still needs adult support to cope with difficult situations. Well developed imaginative play helps to cope with strong feelings. Still fears loss of parents or carers.

5–7 years   Becoming increasingly confident and independent. More aware of right and wrong and will feel guilty if behaving in unacceptable fashion. Often argumentative and dogmatic.

Promoting emotional development

The adult's role in the promotion of healthy emotional development can be expressed in the following interdependent areas which are discussed below:

- Development of independence and trust and confidence in others through firm attachments or emotional bonds.
- Development of self-confidence and self-esteem through praise, encouragement and positive messages to the child.
- Establishing control of powerful feelings and overall emotional balance is a major task of the young child and is facilitated by the support and care of significant adults.

Attachment theory

Babies are vulnerable, and their development is dependent on receiving adequate love and care. Research has indicated that forming close emotional bonds with carers who remain consistent in the child's life forms the basis of healthy emotional development.

In the first years of life a baby will form an enduring emotional attachment or bond with those who give love and care. The processes of feeding, bathing, cuddling, and the responsiveness of the carers to the developing child give opportunity for this bond to become strong. This requires prompt and appropriate responses to the baby's signals. As well as giving physical care to meet basic needs, babies respond to sensory contact and develop socially through turn-taking communication between themselves and carers.

From the earliest weeks of life a baby can recognize its primary carers. often the parents, and begins to respond positively to their voices and presence. Where there are problems in establishing emotional bonds with primary carers for whatever reasons, it is likely that the baby may not be so emotionally secure and well settled. However, babies are all different: some are able to tolerate delay and frustration better than others, and it is a mistake to assume that all babies who seem fretful and difficult have not received sensitive care and handling.

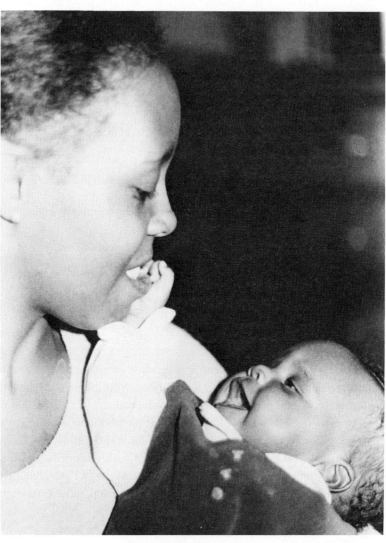

Figure 1.11 Attachment

The work of John Bowlby

The work of Bowlby (1975, 1979) has been influential, his main hypothesis is that babies will do best if they receive consistent care from one adult carer, usually the mother. If the child receives care outside the home from other adults, then, suggests Bowlby, the child suffers maternal deprivation, and this will ultimately harm the child's emotional development and may lead to higher levels of delinquency in later life. This work seemed to be supported by work such as that of the Robertsons (1969). In this piece of work the child's reaction to separation from his mother was starkly recorded in a very moving way, but of course this does not demonstrate that good bonds cannot be made with other important adults. The work of Bowlby is discussed further in chapter 6.

Modern practice is based on the conclusion that babies are able to thrive and develop even when cared for by several adults, but this care must be stable, high quality and consistent in order to promote emotional health and good overall development (Hennessy *et al.*, 1992). Often, for example, babies will turn to their mothers for comfort and to their fathers and others for play. However, there does not need to be a biological link in order to make effective attachments. It is important that attachments are encouraged with other family members, close friends and other carers. This will make it possible for mothers to leave their babies knowing that they will experience minimal distress.

If, as indicated, a baby can make several attachments, then there is much less pressure upon mothers to stay at home. There is an obvious political and ideological point to make here: if mothers do not harm their children by going out to work, and they wish to return to employment, then there should be adequate child care provision to facilitate this. Work such as Bowlby's has given us tremendous insights into the needs of babies and young children for consistent care, but has also been used to justify keeping mothers in the home and reducing state child care provision.

Separation anxiety

During the first few months of life a baby will smile and make eye contact, attempt to reach out and to babble in response to people around. Although the process of bonding is gradual, by around eight months most babies will be firmly attached to their primary carers. They will become increasingly distressed at separation and will demonstrate fear of strange adults, although they are less likely to demonstrate fear of unknown children at this stage. This is known as 'separation anxiety'. Research in Uganda found that, on average, babies from the Ganda tribe were showing separation anxiety by five to six months. This was attributed to the fact that these babies spent far more time in close contact with their mothers: the babies slept with their mothers, were carried in a sling and rarely separated even for short periods.

At around two years of age, fears of separation and strange adults tend to diminish, although this depends on the individual child and circumstances. Children who have had a secure base and firm attachments are generally confident and willing to explore the world around as well as being able to give and receive affection. However, they still experience temporary shyness and difficulties with separation. For example, when starting playgroup or nursery it is often the well attached child who displays initial clinging behaviour before settling in well and taking full advantage of the opportunities offered. At the age of three to five years these children become more independent and begin to make attachments to other children and adults who spend time with them. However, the initial primary attachments, usually with parents, remain very important, and when these are secure and positive the child is likely to continue to develop a good self-image.

Comfort objects

Babies become attached to favourite comfort objects such as soft toys or blankets. They can sometimes be seen staggering along with a large blanket in one hand whilst sucking the thumb of the other. These are usually abandoned when the child has no further use for them and it is generally better to allow this to happen naturally.

Babies prefer human faces

Research has shown that babies have an inbuilt preference for relationships with human beings rather than objects (Fantz, 1961, and see below). It has been found that babies prefer round shapes and especially the human face. Other experiments have been carried out to test babies' reactions to speech as opposed to other sounds, and also to test if very young babies prefer their mother's voice or smell to that of others. Most babies preferred human contact and particularly their mother's. This indicated that the process of attachment or expressing preference for primary carers does start within the first weeks of life.

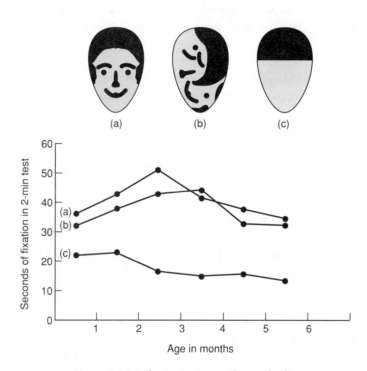

Figure 1.12 Infant's viewing preference for faces

Poor attachments

There are many reasons that parent/carers may have poor attachments to their children. The source of this can sometimes be traced to separation soon after birth, or if the baby is unplanned and unwanted. Some babies are harder to love than others: they may cry a lot or seem to give little back to their parents who may themselves have unrealistic expectations. Research into babies with handicaps shows that it is sometimes difficult for parents to bond with apparently unresponsive or unlovely babies, although most do so satisfactorily. Social conditions such as poverty, large families and overcrowding can sometimes play a part. Some parents simply have too many personal difficulties, may be mentally ill or themselves have received poor parenting. It is important to note that most parents do bond with their children and care for them lovingly, despite difficulties. The quality of that bonding is variable, and all workers with young children and their families should note where attachments seem weak and undeveloped.

Babies who are not developing firm attachments will feel insecure and appear fretful and difficult. In extreme cases, where very little love and contact is made, they will become emotionally 'starved' and exhibit bizarre behaviour such as head-banging or repetitive movements. Babies in large institutions with minimal attention will lie for hours doing these things or just gazing into space hopelessly, sometimes whimpering but not bothering or having the energy to cry, having already learned that their needs will not be met. Sometimes parents or carers cannot discriminate amongst signs of hunger, fatigue and other distress, and the baby may be left in a distressed state for some time. As the child gets older, it is less confident and may not leave its mother's side to explore and experiment or show any emotion if she leaves the room. As a result, these children are less likely to take advantage of the learning opportunities in their environment, their all-round development may be held back and they will be less likely to make trusting relationships. In extreme cases, children may exhibit 'indiscriminate affection' where they make superficial contact with whoever is available and show no fear of strangers. It does seem that, to some extent, early deprivation can be overcome when children do receive consistent loving care, but it is difficult to assess the long-term effects.

Self-esteem

For many children, the development of a positive self-image is difficult, but if they do start life with a good degree of confidence and self-esteem, they will be better able to cope with what lies ahead. Development of this good self-image depends on a child receiving positive messages about its own worth and loving acceptance when mistakes are made. If a child receives negative feedback such as important adults continually criticizing behaviour or being called clumsy, stupid, skinny, and so forth, it is likely that the child will believe itself to be less than worthwhile. Often children with the poorest self-image are those who have been abused or neglected. Also, whilst many children receive positive images regarding themselves from their own family, there are situations which occur where this may become damaged. Children who receive negative images regarding their skin colour, language, cultural background, social class, gender, disability, physical characteristics and so forth will develop poor self-esteem, and measures have to be taken to minimize the damage. Children also learn through identification with positive role models, and it is important both that significant adults in their environment are able to provide these and that they are available in books or through visitors to the nursery. For example, if girls can see older girls or women achieving success in a leadership role, they are more likely to feel that they too can be leaders.

It is vital that those who work with young children and their families recognize the importance of their role in helping to build self-esteem. This is not always easy as workers themselves often have to struggle with these very issues in their own lives.

- Children should be valued for who they are, not what they look like or can do. It is important to praise and encourage children and not to criticize in a destructive manner.
- Children should be offered choices in their daily lives and opportunities to feel in control of their environment, within the limits of safety and consideration for others.
- Children should be given opportunity to succeed in what they are setting out to do, and unrealistic expectations should be avoided.

- Behavioural boundaries should be set and consistently applied so that children are not confused and uncertain regarding what is expected of them.
- The environment should be carefully organized to allow children maximum autonomy.
- Children should receive consistent care, preferably using a key worker system (where a very small number of named adults are responsible for the total care of the child). This enables attachments to be made.
- Materials, activities and resources should reflect positive images of all children regardless of ethnic origin, gender or disability.
- Children's basic needs for food, rest, shelter, love, care and stimulation should be met.
- Children and families should be shown respect in order to develop self-respect.

Powerful feelings

There are aspects of children's lives which do provoke powerful feelings in them, for example major transitions such as weaning, toilet training, arrival of siblings or separations such as illness or starting school. Helping children to cope with these events and to develop in a stable and positive manner requires adults to provide a safe base of love and acceptance from which children can feel secure. From this position of safety it is easier for a child to cope when feeling out of control. The behaviour resulting from feelings such as anger, temper tantrums and jealousy is covered in chapter 9.

Ways of helping children to cope with powerful feelings

It is important to give the child appropriate language to express feelings and a range of appropriate equipment, materials and activities to facilitate imaginative play. As adults support this type of play it allows children to experience powerful and potentially destructive feelings in a safe environment. For example, the child who is feeling jealous of a new baby will often express negative feelings towards a doll or soft toy, this can give adults an insight into those feelings and opportunity to support the child and channel the aggression. Channelling aggression can take many forms. For some children, vigorous outdoor play will help, others find pummelling clay or dough offers a release. Certain toys such as a hammer and pegs also give the child a chance to express anger or frustration.

Fears and anxieties

Children who do experience a wide range of strong fears and can easily become anxious. Babies and toddlers can be frightened of strangers and of losing their primary carer. They can also show fear of loud noises, high places, sudden movements, strange places, animals and so on. Young children's fears are very real and must be taken seriously. It is easy to laugh at a child's fear of disappearing down the bath drain along with the bath water, but is kinder and more sensible to recognize the fear and devise strategies for overcoming it. Many children are frightened of the dark and it is important that they are given night lights and not ridiculed or terrorized.

Childhood fears are often irrational and adults must be patient and sensitive in handling them. It is usually better to face the fears and discuss them appropriately with the child. If children feel defenceless, they may be overwhelmed by feelings of hopelessness, and adults must endeavour to give them the inner resources to cope.

Imaginative play can offer the child an opportunity to 'play out' fears. For example, if they have had painful experiences at the doctor's surgery or in hospital, the setting up of a hospital corner with appropriate resources gives the child a chance to explore feelings, to become the powerful adult, to give the painful treatment. This kind of role play helps to express fears and to control them.

Magical thinking

Children under school age can mix fact and fantasy very easily and many engage in 'magical' thought in which they feel that they can alter reality by their thoughts and wishes. For example, children who are jealous of one parent may feel it is their fault if the parents separate. Their thoughts and feelings are very real to them and 'magical' thinking can leave them feeling guilty, frightened and insecure. As well as this, a child can believe itself to be a person or thing, and can act with conviction and authority within that role. It has been known for children taking on a 'super-hero' role to believe themselves capable of jumping from windows without hurting themselves. Where children have real and persistent difficulties sorting out reality from fantasy they may need specialist help.

Imaginary friends

Sometimes children will invent an imaginary friend who expresses all the unpleasant and guilty feelings that the child cannot, or who is simply a companion to them. This is a perfectly normal happening which children eventually outgrow. There is concern, however, when a child is unable to distinguish fact from fantasy in an extreme manner and, again, adults need to be sensitive and able to assess when this is happening.

Emotional stress

Children who are experiencing pressure in their lives which leads to emotional stress will react in various ways. They can become withdrawn and introverted or conversely very noisy, aggressive and attention-seeking. Children under stress often regress and exhibit babyish behaviour. If they are clean and dry they may start soiling or bed-wetting. They may refuse to eat or demand a bottle. Excessive thumb sucking, masturbation or other comfort habits may also occur (see chapter 9). Adults need to be sensitive to the child's needs, note sudden or gradual changes and be able to assess when these occurrences are temporary during a difficult period for the child or whether they are symptoms of a more serious underlying problem. Either way children need help, and action should be taken involving parents and professionals as necessary. This will involve investigating the cause of the distress than concentrating on the symptoms.

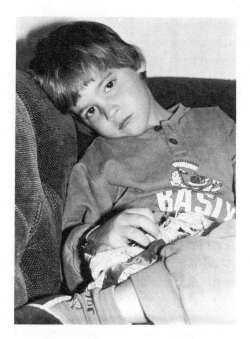

Figure 1.13 Children can feel Sad

Social development

Closely linked to emotional development and the making of attachments is the young child's social development. As good attachments are made, so the baby begins to interact with the world around in a social manner, through reaching, smiling, babbling and so forth. Social development covers:

- Socialization.
- Aspects of socialization.
- Relating to others.
- Developing social skills.

Socialization

Every society has its own code of acceptable behaviour based on its values and beliefs. Within that society, smaller sections will have their own variations which usually stem from religious, cultural or environmental factors and family beliefs concerning what is appropriate and acceptable. Every child has to learn what the code is and to base their behaviour and attitudes on the example of significant adults in the world around. As well as this they must learn their own role within this often bewildering set of expectations. This process is called socialization. It is considered essential that children are socialized into the values and behaviour of their society in order to maintain stability and order. Where this can be seen to be beneficial to all members of that society and is based on mutual respect and consideration this is acceptable to most people. However, it is the case that children can be socialized into accepting values which might be seen to be against human rights, for example the values of the Hitler Youth earlier this century. There is widespread discrimination on the basis of skin colour or gender in many societies and this is perpetuated through the attitudes and values transmitted through socialization.

Socialization is an enormous piece of learning for the child, and although it is difficult to divide up, the following are useful ways of viewing the process:

- Learning to behave in socially approved ways. This involves knowing what is approved and modelling behaviour on these lines.
- Playing approved social roles including gender roles. This involves knowing what your role is and how it is customary to behave, e.g. being a daughter, pupil, brother, friend.
- Developing appropriate social attitudes. This is helped if children like and trust people and enjoy joining in with groups.

Agencies of socialization

There are many socializing influences on young children, but most can be grouped in the following broad categories:

- The family or primary agency whose influence remains throughout childhood and often into adulthood.
- Schools or other form of day care and education become more important as the child grows older and relates to other significant adults.
- Friends and friendship groups become increasingly important influences throughout childhood and adolescence.
- The media becomes increasingly influential as the child grows up. Children today watch a good deal of television, this can be seen reflected in their play.

Aspects of socialization

Social learning

There are many different points of view concerning how children become socialized. One influential view is held by social learning theorists, who feel that children learn who they are and what is expected of them through observing others and their experience of the way adults interact with them. They respond to important adults in their lives by modelling their behaviour upon those adults. It is pointless telling a child what to do and expecting them to behave appropriately if the adult concerned consistently does something different for the child is much more likely to copy the adult's behaviour than listen to their words. Attitudes may also be learned, such as when a child is told to love and care for granny, but picks up the tension and upset in the family if granny is coming to visit. This learning, whether good or bad, will be helped if it is positively reinforced. For example, when a child is aggressive to another boy and the carer rewards this aggression by comments such as, 'Good boy, you really showed him what a wimp he is'.

Bandura (1973) a social psychologist, tested children to see how they modelled themselves on adults. Three groups of young children watched a short film with three different endings. Each group saw an adult attacking a 'bobo' doll. He would hit and punch the doll, sit on it, and kick it whilst shouting aggressively. The different endings were seen by different children, the first group saw the adult being rewarded for his aggression, the second group saw the adult punished and the third or control group saw no reward or punishment given to the adult. After watching this the children were given opportunity to play with a bobo doll and their behaviour recorded. Those who had seen the aggressive adult being rewarded and the control group were equally aggressive to the doll. The group who had seen the adult punished were significantly less aggressive. Bandura concluded that through watching the films children had learned new ways of being aggressive and had become more so.

It is difficult to be certain how far Bandura's finding would be true in a less artificial situation and there are many criticisms of this type of experiment, but there are lessons to be learned from it. Bandura suggested that for children really to learn from models they will need to be seen as powerful, competent and similar to the child and have a good nurturing relationship with the child.

Attachment and separation

Whatever language is used to describe it, most research shows that early socialization takes place through attachments to carers. Good attachments lead to effective socialization as children soon learn what pleases their carers and in general try to behave positively. If attachments are poor there is less incentive for children to try to please, as their efforts are often ignored or misunderstood. Where children experience multiple separations from their carer, this can lead to poor attachments and problems in socialization. If children cannot interpret their carer's expectations, either because they are unable to respond because of learning difficulties or sensory impairment, then there may also be difficulties in socialization.

Attitudes and prejudice

Attitudes and prejudice are formed early in the process of socialization, as are stereotypes of black people, women and so forth. All workers with young children must avoid stereotypical assumptions which, in the case of black children for example, are often negative and lead to poor expectations of those children. Research by Rosenthal and Jacobsen (1968) and others has shown that where expectations are low, children often perform badly (the self-fulfilling prophecy).

Gender roles

Children know what gender they are between the ages of two and a half and three years, although they may not be certain if their gender is permanent. During the whole of the pre-school period they are learning through the various agencies of socialization what it means to be masculine or feminine and are beginning to associate each with various characteristics and valuing each differently. Girls are often taught through socialization that it is better to be pretty and passive, and wrong to be noisy, dirty or inquisitive.

Some theorists think these differences are due to biological reasons but much research disproves this. Work has been done which shows that carers react very differently towards boys and girls. Boy babies are given more attention and they learn to demand more, they are also played with in ways which are likely to encourage assertiveness and independence.

Gender stereotyping prevents boys and girls developing as whole people and restricts their choices. For example, girls may not feel free to tackle woodwork or are intimidated by the boys when they try to use outdoor equipment. Boys may be teased when they show interest in music or dancing. Stereotypes of masculinity and femininity are reinforced through the media and often encouraged by peer pressure. Schools and other institutions are beginning to be aware of the damage that is done through gender stereotyping and some are taking measures to counteract it. Girls are being encouraged to be more assertive and adventurous and to tackle traditional male areas such as technology and engineering. Boys are being encouraged to become more caring and reflective, but there is still a long way to go.

Figure 1.14 Boys bathing 'babies'

Children and race

Research (Milner, 1983) shows that by the age of two years children notice differences in skin colour, and between three and five years they attach a value to that colour. Through the media, family, their peer group, and the world around they receive messages, both non-verbal and verbal, that children with white skin are more beautiful and valuable than those with dark skin. Many workers have experience of very young children trying to scrub their skin white. Workers can do much to aid developing awareness of race by reinforcing positive messages concerning black skin using whatever resources are available. Confronting racism amongst and against children and acting as a positive role model will also assist.

Relating to others

The basis of healthy social development is the establishment of trust which occurs as the babies needs are met in the earliest months of life. Babies begin to associate interaction with adults as both pleasurable and as a means of removing their frustration, whether caused through hunger, discomfort or feeling alone.

Part of social development is the baby's response to its primary carer, usually the mother. Research has shown that babies under six months will explore and play with toys but their reactions to their mothers are quite different. With her, babies hold what could best be termed a 'conversation' which involves encouraging communication by means of making responsive sounds and elaborate body movements. This communication was not linked primarily with the satisfaction of needs but seems to be a mutually enjoyable activity performed just for the pleasure of it and it is known as 'interactional synchrony'. Social interaction is important because it is part of how children discover who they are and what they can do.

Babies begin to show some interest in other infants as young as six months of age. They will smile at each other and explore the other's face and body much as they would an object or plaything. As they become older they become more interested in making social contacts with other children, but how soon real social interactions take place depends on the amount of time they spend with other children and their early experiences and individual personality.

The following table indicates the sequence of social development in play between birth and seven years. All children are likely to go through these stages but some will take much longer than others and will require greater adult support. The age at which children reach each stage can vary widely depending on individual children and their experiences. Each stage is not clear-cut and, for example, children capable of co-operative play may still prefer to play alongside others (parallel) or alone.

Social participation in play 0–7 years	*Approximate age*
Solitary play (child plays alone)	0–2 years
Spectator play (child watches play of those around)	2–2 $^1/_2$ years
Parallel play (child plays alongside others not *with* them)	2 $^1/_2$–3 years
Associative play (a child is beginning to interact with others)	3–4 years
Co-operative play (children playing together cooperatively with shared goals)	Possible from 4 years on

During the pre-school years play will become more socially-oriented and children will begin to demonstrate more pro-social behaviour. At the age of two to three years, when they are entering nursery or playgroups, children's social development depends on the home and environment. If, for example, they live in high-rise flats, with little opportunity to play with other children or meet other adults, they are likely to take some time to settle in at nursery and will need to be given space before they are ready to play with other children or even begin to understand how to share. It is a mistake to expect children of this age to find it easy to share toys and playthings and the demand to share often leads to conflict and tension. It is much better to avoid confrontation with a child by introducing distractions. Many children of three or younger do seem able to show caring behaviour towards other children showing distress even though they are not ready to play with them. However, young children under two to three years are said to be egocentric as they see the world only through their own needs and views. For example, a two-year-old observing another's distress might offer a favourite toy, assuming that what would comfort them would also comfort others.

Figure 1.15 Children playing together

Most children will be developing greater social awareness between three and four years of age. They will enjoy imaginative play in small groups or in twos and can be heard talking to one another and developing their play in a more co-operative manner. These relationships tend to be fleeting but children do express preference for certain friends and play regularly with them. At this stage there is usually, but not always, some preference for play with children of the same sex, but there is still a good deal of mixed play.

By the time children are established at primary school they should have well-developed friendships which can be remarkably enduring. These will be characterized by an ability to develop complex co-operative play and supportive attitudes towards one another. By the time children are seven, and often well before this age, they play almost exclusively in separate boy/girl groups.

Difficulties in relating to others

Children whose language development is delayed, have sensory impairment or who are difficult to understand will sometimes find social relationships problematic, as may those who do not speak the language of the setting. Children in this situation may retreat into themselves and become isolated or conversely become aggressive and attention-seeking. Such problems require prompt help from staff, parents and professionals.

Some children are much more socially popular than others. Often these children are friendly, supportive and outgoing, physically larger, taller and more attractive than their peers. They may also be more successful at school and good at specific tasks or games. Youngest children in families also seem to be more popular. Conversely, children who are physically unattractive or emotionally immature, less friendly, aggressive and critical are those who will be less popular and even isolated from friendship groups. Children of this age and younger already place a value on skin colour and ethnic or gender group, and children may be more or less popular, valued and likely to take risks or to become leaders as a result of these early attitudes and prejudices.

Where children are having difficulty relating to others it is important that correct assessment and monitoring takes place. If the difficulties are superficial and reflect immaturity or lack of experience, they are often easily rectified. If they indicate a more serious underlying cause this will have to be identified and appropriate help sought. Children will often reflect in their social behaviour problems in the family and it is important that parents feel free to discuss these issues.

Developing social skills

Social skills are those aspect of learning, behaviour and development which facilitate acceptance into the wider world. In some instances it is accepted that these will depend on personal values, for example what constitutes 'good manners' will vary from culture to culture. Universally accepted social norms such as consideration for others are important. These involve learning to share and take turns, being positive in play and relationships, and developing basic skills such as dressing and undressing, using appropriate language, keeping clean, using the toilet, mealtime behaviour and so on. If children cannot cope they often become unpopular and ridiculed by other children. Helping children to develop social skills which allow them to become independent and accepted by their peers and adults is a vital aspect of care and education which, if ignored, causes children's self-esteem to suffer. This is particularly difficult if parents are careless or unaware concerning their children's hygiene or appearance and have not prepared them to mix with others. In these cases, particularly, it is important to involve parents in the work with the children.

It is essential to recognize the social and cultural differences amongst families, and workers need to show sensitivity in handling such situations. For example, some children may be used to eating with their fingers at home and this is their cultural norm. Workers should not assume that this indicates children who have not learned to use cutlery which is the 'correct' way to do things, but should devise strategies along with parents to ensure that other children do not ridicule this behaviour. At the same time it will be helpful for the child to learn to use cutlery, but not with an assumption that this is the only acceptable way of eating.

Children who have problems, for whatever reason, need to be given adequate support and guidance as to what is acceptable behaviour. Providing good role models of behaviour is far better than criticizing children and holding unrealistic expectations. Adults working and playing alongside children helps them to understand by example what is acceptable social behaviour. Children should be encouraged and their achievements praised without concentrating on the negative. A consistent routine enables chilren to develop basic skills in self care. Collaborative approaches which involve children working together also provide good learning opportunities.

Moral development

This is the development of conscience and ideas of right and wrong. There are different views as to how this occurs according to the particular school of psychology involved. Views on how children learn to be considerate, thoughtful and socially aware will determine how workers deal with issues of discipline and punishment as well as how day-to-day situations are handled. For example, Bandura and the social learning theorists consider moral development to be linked to what children learn through observation and modelling.

Piaget felt that pre-school children judge things superficially without reference to motive and are not able to separate right from wrong in a adult way. For example, it seems much worse to them accidentally to break ten plates when being helpful, than deliberately to break one plate when being naughty. Children of this age believe that rules are fixed and unchangeable and that the number of plates broken determines the level of punishment meted out. Piaget thought that as children mature, usually from seven to eight years of age, they learn that rules can be broken and that punishment is not inevitable. This leads eventually to a mature understanding of moral concepts and the development of conscience.

Kohlberg (1969) built on Piaget's views and went further in defining six stages of moral development. The highest of these stages was that of 'post-conventional morality'. This involves awareness of high moral principle; not everyone reaches this stage. Kohlberg's theory has proved controversial and led to other ways of looking at moral development. For example, Gilligan (1982) takes a feminist perspective which challenges some of the more orthodox approaches.

Criticism of Piaget's views is similar to that of his description of cognitive development: namely that he under-estimates the child's capacity to think logically, and in this case to understand motive and to think morally.

Discipline and boundary-setting

The practical implications of Piaget's views are that pre-school children need a firm structure of rules and boundaries as they have not yet developed their own 'internal' sense of right and wrong. After the age of seven the child is increasingly likely to have a more adult way of making moral decisions. As children grow up it is important for them to develop their own internal sense of right and wrong which grows out of their relationships and experiences. Sometimes children are given different sets of expectations at different times, and those who care for them are inconsistent in setting boundaries for behaviour; this leads to confusion for the child who simply does not know how to respond. Extreme punishment will lead to a child being insecure, fearful, and lacking trust. It does not lead to a well adjusted and socially competent child. These issues are further discussed in chapter 9.

Observing and assessing children

Assignments are not included for this chapter as it is assumed that readers will wish to undertake observations and assessments on the developing child. In order to provide for children as individuals and in groups we need to develop skills of observation and assessment. You may wish to observe aspects of children's development, their behaviour, their ability to interact in a group, to check their learning and so forth. Observations should be as objective, valid and reliable as possible; and conclusions should not be drawn from one observation only. It is also important that the rights of children and parents are considered when observations and assessments are planned and they should be consulted. Their input can also be a valuable source of data. The following section provides some basic information concerning this important skill, but it is recommended that further research and reading takes place.

Issues of confidentiality are important, and care must be taken in getting permission to observe and record as well as in the dissemination of the information.

Observations and assessments may be required in many different situations of which the following are examples:

- Mild/serious concern about a particular child's development or behaviour.
- Routine assessments.
- Structured assessments in cases of special needs.
- Assessments for purposes of the case conference or court.
- Students for learning purposes.
- To assist with developing care plans.
- To assist with planning individual programmes.
- To facilitate curriculum planning.
- To understand how children use their environment.
- To assist with structured profiles.

The reason for the observation/assessment will determine the type of strategy and method used.

Type of observation

- *Naturalistic.* These are observations of children in natural surroundings doing what they might normally be doing, with no attempt on the part of the observer to structure the situation.
- *Structured.* Situations organized with a view to gaining specific information.
- *Snapshot.* Descriptions which capture what a child is doing at a particular point in time.
- *Longitudinal.* Observations over a period of time.

Observations may involve a variety of methods and forms of recording such as:

- *Time sampling.* Observing and recording what a child is doing at regular intervals during a set period of time, e.g. every fifteen minutes over a morning.
- *Event sampling.* Observing and recording particular events such as temper tantrums or acts of aggression when they occur.
- *Checklists of development.*
- *Pre-coded categories.*
- *Structured records.* For example, those produced by local education authorities.
- *Sociograms.* Recording how children relate to one another in a group.
- *Anecdotal.* Recording events and situations as they happen.
- *Diaries/log books.* For recording specific events or impressions over time.

- *Target child.* A specialized form of observation which focuses on one child in a group or situation.
- *Use of audio or video tapes.*

Relevant information

It must be emphasized that although every situation is different, observations and assessments should in general contain only that which is considered necessary and should exclude unnecessary, speculative comment about children and families. The following are likely to be necessary points to record:

- Details of the setting, numbers of adults, children, equipment and so on.
- Date and time of day.
- Detail of the individual child as appropriate. This might be a thumbnail sketch or a detailed description including family background.
- Purpose/intention of observing.
- Actual observation/data recording.
- Interpretations/conclusions.
- Recommendations for further action.

Pointers towards good observation

- Be clear about why, what and how you are observing.
- Check that you have everything you need to avoid moving once settled.
- Be as unobtrusive as possible.
- Avoid eye contact (in most cases) with those you are observing.
- Be aware of factors in the environment which might affect your judgement or upset the children, e.g. change of routine.
- Leave the interpretation till later.
- Check that your previous knowledge or reports from other workers do not influence your observation, descriptions or interpretations.
- Remember that being observed can change behaviour.
- Remember that children and parents have rights and their feelings should be considered.

Assessments

Assessments should not be judgemental and negative but should accurately reflect your findings, based on observational and other sources of information where relevant. In some cases such as court reports it may be appropriate only to record what children actually say and do and how they behave, including changes over time. In other circumstances, again including court reports, it is necessary to state your professional opinion but it must be based on accurate records which you can utilize to justify your view.

Your data should be discussed with appropriate persons and parents, compared, cross-checked and further assessments done where necessary. When assessing children and families, care should be taken that comparisons against 'the norm' take into account individual variation within the wide range of normality. Assessments should actively consider possible forms of bias related to gender, race, disability, culture, religion, social class, family pattern and so forth.

References and further reading

Bandura, A. 1973. *Aggression: A Social Learning Analysis.* Englewood Cliffs, NJ: Prentice Hall.

BBC Education. 1990. *All Our Children.* London: BBC Publications.

Bee, H. 1987. *The Developing Child.* New York: Harper and Row.

Belsky, J. and Rovine, M.J. 1988. Non-maternal care in the first year of life and the security of infant–parent attachment, *Child Development,* 59: 157–67.

Bernstein, B. 1961. Social class and linguistic development, in *Education, Economy and Society*, edited by Halsey, Floud and Anderson. New York: C.A.

Bowlby, J. 1975. *Attachment and Loss. Vol. 1: Attachment.* Harmondsworth: Pelican.

Bowlby, J. 1979. *The Making and Breaking of Affectional Bonds.* London: Tavistock.

Bruce, T. 1987. *Early Childhood Education.* Sevenoaks: Hodder and Stoughton.

Bruner, J. 1980. *Under Five in Britain: The Oxford Pre-school Research Project.* Oxford: Grant McIntyre/Blackwell.

Chomsky, N. 1968. *Language and Mind.* New York: Harcourt, Brace and World.

Davenport, G.C. 1988. *An Introduction to Child Development.* London: Unwin Hyman.

Donaldson, M. 1978. *Children's Minds.* London: Fontana/Collins.

Donaldson, M., Grieve, R. and Pratt, C. 1983. *Early Childhood Development and Education: Readings in Psychology.* Oxford: Basil Blackwell.

Equal Opportunities Commission. *An Equal Start: Guidelines for those Working with the Under Fives.* Manchester: EOC.

Falhberg, V. 1982. *Child Development.* British Agencies for Fostering and Adoption.

Fantz, R.L. 1961. The origin of form perception, *Scientific American,* 72 (May).

Garvey, C. 1984. *Children's Talk.* London: Fontana.

Gilligan, C. 1982. *In a Different Voice: Psychological Theory and Women's Development.* Cambridge, Mass.: Harvard University Press.

Henessy, E., Martin, S., Moss, P. *et al. Children and Day Care: Lessons from Research.* London: Paul Chapman.

Kholberg, L. 1969. *Stages in the Development of Moral Thought and Action.* New York: Holt, Rinehart and Winston.

Milner, D. 1983. *Children and Race: Ten Years On.* London: Ward Lock Education.

Open University School of Education. 1991. *Working with Under Fives.* Milton Keynes: Open University Press.

Piaget, J. 1926. *The Language and Thought of the Child.* New York: Harcourt, Brace.

J. and J. Robertson Film Services. 1969. *John: Young Children in Brief Separation.*

Rosenthal, R. and Jacobsen, L. 1968. *Pygmalion in the Classroom.* New York: Holt, Rinehart and Winston.

Rutter, M. 1972. *Maternal Deprivation Re-assessed.* Harmondsworth: Penguin.

Sheridan, M. 1980. *From Birth to Five Years: Children's Developmental Progress.* Windsor: NFER/Nelson.

Skinner, B.F. 1953. *Science and Human Behaviour.* New York: Macmillan.

Tizard, B. and Hughes, M. 1984. *Young Children Learning: Thinking and Talking at Home and at School.* London: Fontana.

Vygotsky, L.S. 1962. *Thought and Language.* New York: Wiley.

Wells, G. 1985. *Language, Learning and Education.* Windsor: NFER/Nelson.

Wells, G. 1987. *The Meaning Makers.* Sevenoaks: Hodder and Stoughton.

Wood, D. 1988. *How Children Think and Learn.* Oxford: Basil Blackwell.

Chapter 2
Promoting children's learning through play

Chapter objectives_____

What is play? | Stages of play experience
Purposes and functions | The play environment
Theories of play | Adults' role in promoting play
Types of play | **Links with units C2, C3, C5, C10, C11, E1, M7**

This chapter is not about the philosophy of play but takes as its start point a commitment to play as the young child's right and principal means of learning and self-expression. Research into play has shown that a 'common sense' approach to children's play is not enough, and that workers with young children must understand the central importance of the play experience for a child in order to provide for it effectively.

The importance of play _____

'Deprived of play the child is a prisoner, shut off from all that makes life real and meaningful. Play is not merely a means of learning the skills of daily living. The impulse to create and achieve, working through play, allows the child to grow in body and mind ... Play is one of the ways in which a child may develop a capacity to deal with the stresses and strains of life as they press upon him. It acts too, as a safety valve, allowing him to relive and often come to terms with fears and anxieties which have become overwhelming.' (Organization Mondiale pour L'Education Prescolaire/World Organisations for Early Childhood Education Play in Hospital 1966. Reproduced in *Hospital: A Deprived Environment for Children?* Save the Children Fund 1989)

Figure 2.1 Playing Together

Defining play

There are many definitions of play, none of which is really satisfactory. This is because the subject of children's play is a political one, in that some will see play as unimportant, or worse as a waste of children's time, whilst others will see it as a central vehicle for learning. In general there is a clear division between adult 'play' and that of children. The former usually refers to leisure or recreation activities undertaken by adults when they are not working. These activities have no particular purpose but they are usually pleasurable and adults choose their play activity to suit their individual needs.

To define children's play is much more difficult. In the past, play has been seen as the child's way of getting rid of surplus energy or as a preparation for life. This chapter regards play as a child's work, and there is no doubt that children learn and are motivated through their play and that play can involve intense concentration and commitment of time and energy. In other words, although it is play it is not always 'fun' in the accepted sense. The learning curriculum offered to children in the early years is usually based on play, and it has long been accepted that children learn basic skills and concepts and enhance their development through play.

The definition of play based on an adult model can lead to it being viewed as trivial or un-important. For example, adults often say, 'Run along and play, I'm busy now.' It is important never to trivialise children's play and feel it is of lesser importance than routine or structure. Adults working with young children should avoid using language in ways which devalue what the child is doing in play by separating what is conceived as 'work' from play. For example, 'when you have done this [a set task] you can go and play.' If play is seen as separate from 'work' for young children this can lead to an unnatural division in that it rejects the important principle that play is the main vehicle for children's learning.

Play builds on first-hand experiences, in other words a child cannot play by proxy. Play demands hands-on activity which is immediate and relevant. Although television may stimulate play, watching television is a passive activity which cannot be described as play. Listening to stories is likely to involve children more directly, depending on the telling, but is also not play in an active sense.

Play has also been viewed as all that a child does of its own free-will, in other words activity which is not directed by adults. However, if this line is taken it is often impossible to separate what a child does within the constraints of an adult-directed task from the task itself. For example, if children are sent to the bathroom to clean their teeth, they may spend two minutes on the task and five minutes exploring the toothpaste, feeling its texture, smelling it and enjoying the squiggly patterns it makes on the side of the washbasin. In this case play occurs and is inextricably mixed with other activity. Sitting at a desk and copying letter shapes or doing sums is more easily identified as 'work' for a child, but most situations are less clear-cut and a young child's everyday activity will contain a mixture of both. Given the freedom and materials to do so, most children will turn even the most highly structured activity into an opportunity to play.

Tina Bruce (1991) has attempted to identify what is 'pure' play and uses the term 'free-flow' which has no neat definition and is closely linked to 'imaginative, free or creative play' but not exclusively so as this type of play acts as a catalyst for other activities. Bruce identifies the need for children to 'wallow in ideas, feelings and relationships' and to become 'technically proficient' through free-flow play.

> The following equation states the essence of free-flow play [Bruce 1991]
>
> free-flow play = wallowing in ideas, feelings + application of developed
> and relationships   competence, mastery and control

This is potentially a useful, if somewhat academic way of viewing the type of play which expert practitioners with young children have attempted to promote as a vital component of learning and experience, but which has never been clearly identified. The important message is that children should be permitted to play in a free and unfettered manner, should be given support in their play and resources for their play which should be highly valued and central to their care and education.

Perhaps the most useful way of defining play in a practical sense is by looking at its commonly accepted characteristics. These are:

- It is usually pleasurable.
- It is spontaneous although it may be stimulated by an adult.
- It comes from the child's own intrinsic motivation.
- It usually concentrates on a process not a product.
- It has no explicit rules and no right or wrong way of performing.
- It is an activity where children have ownership of what takes place.
- The child is a willing and active participant.
- It builds on the child's first-hand experiences.

Who plays?

As soon as babies begin to explore and interact with their environment they begin to play. Often their first plaything is their carer's face or mother's breast. As children develop, they learn to play with their own hands and to explore objects around using all their senses. Playing and interacting with the world helps them learn where they end and the world begins. Every healthy child will play spontaneously if not prevented in some artificial manner, although the play will vary in quality and quantity according to the stage of development reached and the life experiences of the child and family. When children do not, cannot or will not play, there is usually cause for concern and the child and parents or other carers will need professional help.

Purposes and function of play

Play is a vital part of the growth and development of a young child it is as necessary for healthy development as is food and rest. Children learn about themselves and their world through the medium of play. Through play, children are helped to develop physically, and are encouraged to explore, experience, discover, practise skills and ideas, and interact socially. Play acts as an outlet for feelings and concerns. Playing goes ahead of serious 'doing' as children experiment and become confident with new skills and concepts. Play acts as an integrating mechanism for every aspect of experience. Through play, children create other worlds where they can test out reality and discover who they are.

Scenario 1	Hannah is three years old. She lives at home with her mother, older sister Katherine aged five, and baby brother Phillip aged six months. Hannah's father has recently moved out of the family home after a difficult period of arguing and bickering with her mother. Hannah spends three mornings a week in a local nursery where she can always be found either playing with dolls or other domestic play in the home corner or 'bathing babies' in the water tray.

Hannah is often aggressive in her doll/domestic play, both to the dolls and to other children. Conversely, she normally shows considerable love and care when bathing her 'babies'.

How might both play situations help Hannah to cope with the situation at home? How could staff extend her play to deal with the strong emotions she is currently experiencing?

Theories of play _____

There are many competing theories of play which the practitioner can draw upon. Some of these are relatively minor differences within a particular theoretical perspective.

Psycho-analytic theories

Psycho-analytic theory derived from the work of Freud or later thinkers such as Winnicott (1971) who view play as the means by which children are helped to cope with their anxieties and fears, and by which they are able to integrate and interpret both positive and negative experiences. Freud saw play also as a means of children fulfilling their deepest wishes. Play is thought to be used by the child to gain mastery over painful anxieties, and this has been viewed as a basis for the development of play therapy techniques.

Cognitive development theories

Cognitive theorists such as Piaget (see chapter 1) also stress the importance of play as an integrating mechanism which helps children to come to terms with the world. Piaget viewed play as a process in which the child is active and through which they learn. He felt that play went through stages of development: for example, the young baby will play using the senses and its own activity (sensori-motor play). Piaget felt that through practice, play develops finally into 'play with rules' which is a higher level of co-operative play when children are able to make and use rules in group play situations.

Piaget has been criticized as seeing play in a narrow form: merely practising and perfecting new skills rather than acquiring them through play. Others see play as much more important in the acquisition of new information and the construction of new concepts and ideas.

Free versus structured play _____

Workers with young children often use the term 'free play' and view it as a benefit to children. It is a term which has been used extensively in recent years but seems to have no common interpretation. Increasingly, it seems a less than useful term which often refers to play where children are free to decide what they will do, who and what they will play with, and where they want to play. Free play can mean the type of play which is superficial, time-wasting, and meaninglessly repetitive, but it can also mean play in a carefully structured environment where learning opportunities are maximized within a framework of a child's free play choices. Exactly when this becomes 'structured play' can be difficult to decide. Often adults do not value free play as it is seen as lacking structure, superficial and without learning objectives. However, children do need to explore and examine materials selected by them in their own way and time. The Oxford Pre-School Project (Sylva, Roy and Painter, 1980) compared children in Oxford pre-school centres with children in

Miami. The children in Oxford were presented with a large range of equipment and materials from which to select whereas the Miami centres offered a more limited range of equipment at any one time chosen and set out by the teacher even during free play periods and with a greater emphasis on the three 'R's. The findings of this investigation revealed that the Miami children were less intellectually involved in their activity despite its apparently more formal educative nature.

Structured play is more likely to refer to play which takes place under adult guidance or facilitation. It implies that the play is carefully organized to extend and consolidate children's learning and experience. It is a term often used to cover so-called work activities which have a more cognitive base such as those linked specifically with language, literacy, arithmetic, technology and science. When talking about free or structured play, workers must themselves be clear what this means and the relative value to the child's education and development.

When to intervene?

In terms of play provision, it is important to provide a balance between free and structured play and to ensure that free play contains within it elements of structure which extend learning. Children who are left to occupy their time without support or resources often do play in a superficial and repetitive way. Adults should intervene sensitively not to dominate the play nor necessarily to change its direction, but to extend it and offer resources and support which enable the children to develop and elaborate their experience.

Scenario 2	Two boys, aged three and four years, have built a long line of blocks across the carpet. They are beginning to make a square enclosure, but are in dispute about whether to do so or not. One of the boys wants to build the line of blocks till it reaches the wall. The other would like to finish the enclosure and make it into a garage. Tempers are beginning to fray. An adult appears on the scene and suggests that if they do not stop squabbling the blocks will be put away.

(a) Is this the most useful form of intervention?
(b) How else might the adult intervene to help with the dispute?
(c) How might the play situation be extended to satisfy both boys?
(d) Are both forms of intervention necessary?

Types of play

Play can take many forms, and many so-called serious learning activities become enjoyable play events for children. Play is often categorized into types, and this can be a useful method of making sense of the variety of activities which might come under this umbrella heading. The following sections list the main categories of play although the lists are not exhaustive. More usually, too, children's play will encompass several types of play within one activity. For example, a child will construct a road or bridge with bricks and this then becomes a part of imaginative play; children playing with basic materials such as sand and water often use imaginative and investigative play.

Vigorous physical play

Activity involved

Crawling	Balancing	Rolling	Rough and tumble
Running	Hopping	Cycling	Digging
Jumping	Skipping	Kicking a ball	Pushing and pulling
Climbing	Chasing	Throwing	
Scrambling	Sliding	Catching	

Development/behaviour encouraged

- Large muscle development.
- Balance and co-ordination
- Spatial awareness.
- Body awareness.
- Physical challenges.
- Learning to take risks and pushing/extending physical development to its limits.
- Healthy exercise encouraging blood circulation and overall better functioning of body systems.
- Social relationships, turn-taking and helping others. Release of tension.
- Practical concepts of area, energy, weight, forces, mass, inertia.

Resources/equipment/environment

- Open space as large as possible within bounds of safety.
- Ensure the surfaces are safe and mats are used as appropriate.
- Indoor or outdoor.
- Natural or manufactured equipment.
- Climbing frames, swings, slides.
- Bicycles/trikes, scooters.
- Large construction.
- Trees, tree trunks, rocks and boulders.
- Earth/sand to dig.
- Balls, hoops, ropes to climb, skipping ropes.
- Wagons, carts and wheelbarrows to push and pull.
- Barrels and tunnels.

Figure 2.2 Group of children playing out of doors

Creative play

Activities involved

Painting and other creative activity with tools or fingers	Drawing Cutting Sticking Modelling	Junk play Printing Collage Cooking	Sewing Threading Lacing Puzzles

Development/behaviour/learning encouraged

- Hand–eye co-ordination, manipulative skills.
- Representation of different types (making something which stands for something else).
- Creativity, divergent thought.
- Sensory learning.
- Self-expression, emotional release, sense of achievement.
- Discovering the properties of different materials.
- Learning about colour, textures, shapes, patterns, two- and three-dimensional experiences.
- Confidence, satisfaction and self-esteem through achievement.

Figure 2.3 Learning to Use Tools

- Greater freedom to experiment as the process of doing is more important than the product which should not be judged against a predetermined adult standard or model.

Resources/equipment/environment

It would be impossible to itemize everything which could be used in creative play as almost anything could. The environment should be encouraging, clean, well presented and maintained with a choice of materials. Children should be provided with overalls and facilities to wash. Wherever possible a workshop approach should be used where adults are available to facilitate a child's creative play, but not to dominate or impose their own ideas of how things should be done at the expense of the child's creativity. Materials should always be accessible to children so they are not dependent on adults. The following items constitute a basic list for creative play:

- Paints, crayons, pens, brushes of different colours and sizes.
- Paste, glue, paste/glue spreaders.
- Sponges, scissors, rulers, staplers, sticky tape.
- Paper of all colours, shapes, textures and sizes.
- Tissue paper, card, corrugated paper, crepe paper, coloured foil.
- Straws, string, beads for threading or lacing.
- Sewing equipment.
- Material for collage.
- Junk which should be sorted and graded.
- Cooking equipment, bowls, rolling pins, wooden spoons, scales, cookers, cutlery.

Play with basic or natural materials

Activity involved

Dough	Sand play	Sawdust	Natural environment
Clay	Earth play	Wood shavings	Pets
Plasticene	Woodwork	Soap flakes	Plants
Cornflour	Peat	Gardens	Insects
Water play			

Development/behaviour/learning encouraged

- Manipulative skills, small muscle development.
- Sensory development.
- Exploration/investigation of natural materials and their properties.
- Release of tension through hammering, pummelling, squeezing and so forth.
- Soothing and relaxing in water play.
- Basic science and mathematical learning such as capacity, volume, change of state (e.g. whisking eggs).
- Life cycles.
- Care of other living creatures.
- Hygiene.

Figure 2.4 Water play

- Planting and growing.
- Enrichment of play through use of 'organic' material especially useful for children in hospitals or restricted urban environments.

Resources/equipment/environment

It would be impossible to itemize everything which could be used in play with basic materials as almost anything could. The environment should be encouraging, well presented and maintained with a choice of materials. Children should be provided with overalls and facilities to wash.

- Indoor and outdoor.
- Tools for use with clay or dough, shapes, rolling pins, boards.
- Woodworking equipment, bench or table, nails, hammers, vice, saw, wood off-cuts.
- Sieves, colanders, different sized containers, jugs, tubing of different diameters for water play, food colouring, liquid detergent/soap for bubbles, items for floating and sinking experiments.
- Buckets, spades, containers with holes, shells, boats, shapes, moulds, sieves, combs, wheels for sand play.
- Zoo and farm animals, dinosaurs and so forth to set up play scenarios in water or sand.

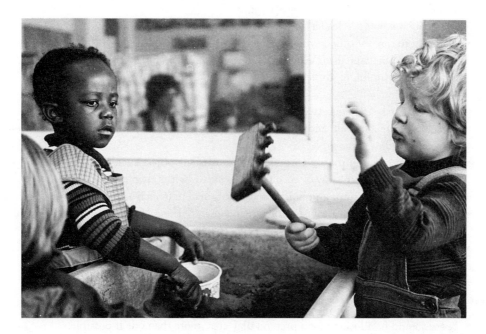

Figure 2.5 Sand play

Pretend play

Activity involved

General role play when children act
  the role of another person

Socio-dramatic play when children in
  groups take on roles and co-operate together

Domestic or house play

Doll play

Pretend play around painful situations such
  as going to the dentist or accommodating
  a new sibling

Advanced fantasy play such as playing
  out stories

Dressing up and pretending

Talking on the play telephone

Puppets

Masks

Small-scale toys such as a car
  track or train set

Development/behaviour/learning encouraged

- Developing an inner 'thought' world through reliving and reorganizing experiences and events.
- Coming to terms with the world around and understanding everyday events, trying out new ideas, practising new words and behaviours in a 'safe', pretend situation.
- Exploring own feelings and experiencing those of others through acting out roles such as mothers or teachers.
- In pretend play, functioning at a more advanced level than would be the case in everyday life.
- Facilitating symbolic and creative thought.
- Experiencing being a 'leader' or person with authority.
- Learning to care for others who are smaller or weaker.
- Developing language using new forms of speech and vocabulary.
- Acting out painful or difficult situations and coming to terms with their own strong emotions.
- Relieving stress and aggressive feelings.
- Developing imagination and fantasy worlds and learning the difference between these and the real world.
- Talking and communicating through an intermediate object such as a telephone or puppet (often a very successful way of encouraging a shy or withdrawn child).
- Early mathematics through grading and sizing materials such as plates or dolls' clothes.
- Early literacy through provision of writing material, e.g. for shopping lists or message-taking, labelling of storage drawers, shelves, play equipment and so forth.
- Co-operative/collaborative play with others and increased social skills.
- Domestic play can help to counteract gender role stereotyping.

Resources/equipment/environment

- Space should be allocated for a pretend play area, more than one if possible.
- Pretend play can be both outdoor and indoor and equipment can be placed outside.

Figure 2.6 Pretend play

- Outdoor areas such as sand pits can become building sites or even ships with a little adult help.
- Pretend play areas such as dens or small corners where children can escape from view and where they feel safe. This enriches language and encourages high quality pretend play.
- Dressing up clothes (should be easily accessible, graded and sized and include a wide variety of everyday clothing such as hats, shawls, trousers, dresses, skirts, saris, shalwar-khamis and so on).
- Other dressing up materials, for example animal or clown costumes or attractive pieces of cloth of all sizes and possibilities.
- Home corners with a wide range of real, yet child-sized equipment from a variety of cultures which acts as a link between home and the care/education environment.
- Material for other pretend play areas such as hairdressers, building sites, garages, offices, hospitals, dentists, clinics, shops.
- A selection of small-scale toys such as garages and cars, road lay outs, train sets, dolls houses.

Construction play

Activity involved

Exploring and experimenting with construction of all types

Making towers, roads, bridges, houses and so forth with blocks

Learning to use Lego™ and similar types of construction toys, at first to familiarize and acquire the technique then actually to make something

Development/behaviour/learning encouraged

- Large and small muscle development.
- Manipulative skills.
- Imaginative use of construction.
- Emotional release (building up and knocking down).
- Sense of achievement.
- Spatial awareness.
- Early mathematics through measuring, lining up, counting, estimating and assessing.
- Design and elements of technology.
- Co-operative play.
- Can help to counteract gender role stereotyping especially for girls.

Figure 2.7 Construction play

Resources/equipment/environment

- Space to use construction. Some should be available at a table, others should be in a safe floor area not used as a passageway. Avoid uncarpeted areas and cover tables with blankets to minimize the potential for noisy play which can disrupt concentration.
- Large construction can take place outdoors, preferably on a safe surface.
- Large and small blocks, wooden or other material, all shapes, colours and sizes.
- Lego™ and similar construction toys.

- Junk.
- Large and small boxes.

Games play

Games playing takes many forms, from simple peek-a-boo or I-Spy through to complex invented games, board games or sports-based games which take place in a playground. Although many modern researchers and practitioners would not agree, according to Piaget and Vygotsky, games with rules are the pinnacle of children's play experience towards which they develop during the pre-school years. In these early years, children learn what rules are, who makes them, how they can be safely broken, and their overall purpose.

Games playing introduces children to their culture, whether it is through playground games which may have their roots in history but have evolved to suit the times, or the highly competitive games which prevail in our culture and suggest to children that to win is all-important. Games imply rules and turn-taking, and in this sense help children to develop socially. Children also have to learn to cope with losing in competitive games but should not be placed in situations with which they cannot cope. Help should be given in a positive manner to children struggling to accept the reality of losing.

Playing board games is usually an enjoyable experience for children and one from which they can learn, or extend and consolidate learning. For example, a learning theme on food may use a simple, home-made board game based on the story of 'The Very Hungry Caterpillar'. Mathematical skills, and concepts such as counting, one-to-one correspondence, matching, seriation and so forth are also part of playing board games such as the above or snakes and ladders or ludo. Children have to learn to cope with losing in competitive board games, and that is why it is often better to make simple, home-made games which can be adapted to ensure that no-one loses in a very destructive manner. Children will, of course, often make their own rules which are kept to in a rather erratic way. Young children will vary in their capacity to lose a game and many will find it very painful.

Messy play

This is an unfortunate title and sometimes leads to a misunderstanding of the value of messy play. Many types of play will come into this category which has a tremendous value for children. Playing with earth, sand and water can be delightfully messy, as can finger painting. Children enjoy playing with cornflour and water or whipped soapflakes and many children spend lengthy periods just feeling and exploring the textures. Messy play allows children to explore through their senses a variety of interesting textures, colours and smells without being thought 'naughty'. Some children find it difficult to enter wholeheartedly into this play for a variety of reasons but they should be given overalls and sensitively encouraged to do so. For example, children vary enormously in their initial reactions to cornflour and water play. Some look at the mixture with suspicion and say 'yuuk'; others delve straight in. Most children enjoy this play and find it tension-releasing, soothing and satisfying. Messy play is particularly important in today's urban environment where children seem surrounded by clinical, dehumanized buildings where cleanliness is valued and there is nothing messy yet safe to explore. Hospital play-workers find safe messy play an important antidote to the extreme version of the above found in a hospital. Children are often worried about being dirty and their own bodily functions and can be highly embarrassed, especially in a hospital setting. Children involved in messy play, touch and explore organic materials, and this seems to help them cope with this kind of urban sensory deprivation.

Super-hero play

Super-hero play (for example, pretending to be Superman or Batman) is common at the nursery/reception stage and usually influenced by watching television. This pretend play is often carried out by boys who perceive themselves as powerful beings taking on the characteristics of their heroes. All that is needed for this play is a piece of material large enough to be tied around the neck as a cape and perhaps some kind of weapon. Although boys particularly enjoy this play, it is very stereotyped and aggressive and usually excludes girls who are portrayed in a rather patronizing and passive manner by these programmes. It is difficult to deal with this and it is almost impossible to discourage it completely; however, attempts should be made to interest boys in other forms of pretend play wherever possible.

Exploratory/experimental play

Young children have an innate curiosity and a fierce determination to explore the world around them. All play should challenge, give first-hand experiences and encourage exploration, discovery and experimentation. With babies and toddlers this is very clear as they go through the stage of 'being into everything'. Their curiosity seems insatiable and they need a constant supply of new and ever more interesting materials to explore. With older children this intense curiosity, although present, is often less obvious. In nursery it can often be seen in, for example, scientific investigative play with mirrors, lenses, circuits, magnifiers, magnets, growing things and keeping pets. Children also enjoy technological investigative play with, for example, windmills or hoists and pulleys, or a table with articles such as old telephones or clocks to dismantle or make up using tools such as screwdrivers. The use of information technology (IT) might also come into this category as many young children are computer-literate and enjoy experimenting with various pieces of software. As children explore and investigate they store away the information and experience gained for later use; the more experiences they have, the more their learning will be generalized to cover other situations and events.

Stages of experience with new materials or objects for play _____

When children explore new materials or objects they first investigate using their senses. This applies to every type of play material and situation including the use of their own bodies and

Figure 2.8 Observing the world outside

other people or children. Babies will look at, listen to, handle and mouth any new object. They will throw it to the ground and watch what happens and repeat/practise the activities over and over again. Through trial and error, much repetition, further exploration and experimentation, children will achieve mastery in the use of various materials, activities and equipment. As they understand the properties of new materials and objects and master the basics in their play, the materials are used in a more controlled manner. Children will elaborate the activity and use it cre-atively as it becomes a commonplace everyday part of their experience. For example, a toddler will explore a cardboard box by looking, touching and watching what others do with it. It may then push the box around, pour juice over it, turn it upside-down and on its side, and push its fingers though a small hole in the side. The toddler may climb inside many times until this can be done without difficulty, and then might use the box as a receptacle for toys which could go in and out of it all day long. After all these uses have been mastered and elaborated upon in play, the box might then become a vehicle for pushing other children around or a bed for a much-loved teddy.

Play tutoring

One of the main features of play is said to be its spontaneity, particularly in pretend play; but it is always important to note who initiates and develops the play. Some children seem much more able to enter into a rich variety of dramatic sequences than others, some of whom need help and encourage-ment. Pretend play is thought to be a vital part of children's experience which has many benefits (see list above). There have been studies which suggest that adult interaction and sensitive intervention in this stimulates, deepens and improves the play (Smith and Sydall, 1978; Sylva *et al.*, 1980). This intervention is often called play tutoring. Some research (e.g. Smilansky, 1968) suggests that there may be social class differences in the quality of pretend play, or that it could be linked with improved creativity, symbolic thought or intelligence (Lieberman, 1977; Singer, 1973). Singer categorized children into those with high fantasy (HF) disposition and those with low fantasy (LF) disposition and found those who were HF were more creative or imaginative. Some of these studies have been criticized as leaving out important factors or being methodologically suspect. Nevertheless it is important for workers with young children to be aware of the central importance of pretend play.

Play tutoring enables adults to assist children in moving on in their play, and modern practice is to intervene sensitively. Workers should develop the ability to 'tune into' the play and expand the activities or concepts through discussion as well as providing a varied and rich range of materials and equipment. This can take the form of offering advice or support outside the play (outside intervention), or involve taking on a role within the play (inside intervention).

| Scenario 3 | There is a mixed-gender group of four children, aged three and four years, playing in the home corner. They have played at serving sandwiches and cakes to each other, clearing the table, and then offering tea. The conversation is sparse and dominated by one girl being a 'Mummy' and saying over and over again 'it's time for dinner'. This same group often plays together in the home corner enacting similar events and seems to have got 'stuck' in their play. |

(a) How could the worker enrich and extend this play?
(b) What new props could be introduced?
(c) What forms of outside or inside intervention could be used?
(d) How could this play be used to extend mathematical concepts?
(e) How could this play be used to develop a multi-cultural perspective?

Equal opportunities

The full range of play experiences should be available to all children and not constrained by stereotypic attitudes toward race, culture, gender or disability (see chapter 1). Workers should be sensitive to children's backgrounds and cultures in their play provision.

The play environment

The play environment should be carefully planned, safe, age/stage appropriate, encouraging, stimulating and interesting with variety of equipment and activity available, at different skill and conceptual levels to offer a challenge. Out of sight is often out of mind with young children, and they will need to be able to see and reach the equipment. Equipment should not be frequently moved or stored in different places as children need to know where to look for things to continue their play from day to day. This is difficult in certain situations where everything has to be packed up after each session, but the general principles can be adhered to.

Thought should be given to carpeting areas where children will be on the floor or where noise needs to be minimized. Play areas should not be used as passageways by other children or adults. Small play spaces and dens should be encouraged within the bounds of safety. It is important to concentrate activity or equipment in general areas within a given space. For example:

- Quiet areas.
- Book areas.
- Graphics areas.
- Messy areas.
- Science areas.
- Pretend play areas.
- Construction areas.
- Table areas for construction, puzzles, creative activity and so on.

All space and room features should be exploited to their best advantage, adjacent corridors should be used where possible. Walls, windows, ceiling beams and partitions can be used for display purposes. Children should have a coat hanger, drawer or storage space which is exclusively theirs and where they can store their creative work or other precious objects in safety.

Bruce (1991) suggests that double provision on such items as sand trays or pretend play areas can facilitate learning by allowing children to play at different levels through varying the provision.

The environment should provide a link between the care/education settings and the child's home. Large, open spaces are threatening at first, as are groups of noisy children. Young children should have places to escape from the hubbub and where there are items which provide a link with home. For example, a home corner should contain dressing up clothes or cooking equipment which reflect the home cultures of all the children and with which they can identify as well as those which extend their immediate experience.

A workshop-style of provision where children are independent and help themselves to materials will facilitate children's choice, rather than adults deciding on what should be available. Where there is an overall curriculum plan, a variety of play materials supporting the plan should be available. Clearing away and storing equipment should be an extension of play, and the children should be clear where things are kept and learn how to keep their environment clean and tidy.

Equipment should be adapted as necessary to enable children with special needs to participate as fully as possible. Sometimes specialist equipment is necessary and available but often a simple adjustment is all that is required: for example, to stabilize table equipment and stop it rolling away when children cannot grasp or reach effectively.

Outdoor play

This can provide a form of double provision and is a good means of extending play. Play should move smoothly from indoor to outside, and the environment planned for continuity. For example, if the theme is 'the seaside' there can be a water tray indoors with water, pretend fish, boats, nets, seaweed made from coloured paper. Outdoors the theme may be continued by creating a 'beach' with sand and water, buckets and spades, rock pools and pebbles.

It is important that children have continuous access to outdoor play and it is not confined to set times and good weather. Children can wear boots and warm clothes and organization can allow for adult supervision in most cases. Outdoor play gives excellent opportunity for vigorous physical play (see above).

Adults' role in promoting play

- To extend and support play.
- To support and 'scaffold' play (see chapters 1 and 3).
- To assess children's play and development and sensitively intervene in order to further the play.
- To supervise and sort out disputes.
- To ensure all children have access to the full range of play facilities regardless of race, gender, disability, cultural or religious factors.
- To provide a safe and healthy play environment.
- To provide a stimulating play environment where choice is maximized.
- To maintain the play environment to an acceptable standard.
- To maintain equipment to an acceptable standard.
- To maintain stocks of consumables and note where and when new equipment will be needed.
- To communicate with parents and other workers concerning children's play and development as appropriate.
- To ensure continuity between indoor and outdoor play.

Assignment 1

Objective   Observe and assess the use of play space and equipment.

Task

1. Draw a rough plan of the play area (indoor and/or outdoor).
2. Observe several children (one at a time) and 'map' their movements on the plan, noting what they are doing and how long they spend at each play activity. Choose the same time of day and a time of 'free play'.
3. Draw on the plan the route the child takes and how long it spends at each activity.
4. Compare your results from different children/ages.

Discussion

(a) Are there certain areas which few children use or cannot easily access?

(b) Are certain children 'flitting' around and not spending time profitably anywhere?

(c) What are popular play areas and why?

(d) Which materials encourage long spells of concentrated play?

(e) How could the equipment and materials be changed to allow more elaborated play?

(f) Can you tell what made each child stop and play?

(g) How could the room layout be improved?

(h) Did the presence of an adult in a particular area cause it to be used more frequently.

Assignment 2

You are training to work with young children in a community playgroup and have in your care the following children:

1. Three-year-old Jason who has difficulty in fine manipulative tasks.

2. Four-year-old Anna who find difficulty settling to any play activity and dislikes getting her hands dirty.

3. Three-and-a-half-year-old Samuel who shows exceptional ability in creative activity.

Discussion

(a) Describe how you would assess each child's skills and abilities.

(b) Describe how you would identify goals for the children.

(c) Devise a play-based programme for each of them to encourage learning and development through play.

Assignment 3

Objectives To extend and elaborate children's pretend play.

Task In consultation with your supervisor and preferably following the interest of the children, look for a way of developing and extending children's pretend play. Building on what is already taking place or introducing a new theme, help to create an environment where children can enjoy exploring new roles and playing together in an exciting and imaginative way.

Discussion

    (a) Discuss how you would introduce the new materials and link with previous or ongoing experience.

    (b) Outline your objectives for individual children and/or the group.

    (c) Carefully observe the children's reactions, language, interactions and behaviour.

    (d) Note how the activity might be developed and extended into other areas of play.

    (e) Review and evaluate the overall results.

Assignment 4

Objective   To promote learning through sensory play.

Task   Bearing in mind health and safety, make a toy or devise a game or activity which will extend a young child's sensory play experience. Provide a description of its potential use, the rationale for your choice and how the toy/game was made.

Discussion   Where possible, discuss the reaction of children with whom you have used the item.

References and further reading

Bruce, T. 1991. *Time to Play in Early Childhood Education*. Sevenoaks: Hodder and Stoughton.

Bruner, J. 1980. *Under Five in Britain: The Oxford Pre-School Research Project*. Oxford: Grant McIntyre/Blackwell.

Cohen, A. and Cohen, L. (eds). 1988. *Early Education: The Pre-School Years*. London: Paul Chapman.

Donaldson, M. 1978. *Children's Minds*. London: Collins/Fontana.

Garvey, C. 1977. *Play*. London: Collins/Fontana Open Books.

Isaacs, S. 1950. *Intellectual Growth in Young Children*. London: Routledge and Kegan Paul.

Lieberman, J.N. 1977. *Playfulness: Its Relationship to Imagination and Creativity*. New York: Academic Press.

Matterson, E. 1989. *Play with a Purpose for Under Sevens*. Harmondsworth: Penguin.

Moyles, J. 1989. *Just Playing? The Role and Status of Play in Early Childhood Education*. Milton Keynes: Open University Press.

Newsom, J. and Newsom, E. 1970. *Four Years Old in an Urban Community*. Harmondsworth: Pelican.

Piaget, J. 1962. *Play, Dreams and Imitation in Childhood*. London: Routledge and Kegan Paul.

Singer, J.L. 1973. *The Child's World of Make Believe*. New York: Academic Press.

Singer, D.G. and J.L. 1990. *The House of Make Believe*. London: Harvard University.

Smilansky, S. 1968. *The Effects of Socio-dramatic Play on Disadvantaged Pre-school Children*. New York: Wiley.

Smith, P.K. and Sydall, S. 1978. 'Play and non-play tutoring in pre-school children', *Child Development*, **48**: 315–29.

Sylva, K., Roy, C. and Painter, M. 1980. *Childwatching at Playgroup and Nursery School. Oxford Pre-school Research Project*. Oxford: Grant McIntyre/Blackwell.

Winnitcott, D.W. 1971. *Playing and Reality*. London: Tavistock (reprinted 1974 by Penguin Books, Harmondsworth).

Chapter 3
Curriculum in the
early years

Introduction _____

The term curriculum is widely used but often means different things to different people. In this chapter we take our definition of curriculum to include all the activities, interactions and experiences from which young children learn within the broad range of settings where they receive care and education. This may be within or outside the home, in formal or informal settings, and will include the use of their environment and daily care routine as aspects of curriculum. It is also important to acknowledge that all aspects of a child's experiences will have some learning component and the early curriculum is not just that which is structured, formalized and written down or planned. With such a wide definition of 'curriculum' this chapter can only provide a brief overview of the ideas behind the provision, and the likely interpretation by practitioners. References and ideas for further reading are provided at the end of the chapter.

The early years curriculum must be very closely related to a child's sequence and stage of development and should be viewed in a holistic manner as young children do not perceive the world in separate chunks based on traditional subjects such as mathematics or science. For example, counting and sorting the dessert spoons and making sure each person has one includes several concepts: one-to-one correspondence, shape and size recognition, classification, counting and so on. In the context of setting the table for lunch there is a recognizable informal mathematics learning experience, but this is also likely to include language development through mathematics talk and social development through sharing the task and working with other children or adults.

Although the child's chronological age may not match its stage of development, it is frequently the former which dictates the types of activities, experiences and environment offered by those giving care and education. It is important to recognize that children do vary widely in their development and individual needs; differences and prior experiences should always be taken into account in determining the curriculum provided for individual children.

On the basis of convenience, the chapter looks at curriculum over three broad stages:

1. Children 3–5 years (nursery/reception stage)
2. Children 5–8 years (national curriculum stage)
3. Babies and toddlers 0–3 years

Figure 3.1 Starting a movement session in school

Approaches to the curriculum

Many well known historical figures in the world of philosophy and education have influenced the curriculum in Britain today, not least amongst whom are Margaret McMillan, Friedrich Froebel, Rudolph Steiner and Maria Montessori. The highly influential work of Piaget on children's development has been discussed in chapter 1 and can be seen as directly applicable to the early years curriculum. The work of other psychologists and researchers such as Bruner and Vygotsky also has relevance to the curriculum.

Approaches to the curriculum will depend on the philosophy and training of every person involved in providing care and education for young children. There are many different viewpoints which have contributed over the years to a particular view of children and their learning and development. During the 1960s and 1970s the main function of nursery education was thought to be the prevention of later educational failure, especially on the part of working-class and ethnic-minority children, by giving them enriched early experiences which it was thought they were unlikely to receive at home. Today it is generally felt that good practice will provide a curriculum which incorporates and uses in a positive way the children's own cultural and educational experiences from their homes and community.

Modern views on curriculum

The curriculum offered to young children in most mainstream settings generally works from a basis of commonly accepted principles, although these may vary in detail. Many of these principles have been taken from earlier theoretical viewpoints and have incorporated the research from developmental psychologists and others. The curriculum has also had to respond to political and social pressures, with governments and politicians varying in their approaches to the teaching of parts of the curriculum such as reading and mathematics and attempting to influence how these are taught. For example, emphasis on science and technology in the National Curriculum reflects the government's concern that children will become better equipped to develop new ideas and technologies appropriate for the twenty-first century. However, in general, workers with young children have stood out against so-called reforms or pressures which are designed to over-formalize the curriculum and which do not take into account the development of the child.

Often there is a lack of understanding of the aims and goals of the early years curriculum. It is important to recognize that, for some, nursery education is 'just playing' so it is vital to ensure that the curriculum content and method of delivery which is closely linked to the development of the child are clearly understood by practitioners, parents and other carers. This in turn requires all workers with young children to be able to understand and justify the curriculum they offer in both educational and developmental terms.

The spiral curriculum

It can be helpful to consider the concept of the spiral curriculum (Bruner, 1977). At the heart of this concept is the notion that 'any subject can be taught to any child at any age in some form that is honest'. This means that the basic themes at the centre of mathematics, science, literature etc. can be within the reach of any child at an appropriate level for their stage of development. Bruner has further developed these ideas to say that if what we offer children does not have within it possibilities for future learning, it should be considered to be unhelpful 'clutter'. In assessing the early years curriculum it is an interesting exercise to view the activities and experiences traditionally offered to children at this stage and assess whether or not they are laying the foundations for future learning. It is not always obvious that children cooking are laying foundations for understanding physics and chemistry, or that classifying through sorting and matching objects is a prerequisite for higher-order mathematical thinking. Equally, there are traditions in care and education which may not meet Bruner's criteria. For example, adult-centred 'creative' activity, designed and presented to please adults, by adults and where the children play a peripheral role such as repetitively sticking one pre-cut shape onto another.

The hidden curriculum

This term is used to refer to aspects of our provision through which a child may learn attitudes, values, stereotypes and behaviour which may or may not be those which are generally considered beneficial and positive for themselves or others. This 'hidden' curriculum is concerned with the indirect messages children receive concerning themselves and others. For example, workers may indirectly reinforce sexism by valuing a quiet submissive attitude in girls whilst encouraging the boys to be noisy and boisterous. Toys, games, books and equipment often show white, middle-class boys taking active dominant roles with girls and black children taking a more passive, secondary role. How we view or judge children and our own attitudes and prejudices will be reflected to some extent in our dealings with them, often in ways which are quite unconscious. It is important that workers with young children do examine their own values and attitudes to ensure that they can see where the 'hidden' curriculum is active. If this is not taken seriously, conscious or unconscious discrimination may block children's full access to the formal early years curriculum. Although there are still many parts of the country where there may not be representatives of different ethnic groups, recognition that we live in a multi-cultural, multi-lingual, pluralist society and the need to promote a positive world-view should be integrated throughout the curriculum, and efforts should be made to ensure that all children receive positive images of themselves.

The following are examples of ways in which workers can check whether or not they are providing a non-sexist curriculum or whether aspects of sexism creep in under a 'hidden' curriculum.

- Do you use gender specific descriptions of people's jobs such as 'fireman', 'waitress', 'policeman', 'postman'?
- Do you have story books that depict people in non-stereotypical jobs?
- Do you encourage both boys and girls to use the bicycles and outdoor equipment?
- Do you discourage boys from activities such as dressing up or playing in the home corner?
- Do you intervene if boys are dominating the wheeled toys in the outdoor area?
- What is your reaction if you find a boy playing with a doll?
- What is your reaction to boys when they are crying?

- What is your reaction when a boy dresses up in female clothes from the dressing-up corner?

Naima-Browne and Pauline France (1986) offer practical ways of dispelling the myths attached to some areas of play. For example, the idea that boys do not like playing in the home corner and that it is really a female domain is usually due to staff discouraging boys from this type of play.

It has been argued by feminists that the very existence of a home corner only succeeds in reinforcing gender roles at an early stage, but this could be said about other activities such as riding bicycles, cooking, hospital corners and so forth. it is not the activity that is at fault but the attitudes of adults who label activities as 'for boys' or 'for girls'. In many instances adults need to encourage girls and boys to try out new activities in order that they may broaden their experience and develop new skills.

When children start in playgroup or nursery they are likely to be entrenched in the role that goes with their gender from their early experiences at home. In our society we still associate blue with boys and pink with girls and buy toys and clothes according to gender. This prevents children developing according to the individual interests and personal strengths, which may contrast sharply with their gender stereotype. Although staff should not be in open conflict with the child's family, opportunities will occur for children to participate in activities which might normally be denied them. This will extend and develop their learning.

Scenario 1	In a nursery school home corner two four-year-old boys have dressed up in a variety of hats, scarves, skirts and waistcoats. One is busy filling up a handbag with small items from the kitchen. A small group of boys of the same age dressed as 'super-heroes' approach and start to comment and whisper together. As they move away a parting comment from one is 'you're a girl', spoken with the intention of offering an insult.
	(a) Would you intervene in this situation?
	(b) If you do intervene, how would you deal with each set of boys?
	(c) What do you think is the underlying learning influencing the attitudes of the 'super-heroes'?
	(d) What messages are the boys playing in the home corner receiving?

| Scenario 2 | A new day nursery worker in a predominantly white, middle-class suburban area becomes concerned because the nursery provides no material, equipment or activities which portray children from other ethnic or linguistic groups in a positive manner. She had noticed that many of the children's books were both sexist and racist. |

(a) Why should she be concerned?
(b) What are the possible reasons for this situation?
(c) Devise a strategy she might use to mention her concerns to her supervisor.
(d) What practical changes might be introduced to remedy the situation in three areas of provision? Provide a rationale for your suggested changes.

Figure 3.2 Girl at the woodwork bench

Example of research findings

Research findings often affect the early years curriculum. An example of some recent work is that of Chris Athey (1990) who suggests that children who were displaying often unconnected behaviour in the nursery situation were in fact working on a closely defined series of schema. These are 'patterns of repeatable and generalizable actions which can be applied to objects or events', and the work draws on Piaget's original conception. Athey has identified many schema and named them according to their characteristics. These activities are repeated over and over again by children using different equipment and materials but with the same underlying theme. Children are motivated to develop their schema which develop from the 'doing' or motor level through to internalized thought. Examples of schema may be:

- Transportation – when the child constantly moves objects from place to place.
- Enclosure – the child builds enclosures with Lego™ or bricks, or in paintings.
- Rotation – the child is absorbed by things which turn, such as cogs and wheels.

Athey suggests that children have particular schematic interests at different times and that the curriculum should reflect a child's current interest. If this is the case, workers will have to observe, identify, assess and extend schematic experience and make provision accordingly. This view of children's cognitive development could influence the nursery curriculum profoundly and encourage a move away from traditional content-centred provision to that based on schema recognition which looks at 'how' children do things rather than what they do. It is an example of how important it is to continue research into the development of the child in the early years.

Characteristics of the early years curriculum

- The curriculum should start from the child's needs and interests. It does not mean that there is no planning or overall strategy, but rather the reverse. Careful planning and evaluation of the curriculum takes place with consideration of the needs of all the children and their age/stage of development, often on an individualized basis. Where children show aptitude or interest which is outside the formal plan, there is sufficient flexibility to incorporate change and include further challenge.
- The curriculum recognizes the importance of this period of a child's life and values it as important in itself, as well as a preparation for school or adult life.
- The curriculum should be broad and balanced. The Educational Reform Act 1988 emphasizes the need for a curriculum which 'promotes the spiritual, moral, cultural, mental and physical development of pupils at the school and of society, and prepares such pupils for the opportunities, responsibilities and experiences of adult life.' This means that the curriculum must consider the needs of the whole child in a balanced way, and should not be narrowly based on traditional academic subjects. At the same time the subject-based National Curriculum must be considered.
- The curriculum should take into account how children learn and the developmental needs of young children and should avoid too much formal learning before young children are able to cope. Comment has been made (HMI, 1989) that 'there is often insufficient exploratory and

practical work to support the children's developing understanding of ideas and language before they start out on the formal work more appropriate to later stages of learning.'

- The curriculum should recognize that play is the best way to integrate and facilitate all aspects of a child's learning.
- The curriculum should emphasize the process of learning, whether skills, concepts or knowledge, rather than the products of learning such as paintings or models which might be evaluated against an adult perception of what is 'correct'.
- The curriculum should be integrated as far as possible and not presented as separate subjects all of the time. In some instances this is not appropriate, e.g. when learning particular mathematical concepts these may need to be taught in a more formal way and the learning backed up with a range of related activities. Learning in the early years often involves working with projects or themes which integrate many aspects of the curriculum.
- The daily care routines such as bath or meal times, visits to the clinic or hairdresser offer security to the child and can all be considered part of the curriculum, presenting important learning opportunities.
- Equality of opportunity for all children regardless of social, cultural, linguistic or ethnic origin, gender or disability should be a central feature which is reflected in materials, activities, resources and staffing. This is necessary go give all children equal access to the whole curriculum.
- Parents and significant people in a child's life should be encouraged to participate in the delivery and planning of the curriculum. The child's experiences within the curriculum should complement, extend and involve their home and community life.
- There should be continuity and progression between classes, schools, nurseries and playgroups concerning the curriculum on offer.
- Children should be recognized and treated as individuals within their own social context which should be reflected and enhanced within the curriculum, affirming them as valued and unique.

Contemporary views of the child as learner

- There are stages in children's development when they are more sensitive to certain types of skill or concept acquisition, and the curriculum offered should match these stages.
- Children's learning does not 'just happen'. Methods such as discovery learning have their place but modern research indicates a need for adults to structure the learning environment carefully and to provide for direct learning experience.
- Children learn largely through play, and the curriculum should offer a balance between structured or spontaneous 'free' play. Play should be pleasurable and, to gain the maximum in terms of learning, needs to be carefully structured and extended within a framework of individual choice.
- Children learn best through direct experience, handling, exploring through their senses, solving problems, rather than through 'being told'.
- Children's learning is facilitated by their use of language which should be a central aspect of the curriculum.

- Children's learning should be founded on what is familiar to them and build on their individual experience and social and cultural context.
- Children need time to explore and consider in order to produce work of quality, and the time taken will vary amongst individuals. Time is necessary to practise and refine skills; children should not be rushed.
- Children are intrinsically motivated to learn and to explore their environment, their curiosity should be harnessed and utilized by early years workers when planning and implementing the curriculum, not stifled through a rigid and unimaginative regime.
- Children learn best in a secure environment where adults make clear the boundaries for acceptable behaviour and are consistent in their handling of the various conflict situations which arise, and where praise and encouragement are freely and appropriately given. Self-discipline is the goal for children rather than a rigidly imposed set of rules and regulations with which the child has to conform without any basic understanding of why.
- Children who do not have their basic needs met, or who have suffered loss of self-esteem through poverty, abuse, disadvantage or discrimination will find it more difficult to learn and take advantage of opportunities offered to them.

The adult's role in the delivery of the curriculum

- The adult should provide a safe, stimulating and caring environment. This environment should be carefully planned and organized in order to maximize learning opportunities.
- The adult should view the environment and curriculum from the child's perspective and assess how much is simply cosmetic and adult-centred and how much is relevant and accessible for the child.
- The adult should adopt an active role in promoting learning, creativity and development and in the provision of suitable resources and environment both indoors and outdoors. This active role should include supporting and at first directing a child's learning.
- The day-to-day routines and activities should encourage a child's independence of thought and action. The adult should enable the child to take ownership of the environment and feel confident in everyday activity. Through their increasing autonomy and sense of control, children will develop confidence, self-control and enhanced self-esteem.
- The interactions, both non-verbal and verbal, between adult and child are vital and should be of high quality, extending the child's language and thinking.
- Children's learning should be facilitated by careful assessment of their progress and the extension of learning through increased demands and greater challenges. This means workers start where the child is and with what they can do, and build on this rather than concentrating on what the child cannot do.
- Detailed individual records should be kept based on observations of children and assessment of their future needs.
- Adults need a deep knowledge of child development in order to observe and identify children's needs and special needs. They also require a wide range of skills and knowledge including interpersonal skills.

Figure 3.3 Curriculum Delivery can be Formal or Informal

Scenario 3

Imagine a typical class of thirty or forty years ago. Young children are admitted into a large class of perhaps forty other children with one teacher. The day starts at 9 a.m. and parents are not allowed into the school. The desks are arranged in rows, there are few if any toys or playthings, although there are crayons and pencils for drawing, and occasionally paints or modelling materials are allowed.

The morning begins with a formal assembly, followed by a strict timetable of subjects. For example, writing followed by number work where the children are expected to count on their fingers or in their head and then to write down when they are able.

After playtime they might have P.E. followed by nature study. This might involve planting bulbs and putting them in a dark cupboard, or drawing flowers and trees.

After dinner some of the younger children are given a bed to rest on, whether or not they feel tired. Every day they are given vitamin capsules and made to drink their milk.

Afternoon school consists of further subject periods such as reading, history or geography before going home at 3.45 or 4 p.m.

In the light of the information given in this chapter, your own reading and experience, give a short critique of this type of provision. Allowing for lack of resources in those days but utilizing modern views on children's learning, discuss in outline what measures could have been taken immediately to improve the situation?

Other versions of the early years curriculum _____

The High/Scope Curriculum

The High/Scope Curriculum is derived from work with deprived children and families which took place in the USA during the 1960s and 1970s (Hohman *et al.*, 1979). These programmes involved work with parents and were designed to prepare children for school and to maximize future school success. The results of these programmes have been monitored and it is thought that they are effective in the long term in improving children' performance and life chances.

The High/Scope Curriculum involves a highly structured approach to children's learning and reflects much good nursery practice. Working on the premise that children are active learners who learn best from activities they plan and carry out themselves, the session is organized so that children engage in a plan–do–review sequence. The children are notified in advance if the routine is going to vary.

Through careful assessment of the children, developmental programmes based on 'key experiences' are devised for each child. These incorporate adult–child communication and teaching strategies, parental partnership, and detailed record-keeping. Criticism of the High/Scope Curriculum is centred around the tight structure, but there are many useful insights into effective work with children through use of the programme.

Montessori and other highly structured programmes

Maria Montessori (1869–1952)

Maria Montessori was a doctor who worked in Italy during the early part of the twentieth century. She viewed the development of children as a biological programme and believed that children go through sensitive periods in their development when they are more receptive to learning various skills and concepts.

The method involved providing a series of activities, carefully graded from simple to complex and within a planned environment, through which every child must proceed. Children were thought to learn from their own spontaneous activities and, within this highly structured environment, they were encouraged to work alone with the materials presented to them. Although Montessori did consider the whole child, she approached learning and development by concentrating on encouraging separate sensory experiences, and when the relevant learning had taken place she considered that it could be generalized to cover other situations.

There has been much criticism of the Montessori approach with its emphasis on formal work. It is thought to stifle creativity and as there is so little interaction, it does not encourage language development and social skills. Major criticisms are that the child is encouraged to work individually, there is little direct parental involvement and the role of the adult (directress) is limited as the child has a 'teacher within himself'. However, there are variants on the traditional Montessori approach which place emphasis in slightly different ways. In spite of this, aspects of her work are still useful today. The equipment she developed to encourage children's intellectual and sensory development has been modified and is widely used today, and her view of the child as an active, autonomous thinker is also encouraged, although not necessarily by the methods she used.

Other highly structured programmes usually follow particular theories of how children develop, and consist of structured, sequential education activities which are thought to stimulate the child's cognitive and language development. The programmes do seem to have achieved a measure of success in that limited area, and are usually taught in specialist centres and privately funded through fees paid by parents, although they can take the form of postal lessons. Attitudes behind such programmes can be elitist and build on parents' anxieties to give their child the best possible start by providing sometimes misleading or biased information about how children learn.

Criticism of these types of programmes will vary accordingly but often centres around their apparent concentration on intellectual development rather than considering the whole child. Also, the tight structure gives little opportunity for creativity, social interaction, decision-making and problem-solving.

The curriculum for babies and toddlers

Very young babies show a need to be competent and to master their own world. This gives them confidence and high self-esteem. They need to link their interaction with the environment to a change or response in that environment. In other words, they learn that what they do is effective and can change things for them in a positive way. This can range from crying because they are hungry or uncomfortable and being attended to promptly, to swiping at a pram toy and hearing it rattle or seeing it swing at their command. If their attempts to interact or communicate bring little or no response from people or objects, they receive the message that they are helpless and powerless and that response is pointless. This has important long-term effects on their feelings about themselves and about learning. Parents or carers of babies and toddlers often find it difficult to recognize that they are in fact providing a learning curriculum for them. This curriculum involves the routines, activities, interactions, equipment and materials used and the opportunities for learning which are given and stresses the interrelatedness of education and care.

Bruner (1975) found three important features of parents/carers interactions with their babies and young children. These were:

1. Parents are sensitive to their children's needs as learners.
2. Parents provide a flexible framework or scaffold where children can learn.
3. Parents follow the conversational initiatives of their children in a meaningful way.

Bruner found that most of this learning took place in informal interactions and routines such as bathtimes and games such as 'round and round the garden'. These routines, with their repetitive nature, allow children to learn and to talk about regular events that make up their lives, and parents gradually extend this behaviour as they see the child making progress. Bruner adopted the image of a scaffold erected by adults to support a child's learning, which occurs little by little. Eventually the scaffold can be removed and the child has achieved competence. This is important in terms of the curriculum offered to the under-threes which should utilize everyday activities and routines to support learning. The importance of the interaction with the adult cannot be stressed enough, and every opportunity should be used sensitively; careful assessment of the child should reveal when they are ready to move on.

Figure 3.4 Young children playing and exploring

Treasure basket and heuristic play

Research has revealed that very young babies are highly curious and motivated to learn (Goldschmeid, 1989) and shows that babies as young as six months enjoy 'treasure basket' play. This involves them selecting from a basket, handling and mouthing a series of safe everyday, natural (not plastic) objects which are new and interesting such as shells, fir cones, apples, lemons, metal objects such as spoons, items made of wood, leather, rubber, textile or fur. Babies show amazing powers of concentration, but their lack of mobility means they cannot retrieve dropped objects until they have become more mobile. The explorations are facilitated by attentive but not intrusive adults. This type of activity increases not only their manipulative skills and sensory learning, but also, where two or three sit at the treasure basket together, their social learning.

Goldschmeid has identified 'heuristic' play which can occur during the second year of life and is linked with increasing mobility. Children at this stage are constantly putting objects in and out of a container, filling and emptying it. To satisfy children at this stage requires a wide variety of different objects (not toys) with which they will develop and expand their skill. To facilitate this play, adults need to provide quantities of items similar to those used in the treasure basket but which are kept in bags. A set period of time is needed for toddlers to use these, usually about one hour several times a week.

Curriculum for 3–5 year olds

This stage covers the time that many children begin to enter some type of early years provision through to their first year in the reception class at school. Ideally, this period of care and education should not involve any major changes in approach as children enter school but should be characterized by continuity and progression.

The type of curriculum offered before the reception class will depend on the setting. Different settings will vary not only in their staffing and resources but in their emphasis. For example, playgroups have a high degree of parental involvement and a great emphasis on play. Some nursery schools or classes will have much less emphasis on both these aspects and perhaps include a more structured curriculum for the rising fives. However, good practice in all settings and stages will involve careful planning and structuring of an informal curriculum usually based on play. This curriculum should incorporate the principles outlined above.

Four year olds in school

In recent years there has been a tendency to admit children into the reception class soon after their fourth birthday. This was partly as a result of falling school roles, partly a cheap alternative to nursery education and partly reflects the concern that summer-born children had been shown to perform less well academically than those born during the rest of the year who were receiving a longer infant education. This has led to considerable concern, as in some cases children have been plunged into a highly formal and structured environment which is quite unsuitable for their needs (NFER/SCDC, 1987). In part this is a response to parental pressures for their children to begin to learn the three 'R's, but also reflects in some cases inadequate training of staff and poor staffing levels.

Recent advice to schools has been that the numbers in classes containing under-fives should be restricted and that ancillary help, preferably with qualifications such as NNEB, should be employed. However, there is still a problem in many reception classes as there is a shortage of early years specialists and local authorities will not or cannot afford to implement real and effective change.

The National Curriculum

The National Curriculum aims to provide for all children between five and sixteen years an education which incorporates a broad range of subjects and promotes the development of personal and social skills. It is hoped that this curriculum will meet the needs of all children and encourage them to do the best they can as well as informing parents about their child's education and progress. The National Curriculum consists of ten subjects which all children must study at school. These are:

English	Geography
Mathematics	Music
Science	Art
Technology	Physical Education
History	A modern foreign language for 11–16 year olds

These subjects are called foundation subjects, and English, mathematics and science are also known as core subjects as they help children to study everything else.

For each foundation subject there will be learning objectives setting out what children should know and be able to do at each stage of their schooling. These are called 'attainment targets'. Descriptions of what children should be taught in order to achieve attainment targets are called 'programmes of study'.

At the time of writing, it is planned to assess children at ages 7, 11, 14 and 16 against the attainment targets and this has already begun. These assessments are called 'standard assessment tasks' (SATs) and, together with teacher assessments, should provide information for staff about where children may need extra help. However, because the National Curriculum is still not fully implemented and is continually developing, all this is subject to change.

There are four stages for different age groups known as 'key stages':

- Key stage 1 from 5 to 7.
- Key stage 2 from 7 to 11.
- Key stage 3 from 11 to 14.
- Key stage 4 from 14 to 16.

Effect on the early years curriculum

As children in key stage 1 are following the early years curriculum it is important that the principles of good practice for this stage of development are fully incorporated into the National Curriculum. So far, this does not seem to have been a problem as the National Curriculum Council has taken a flexible and positive approach to this age group. The main problem seems to centre on the SATs, as staff have found these cumbersome and time-consuming to apply. At present, further development work is taking place and change is occurring all the time.

Examples of how National Curriculum attainment targets can be incorporated into the on-going classroom work in years 1 and 2 can be found in many new textbooks for schools.

National Curriculum core subjects as part of the early years curriculum

Early literacy (National Curriculum 'English')

This is a very important area of children's learning. The early years curriculum will encompass the four modes of language, i.e. speaking, listening, reading, writing. Workers in care and education need to take every opportunity to encourage children to communicate and should practise active listening in order to understand properly what children are attempting to say. A crucial area of learning and experience is the use of stories and rhymes which help to introduce children to the world of symbols and ideas which underpin much future learning.

Babies and toddlers

Talking and listening games should be used from the first days of a baby's life with time given to gain eye contact and allow the baby to respond. Songs, rhymes, stories, laughter, lively and expressive conversation should feature strongly during these early months and years, with one-to-one interaction being the most important feature.

Figure 3.5 Reading together

Pre-school and reception children

Most children starting at nursery or playgroup can speak and listen very well in their home language but there will be considerable variation according to previous experience, abilities or special needs including bilingualism. Although at this stage there will still be an emphasis on talking, communicating and listening, both on a one-to-one basis and in small groups, early reading and writing skills and other forms of representation are also being developed. It is important that early years practitioners involve parents in what they are doing and discuss why it is appropriate for children of this age. For children who do not speak the language of the setting it is necessary to obtain appropriate support, wherever possible including using parents and community resources. Development of the home language should be encouraged as well as the use of English.

Early writing can be encouraged through the provision of a writing workshop or graphics area where tools and materials are left for the children to explore and/or use with adult helpers. Other opportunities for the children to 'write' could be shopping pads in the home corner, telephone message pads and so forth. Painting, creative work and the development of manipulative skills and hand–eye co-ordination through a whole range of nursery activities helps with the development of writing. Children's early attempts should be explored and discussed with them, and as they develop greater skill they will copy shapes and letters, their own name and so forth. When they enter formal school these activities will become more structured and formalized, but only as the children are able to cope.

Early or emergent reading is helped by encouraging children to understand that print has meaning. This can be done in many ways, for example labelling in the nursery or looking at the print in the environment when outside the nursery or through books and stories especially real life 'home-made' books that feature the children or may be their own stories written down. Children often enjoy pretend 'reading' to each other and this should be encouraged. Success in reading is linked to being read to or told stories, and this is an important part of the curriculum. In many nurseries parents are encouraged to borrow books to take home to read to their children. More formal reading skills should be encouraged as the individual child is ready. There are different ways in which children are taught to read and teachers will use a variety of methods. Some will use structured reading schemes which children have to work through, others use 'real' books which are thought to be more relevant and interesting to children. Some teachers use 'look and say' which involves children in whole word recognition often linked to pictures, other will use phonics which help children to interpret written words by building up from individual sounds. In practice, many teachers will use a variety of different approaches based on the individual child and its needs.

Figure 3.6 A story-telling session by Beulah Candappa at Cherry Orchard School

Scenario 4	You are working as a nursery nurse in a reception class with a group of four-year-olds, many of whom are lively and anxious to learn and explore. The children are offered a full and interesting curriculum, and the class is well resourced and staffed. The parent of a bright four-year-old complains to you that all her child ever does is play, he never brings home any paintings or creative work, his home reading books are too easy and he is just wasting his time. She wants him to get on with some 'real' work such as maths or writing, for which she thinks he is more than ready. You are concerned about this and discuss it with the class teacher.

    (a) Does the parent have a point?

    (b) What would be an appropriate form of action to take?

    (c) How could you explain to this parent that her child was gaining valuable experience and developing skills in these areas of learning?

    (d) Justify three areas of provision which assist in the development of reading and writing.

Early numeracy

Mathematics learning is not just about numbers and counting, but about sorting and grouping, spatial relationships, patterns, problem-solving and understanding that words and symbols convey ideas of quantity. The child is surrounded by mathematical ideas and relationships in the everyday world and adults should take every opportunity to develop these concepts, particularly through discussion and the use of mathematical language. Terms such as 'how much', 'none', 'lots', or 'how many' in practical situations convey ideas of number or volume from the earliest years. Counting the plates at meal times or the number of steps to the front door are valuable routine experiences for children which reinforce numeracy. There are many number songs, finger plays and rhymes which teach children about number in an informal and pleasurable way.

In the pre-school/reception stage, children will be talking about weight and volume as well as classifying materials by colour, shape or other features. The language of mathematics and conceptual development will become more sophisticated as the children are ready and many young children will, for example, weigh out flour for cooking very precisely and understand the need for accuracy.

Many of the practical activities in the nursery will develop mathematics and science concepts, and it is important that these are recognized and used. For example, the home corner will provide opportunities for children to estimate the size of dolls' clothes. The construction area will allow children to explore size, shape and spatial relations. Water and sand play develop ideas concerning volume and density.

Parents and others should be encouraged to understand that in many ways young children are tied to the concrete world of their own experience and sensory learning. Children will move on to deal with more abstract and symbolic number as and when they are ready. It is not appropriate for children to be given formal written mathematics work until they have grasped many basic concrete concepts and staff should be sensitive to where an individual child has developed. In this way children can be encouraged to deal competently with mathematics.

Teachers use a variety of techniques to teach numeracy skills and concepts. They may use workbooks or cards and have an area of the room devoted to mathematics learning, but it is likely that mathematical concepts will also be integrated in a carefully structured way throughout all the curriculum activities.

Early science

Children are interested in the natural world and how things around them work, from a very young age. They enjoy experimenting and exploring, for example mixing earth and water or playing with insects and worms. They are fascinated with the technological world around and can be very sophisticated in their use of computers and calculators. The simple use of magnets, mirrors, or batteries and circuits lay important foundations for understanding the physical world.

The science curriculum should build on children's experiences and interests in the everyday world. As well as using these events, experiments can be carefully set up by adults to stimulate interest, and children should be encouraged to observe closely, discuss and perhaps draw or paint what they see. The introduction or changing of one element in an activity, such as the addition of cocoa powder to colour a cake mixture in a simple cooking activity, introduces another variable and this forms the basis of scientific investigation (what will happen if...?). Planting seeds or bulbs can teach children about the sequence of events in nature and the cycles of growth and development.

Good practice with young children has for many years involved activities which are basically scientific, but which have not been recognized or called science. All work which contains elements of observation, investigation, experimentation, and eliciting ideas and hypotheses from children is likely to have a substantial science component. Workers with young children need to develop confidence in their scientific or technological abilities and to recognize where these can be used and developed.

Figure 3.7 Games with magnets

Organization and environment

The organization of the learning environment means the organization of the total environment for the child. This will depend to some extent on the particular individual situations where children receive care and education. Some situations will be well staffed and resourced, whereas others will be chronically under-funded and in difficult physical circumstances. For example, some inner city or, by contrast, isolated rural playgroups do fine work under very difficult circumstances which often involves removing displays after every session and packing up all the play equipment after usage when using a multi-purpose hall. For those such as childminders or nannies offering full day care and education there are constraints on the usage of the environment. It is not always possible to have messy play areas available every day or regular access to high quality outdoor experiences. However, good organization underpins good practice and frees adults and children to concentrate on the activity or experience without distraction. There are certain basic principles (outlined below) which should wherever possible govern our provision:

- Health and safety are always the first considerations.
- The environment should foster the all-round development of the child.
- Children should be given maximum space and freedom to explore and discover.
- Rooms are divided where possible into areas, well defined by screens, shelves or walls but with doors or openings for children and adults to see within. This encourages children to concentrate and to talk to each other as well as reducing noise. Separate areas may be for messy play, sand and water, quiet areas for using books or puzzles, science and exploration, garden, construction, domestic play, music, imaginative and so forth.
- Provision of a workshop-style environment where adults actively facilitate rather than instruct or do not intervene at all, will encourage learning and should be adopted wherever appropriate. There will, of course, be times when it is necessary to adopt a more formal approach, and sufficient flexibility should allow for this.
- Separate areas are carefully sited in a logical manner, designed to integrate learning and to facilitate easy access. It is also important to discourage through-traffic (other children or adults going from one place to another) and to make the best use of basic facilities such as sinks and other fixtures.
- Flooring is appropriate for the type of area usage.
- Work areas have adequate numbers of child-sized tables and chairs, and children are encouraged not to crowd in.
- Wherever possible, indoor and outdoor play areas should be planned together so that children's activity continues naturally from one to the other. Access to outdoors should not be restricted to certain times and seasons.
- Displays are at child height as far as possible and should involve items which can be handled and explored.
- Children have their own storage space, coat hanger, table mat, flannel, toothbrush, towel and so forth.

- Presentation and preparation of the environment should be attractive to the children, equipment well cared for, and items such as junk carefully sorted and stored.
- Animals should be cleaned regularly and shown respect and care.
- The environment should consider children with special needs and provide for physical, or sensory impairment and children with learning difficulties.
- Good organization derives from good planning, and written plans should be available for adults to use.
- Organization should allow the child time for reflection, prioritizing, forward-planning and predicting.
- Children should be encouraged to work collaboratively.
- Clearing up routines should be used as learning events.

Materials and equipment

- A wide and balanced range of materials should be available and easily seen and reached by the child, all equipment should be child-sized.
- Materials and equipment to promote all types of learning and development should always be available; this applies particularly to basic materials such as sand and water.
- Materials, activities and equipment reflect positive images to all children and actively promotes and uses cultural and linguistic diversity.
- Material and equipment allow for extension and progression of children's learning.
- Equipment and materials are arranged so that children are encouraged to help themselves and do not have continually to depend on adults.
- Tool, equipment and context should be 'real' wherever possible.
- Sets of sized items such as dolls' clothes are hung up or displayed in ways which demonstrate size differences.
- Equipment and materials are labelled and stored in the same place so that children know where to find and replace them and wherever possible kept where they are used. This can be facilitated by providing templates on the storage surfaces for children to match, photographs or colour coding of item. Identical or similar items are best stored close together.

Planning the curriculum

Areas of learning

The National Curriculum has imposed a structure for 5–7 year olds which covers a range of subjects. As a result, curriculum planning must incorporate these but in a way which is meaningful for children of this age. The need for continuity means that it is important that the curriculum for younger children should reflect these general areas but does not move away from the principles behind good practice outlined earlier. Staff working with young children should be broadly familiar

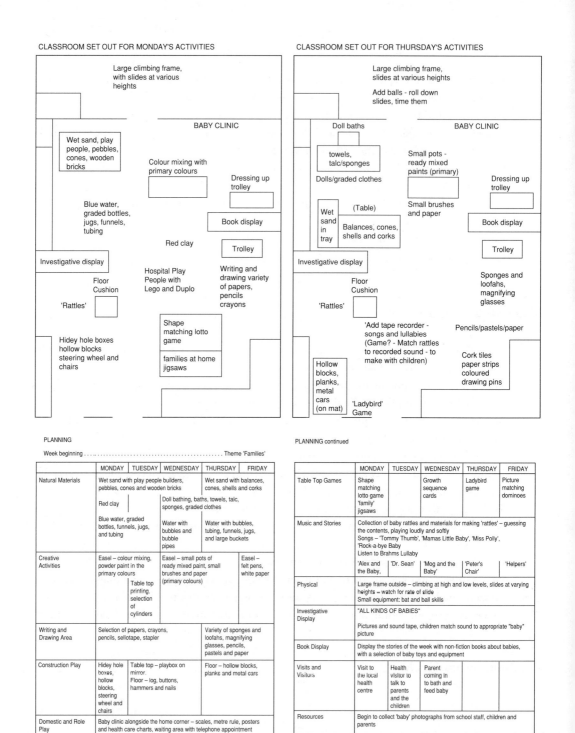

CLASSROOM SET OUT FOR MONDAY'S ACTIVITIES

- Large climbing frame, with slides at various heights
- BABY CLINIC
- Wet sand, play people, pebbles, cones, wooden bricks
- Colour mixing with primary colours
- Dressing up trolley
- Blue water, graded bottles, jugs, funnels, tubing
- Book display
- Red clay
- Trolley
- Investigative display
- Hospital Play People with Lego and Duplo
- Writing and drawing variety of papers, pencils crayons
- Floor Cushion
- 'Rattles'
- Shape matching lotto game
- Hidey hole boxes hollow blocks steering wheel and chairs
- families at home jigsaws

CLASSROOM SET OUT FOR THURSDAY'S ACTIVITIES

- Large climbing frame, slides at various heights
- Add balls - roll down slides, time them
- Doll baths
- BABY CLINIC
- towels, talc/sponges
- Small pots - ready mixed paints (primary)
- Dolls/graded clothes
- Dressing up trolley
- Wet sand in tray
- (Table)
- Balances, cones, shells and corks
- Small brushes and paper
- Book display
- Investigative display
- Trolley
- Floor Cushion
- Sponges and loofahs, magnifying glasses
- 'Rattles'
- 'Add tape recorder - songs and lullabies (Game? - Match rattles to recorded sound - to make with children)
- Pencils/pastels/paper
- Hollow blocks, planks, metal cars (on mat)
- 'Ladybird' Game
- Cork tiles paper strips coloured drawing pins

PLANNING

Week beginning . . . . Theme 'Families'

	MONDAY	TUESDAY	WEDNESDAY	THURSDAY	FRIDAY
Natural Materials	Wet sand with play people builders, pebbles, cones and wooden bricks			Wet sand with balances, cones, shells and corks	
	Red clay		Doll bathing, baths, towels, talc, sponges, graded clothes		
	Blue water, graded bottles, funnels, jugs, and tubing		Water with bubbles and bubble pipes	Water with bubbles, tubing, funnels, jugs, and large buckets	
Creative Activities	Easel – colour mixing, powder paint in the primary colours		Easel – small pots of ready mixed paint, small brushes and paper (primary colours)	Easel – felt pens, white paper	
		Table top printing, selection of cylinders			
Writing and Drawing Area	Selection of papers, crayons, pencils, sellotape, stapler			Variety of sponges and loofahs, magnifying glasses, pencils, pastels and paper	
Construction Play	Hidey hole boxes, hollow blocks, steering wheel and chairs	Table top – playbox on mirror. Floor – log, buttons, hammers and nails		Floor – hollow blocks, planks and metal cars	
Domestic and Role Play	Baby clinic alongside the home corner – scales, metre rule, posters and health care charts, waiting area with telephone appointment book and pens				
Small Imaginative	Play people – hospital, include Duplo and Lego				
Manipulative		Pegs and peg boards		Cork tiles paper strips and coloured drawing pins	Threading cards

PLANNING continued

	MONDAY	TUESDAY	WEDNESDAY	THURSDAY	FRIDAY
Table Top Games	Shape matching lotto game 'family' jigsaws		Growth sequence cards	Ladybird game	Picture matching dominoes
Music and Stories	Collection of baby rattles and materials for making 'rattles' – guessing the contents, playing loudly and softly				
	Songs – 'Tommy Thumb', 'Mamas Little Baby', 'Miss Polly', 'Rock-a-bye Baby'				
	Listen to Brahms Lullaby				
	'Alex and the Baby,	'Dr. Sean'	'Mog and the Baby'	'Peter's Chair'	'Helpers'
Physical	Large frame outside – climbing at high and low levels, slides at varying heights – watch for rate of slide				
	Small equipment: bat and ball skills				
Investigative Display	"ALL KINDS OF BABIES"				
	Pictures and sound tape, children match sound to appropriate "baby" picture				
Book Display	Display the stories of the week with non-fiction books about babies, with a selection of baby toys and equipment				
Visits and Visitors	Visit to the local health centre	Health visitor to talk to parents and the children	Parent coming in to bath and feed baby		
Resources	Begin to collect 'baby' photographs from school staff, children and parents				

NB All these activities can be incorporated in <u>OUTDOOR PLAY</u>

Figure 3.8 Example of planning and organization in a reception class

with the attainment targets for National Curriculum key stage 1 in order to provide experiences which will take children towards, or in some cases to cover, the earlier parts of the work.

Although in some ways superseded by the introduction of the national curriculum, the nine areas of learning and experience discussed in *The Curriculum from 5 to 16* (Curriculum Matters 2, 1985), which are widely recognized as applying to all children including the under-fives, are still useful. These are:

1. Aesthetic and creative (symbolic representation, imagination, drama, making things, music, singing, rhymes, appreciating creativity in others).
2. Human and social (quality and consistency of relationships, how we live).
3. Linguistic and literary (listening, speaking, reading, writing).
4. Mathematics (including all mathematics experiences and language).
5. Moral (considering others, right and wrong, discipline, self-awareness, being a member of a group).
6. Physical (handling tools, large and small muscle development, co-ordination manipulation, spatial awareness, body awareness, health).
7. Scientific (observation, investigation and enquiry, problem-solving, ourselves and living things).
8. Spiritual (understanding each other, religious experience, the meaning of life, festivals, experiences such as joy, warmth, love, conflict).
9. Technological (how things work, designing and testing, forces, movement, energy).

Elements of learning

As well as the nine areas of learning, four elements of learning are considered. These are:

1. Knowledge.
2. Concepts or ideas.
3. Skills.
4. Attitudes.

In planning the curriculum it is helpful to consider these headings as they provide a broad framework within which the needs of the whole child may be met. In practice, planning a curriculum is done in many different ways, with different emphasis. Nurseries may offer a curriculum which is skills-based, whereas children in the second year of formal school may work far more in the realms of ideas and concepts. The important thing is that the curriculum has breadth and balance. This means that nursery children need not concentrate wholly on, say, using tools or developing physical skills but should also be given the opportunity to develop concepts such as shape, time, spatial awareness or those associated with early reading and writing. Equally, older children need to continue with the skills curriculum. In planning a curriculum it is important to make sure that the four elements of learning are considered. By using the nine curriculum areas as a check it is also possible to make sure that there is sufficient breadth and balance.

Planning may need to concentrate on specific aspects of the curriculum which support the

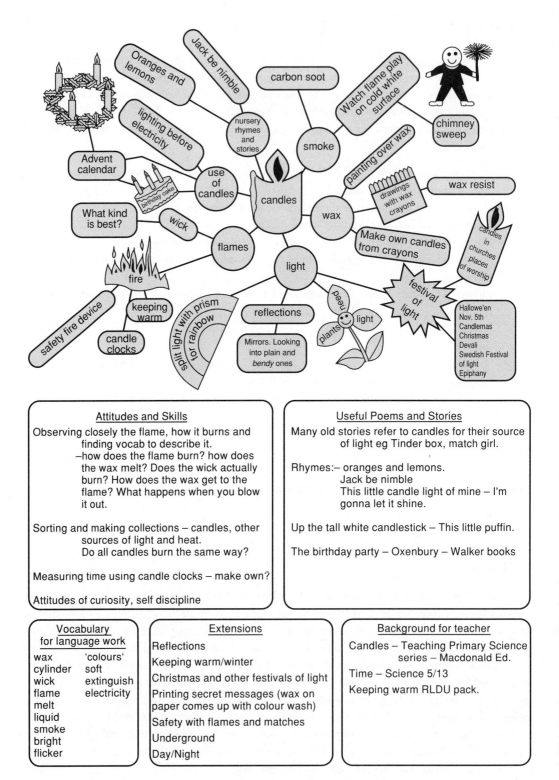

Attitudes and Skills

Observing closely the flame, how it burns and finding vocab to describe it.
  –how does the flame burn? how does the wax melt? Does the wick actually burn? How does the wax get to the flame? What happens when you blow it out.

Sorting and making collections – candles, other sources of light and heat.
  Do all candles burn the same way?

Measuring time using candle clocks – make own?

Attitudes of curiosity, self discipline

Useful Poems and Stories

Many old stories refer to candles for their source of light eg Tinder box, match girl.

Rhymes:– oranges and lemons.
  Jack be nimble
  This little candle light of mine – I'm gonna let it shine.

Up the tall white candlestick – This little puffin.

The birthday party – Oxenbury – Walker books

Vocabulary for language work

wax	'colours'
cylinder	soft
wick	extinguish
flame	electricity
melt	
liquid	
smoke	
bright	
flicker	

Extensions

Reflections
Keeping warm/winter
Christmas and other festivals of light
Printing secret messages (wax on paper comes up with colour wash)
Safety with flames and matches
Underground
Day/Night

Background for teacher

Candles – Teaching Primary Science series – Macdonald Ed.

Time – Science 5/13

Keeping warm RLDU pack.

Figure 3.9 Using the topic of candles to plan a cross-curricular theme in the nursery

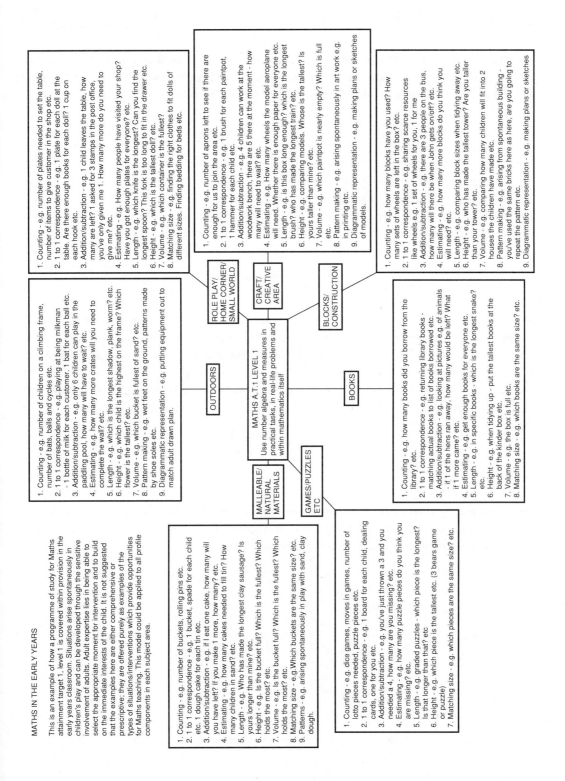

MATHS IN THE EARLY YEARS

This is an example of how a programme of study for Maths attainment target 1, level 1 is covered within provision in the early years classroom. Situations arise spontaneously in children's play and can be developed through the sensitive involvement of adults. Adult expertise lies in being able to select the appropriate moment for intervention and to build on the immediate interests of the child. It is not suggested that the examples here are either comprehensive or prescriptive; they are offered purely as examples of the types of situations/interventions which provide opportunities for Maths teaching. This model could be applied to all profile components in each subject area.

OUTDOORS

1. Counting - e.g. number of children on a climbing frame, number of bats, balls and cycles etc.
2. 1 to 1 correspondence - e.g. playing at being milkman - 1 bottle of milk for each customer, 1 bat for each ball etc.
3. Addition/subtraction - e.g. only 6 children can play in the paddling pool, how many will have to wait? etc.
4. Estimating - e.g. how many more crates will you need to complete the wall? etc.
5. Length - e.g. which is the longest shadow, plank, worm? etc.
6. Height - e.g. which child is the highest on the frame? Which flower is the tallest? etc.
7. Volume - e.g. which bucket is fullest of sand? etc.
8. Pattern making - e.g. wet feet on the ground, patterns made by shoe soles etc.
9. Diagrammatic representation - e.g. putting equipment out to match adult drawn plan.

ROLE PLAY/ HOME CORNER/ SMALL WORLD

1. Counting - e.g. number of plates needed to set the table, number of items to give customer in the shop etc.
2. 1 to 1 correspondence - e.g. 1 plate for each doll at the table. Are there enough books for each doll? 1 cup on each hook etc.
3. Addition/subtraction - e.g. 1 child leaves the table, how many are left? 1 asked for 3 stamps in the post office, you've only given me 1. How many more do you need to give me? etc.
4. Estimating - e.g. How many people have visited your shop? Have you got enough plates for everyone? etc.
5. Length - e.g. which knife is the longest? Can you find the longest spoon? This fork is too long to fit in the drawer etc.
6. Height - e.g. which is the tallest doll? etc.
7. Volume - e.g. which container is the fullest?
8. Matching size - e.g. finding the right clothes to fit dolls of different sizes. Finding bedding for beds etc.

CRAFT/ CREATIVE AREA

1. Counting - e.g. number of aprons left to see if there are enough for us to join the area etc.
2. 1 to 1 correspondence - e.g. 1 brush for each paintpot, 1 hammer for each child etc.
3. Addition/subtraction - e.g. 4 children can work at the woodwork bench, there are 5 there at the moment - how many will need to wait? etc.
4. Estimating - e.g. How many wheels the model aeroplane will need. Whether there is enough paper for everyone etc.
5. Length - e.g. is this box long enough? which is the longest brush? who has made the longest train? etc.
6. Height - e.g. comparing models. Whose is the tallest? Is yours taller than mine? etc.
7. Volume - e.g. which paintpot is nearly empty? Which is full etc.
8. Pattern making - e.g. arising spontaneously in art work e.g. in printing etc.
9. Diagrammatic representation - e.g. making plans or sketches of models.

BLOCKS/ CONSTRUCTION

1. Counting - e.g. how many blocks have you used? How many sets of wheels are left in the box? etc.
2. 1 to 1 correspondence - e.g. sharing scarce resources like wheels e.g. 1 set of wheels for you, 1 for me
3. Addition/subtraction - e.g. there are 3 people on the bus, how many will there be when John gets on/off? etc.
4. Estimating - e.g. how many more blocks do you think you will need? etc.
5. Length - e.g. comparing block sizes when tidying away etc.
6. Height - e.g. who has made the tallest tower? Are you taller than your tower? etc.
7. Volume - e.g. comparing how many children will fit into 2 houses the children have made etc.
8. Pattern making - e.g. arising from spontaneous building - you've used the same bricks as here, are you going to repeat the pattern etc.
9. Diagrammatic representation - e.g. making plans or sketches

MATHS A.T. 1 LEVEL 1
Use number algebra and measures in practical tasks, in real-life problems and within mathematics itself

BOOKS

1. Counting - e.g. how many books did you borrow from the library? etc.
2. 1 to 1 correspondence - e.g. returning library books - matching actual books to list of books borrowed etc.
3. Addition/subtraction - e.g. looking at pictures e.g. of animals - if 1 of the hens ran away, how many would be left? What if 1 more came?
4. Estimating - e.g. get enough books for everyone etc.
5. Length - e.g. in specific books - which is the longest snake? etc.
6. Height - e.g. when tidying up - put the tallest books at the back of the kinder box etc.
7. Volume - e.g. the box is full etc.
8. Matching size - e.g. which books are the same size? etc.

MALLEABLE/ NATURAL MATERIALS

1. Counting - e.g. number of buckets, rolling pins etc.
2. 1 to 1 correspondence - e.g. 1 bucket, spade for each child etc. 1 dough cake for each tin etc.
3. Addition/subtraction - e.g. if I eat one cake, how many will you have left? If you make 1 more, how many? etc.
4. Estimating - e.g. how many cakes needed to fill tin? How many children in sand? etc.
5. Length - e.g. Who has made the longest clay sausage? Is yours longer than mine? etc.
6. Height - e.g. Is the bucket full? Which holds the most? etc.
7. Volume - e.g. Is the bucket full? Which is the fullest? Which holds the most? etc.
8. Matching size - e.g. Which buckets are the same size? etc.
9. Patterns - e.g. arising spontaneously in play with sand, clay dough.

GAMES/PUZZLES ETC

1. Counting - e.g. dice games, moves in games, number of lotto pieces needed, puzzle pieces etc.
2. 1 to 1 correspondence - e.g. 1 board for each child, dealing cards, one for you etc.
3. Addition/subtraction - e.g. you've just thrown a 3 and you needed a 4, how many are you missing? etc.
4. Estimating - e.g. how many puzzle pieces do you think you are missing? etc.
5. Length - e.g. graded puzzles - which piece is the longest? Is that longer than that? etc
6. Height - e.g. which piece is the tallest etc. (3 bears game or puzzle)
7. Matching size - e.g. which pieces are the same size? etc.

Figure 3.10 National Curriculum planning

overall policy of the school, nursery or playgroup or where assessment of the children reveals a specific need. For example, where there has been much good work done in the area of language and literacy, but little on technology, obviously this should feature strongly in forward-planning.

Cross-curricular themes

Cross-curricular topics or themes are commonly used as means of delivering the curriculum in an integrated way. These themes can be developed in a variety of ways using the children's own interests, stories or nursery rhymes, and many other subjects or situations. The example of a theme on candles in Figure 3.9 is just one way of planning for some work in the nursery.

Planning around different types of learning experience

Some types of learning activity such as learning to use particular tools are not so easily integrated, and may need to be taught as discrete components of the curriculum. Other types of plan will be drawn up according to different needs or if it is felt the children lack experience in particular skills which need some work. For example, the centre of the planning web above might be 'manipulative skills' and the planning may focus on how these can be developed. It is important to remember that there is no right way of planning, it should always be flexible and responsive to the children and circumstances.

National Curriculum planning

Planning the early years curriculum around the various attainment targets in the foundation subjects already operational can be done as shown in Figure 3.10 and is an alternative to the much favoured cross-curricular approach already discussed.

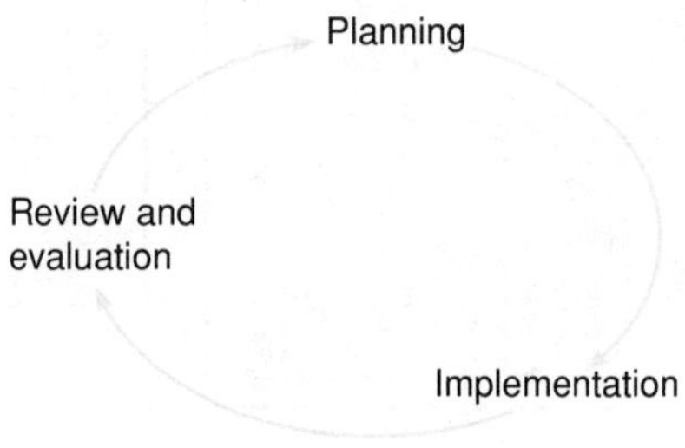

Planning

Review and
evaluation

Implementation

Figure 3.11 The planning cycle

The planning cycle

The planning cycle is a useful tool in preparing for work with young children. It should be applied routinely as part of good practice in care and education settings and can apply on a large scale with a whole group or class of children over a long period of time or for a very small-scale, one-off activity. The planning cycle can cover routines and activities with children, work with parents and so forth. In early years settings it is important to involve the whole team in planning as well as parents/carers and children.

Planning (initial ideas)
Planning any curriculum is an ongoing process. The initial ideas may be stimulated by the children's interest or may be derived from a whole school project. For babies and very young children routines may feature prominently. From this are derived more detailed aims and goals. The plans will reflect a broad and balanced curriculum which considers skills, concepts and factual knowledge and the kinds of attitudes which the work may promote.

Implementation (put into practice)
After the initial planning comes the implementation phase which in the early years is always flexible and responsive to changing needs and circumstances.

Review and evaluation (How did it go? What needs changing?)
The review and evaluation phase is a vital part of the cycle and will inform future planning. Evaluation should consider whether the aims and goals were fulfilled. If they were, how could the activity or experience be extended or improved. If not, the evaluation considers why and how things could be changed. Self-evaluation of performance is a useful exercise.

Assignment 1

Task   Consider several activities taking place in your work setting. These might involve a variety of different ways of learning for the children. Observe the children closely as they engage in the activity and assess what they are doing and learning on an individual basis. After you have done this write up the activity in the following way.

Example: Water play using funnels, sieves and measuring jugs of different sizes

1. Why was this activity provided?
2. How was it presented and introduced?
3. How did it link with other ongoing activity?
4. What previous experience did the children have using this equipment or similar?
5. What were your expectations of how the equipment would be used?
6. What learning/development did you expect to take place (skills, concepts, knowledge and attitudes)?
7. What actually happened?

Discussion

(a) What aspects of development and learning were promoted by the experience?
(b) How could this activity be developed and extended?
(c) Is this activity providing a foundation for future learning?
(d) What would be the next learning steps?
(e) Projecting ahead as far as possible, identify those skills, concepts, knowledge and attitudes which might be linked with identifiable areas of knowledge such as science or technology.
(f) Is it possible to make those links in the areas you have chosen? If not, why not?
(g) Do your findings help you to understand the concept of a spiral curriculum?

Assignment 2

Objectives   To plan, implement and evaluate one aspect of the curriculum in your work setting.

You are training to be a nursery nurse in a depressed inner city nursery school. You have children from many different ethnic groups in your class: several have very little spoken English but converse freely in their home language when they have opportunity.

Task   After discussion with your supervisor, work on a small-scale plan for one aspect of the curriculum in your work setting designed to promote language development. Set out your goals clearly, consider the feasibility of what you are doing and how it will fit in with the overall curriculum plan. Think of ways in which parents or other adults could be involved in the project. Implement and evaluate your plans.

Assignment 3

Objectives   To develop and extend children's love of stories and books.

Task   In discussion with your supervisor or tutor and the children you work with, plan and make a short book suitable for young children. The book may be written by you and the children working together or just by you; it should be relevant to your situation and provide fun for and discussion with the children. It may include photographs or be a group book containing drawings and individual stories by the children. Other ideas may be:

- A book for counting.
- A book for colours or shapes.
- A book about the locality.
- A book about a difficult or challenging real situation.
- A simple story.
- A rhyme book.

Discussion   Evaluate the experience and say how the children responded.

Assignment 4

Objectives   To extend and expand children's scientific understanding.

Task   In discussion with your supervisor, set up an area where children can explore and experiment with natural or created materials. Wherever possible choose new or unfamiliar items for them to explore. Structure the activity so that children can test their ideas in a non-threatening manner.

Discussion

(a) Discuss how you might best introduce the activity/experience.
(b) Outline your learning objectives.
(c) Carefully observe the reactions of the children.
(d) Note how the activity might be developed and extended.

References and further reading

Athey, C. 1990. *Extending Thought in Young Children. A Parent Teacher Partnership*. London: Paul Chapman.

Baker, C. 1988. *Reading through Play*. London: MacDonald.

Blenkin, G. and Kelly V. (eds). 1988. *Early Childhood Education: A Developmental Curriculum*. London: Paul Chapman.

Brown, B. 1990. *All Our Children*. London: BBC Educational.

Browne, N. and France, P. 1986. *Untying the Apron Strings: Anti-sexist Provision for the Under Fives*. Milton Keynes: Open University Press.

Bruce, T. 1987. *Early Childhood Education*. Sevenoaks: Hodder and Stoughton.

Bruner, J. 1975. 'The ontogenesis of speech acts', *Journal of Child Language,* 2.

Bruner, J. 1980. *Under Five in Britain*. The Oxford Pre-school Research Project. Oxford: Grant McIntyre/Blackwell.

Department of Education and Science. 1975. *The Bullock Report: A Language for Life*. London: HMSO.

Department of Education and Science. 1978. *The Warnock Report: Special Educational Needs*. London: HMSO.

Clarke, M. 1988. *Children Under Five: Final Report to the Department of Education and Science*. London: Gordon and Breach.

Commission for Racial Equality. 1989. *From Cradle to School*. London: CRE.

Concern No. 68. 1989. *Creating a Learning Environment: What's Special About Under Fives?* Spring 1989.

Curtis, A. 1986. *A Curriculum for the Pre-school Child*. Windsor: NFER/Nelson.

David, T. 1990. *Under Five – Under-Educated?* Milton Keynes: Open University Press.

Dowling, M. 1988. *Education 3–5*. London: Paul Chapman.

Drummond, M., Lally, M. and Pugh, G. (eds). 1989. *Working with Young Children: Developing a Curriculum for the Early Years*. National Children's Bureau/Nottingham Educational Supplies.

Early Years Curriculum Group. 1989. *Early Childhood Education: The Early Years Curriculum and the National Curriculum*. Stoke on Trent: Trentham Books.

Equal Opportunities Commission. *An Equal Start: Guidelines for those Working with the Under Fives*. Manchester: EOC.

Goldschmeid, E. 1989. 'Play and learning in the nursery', in *Babies in Daycare*, edited by V. Williams. Daycare Trust.

Griffiths, R. 1988. *Maths through Play*. London: MacDonald.

Hazareesingh, S., Simms, K., Anderson, P. *et al*., 1989. *Educating the Whole Child: A Holistic Approach to Education in the Early Years*. London: Building Blocks Educational.

Her Majesty's Inspectorate. 1989. *The Education of Children Under Five*. London: HMSO.

Hohmann, M., Banet, B. and Wiekart, D. 1979. *Young Children in Action*. High/Scope Press.

HMSO. 1985. *Curriculum Matters 2: The Curriculum from 5 to 16*. London: HMSO.

Lancashire County Council. 1986. *Science in the Early Years*.

Minns, H. 1990. *Read it to Me Now*. London: Virago.

National Children's Bureau: *Highlights,* nos 88 and 89. London: NCB.

National Writing Project. *Becoming a Write*r. London: Nelson.

NFER/SCDC. 1987. *Four Year Olds in Schools*. Windsor: NFER/SCDC.

Rouse, D. (ed.). 1991. *Babies and Toddlers, Carers and Educators. Quality for the Under Three*s. London: National Children's Bureau.

Department of Education and Science. 1990. *The Rumbold Report: Starting with Quality*, part 2. London: HMSO.

Wolfendale, S. 1991. *All About Me*. Nottingham: NES/Arnold.

Wray, D. 1989. *Bright Ideas– Writing*. Leamington Spa: Scholastic.

Yates, I. 1990. *Bright Ideas – Language Activities*. Leamington Spa: Scholastic.

Chapter 4
Parental involvement

Chapter objectives_____

Background and definitions
Parental involvement in the
education service
Parental involvement in
social services

Parental involvement in the voluntary
and private sectors
Principles of work with parents
Practical ways of working with parents
Links with units P2, P3, P5

There has been a movement in recent years, particularly since the 1960s and 1970s, towards involving parents as partners in the care and education of their children. Parents are the people who have primary responsibility for caring, and many professionals involved in child care and education have increasingly seen the need to include them as fully as possible. Generally, parental involvement can be viewed as being beneficial to both the family and to the institution. Although there are exceptions, parents today of all backgrounds tend to be well informed and in possession of a great deal of knowledge about the education and social service systems due to the massive amount of media coverage.

The term 'parents' refers to the principal carers of children, whoever they may be and includes those who have 'parental responsibility' under the Children Act 1989. The carer may have any one of a variety of different relationships with the child, such as grandparent, childminder, foster parent, step-parent, older sibling, but, for the purposes of this chapter, it is understood that they usually have the main care of the child. In practice it is mostly the natural parents who care for their young children, especially the mother, and this chapter presupposes this although acknowledging the term 'parent' to refer to a wider grouping.

Parental or family involvement as a concept will also mean different things according to the setting and the ethos of the setting. A psychologist may use the term to refer to planned activities involving parents in educational activities with their children. Social workers may see parental involvement with their child in a group setting as a positive indicator in the rehabilitation of a family. A teacher may see it as referring to the practical help offered in a classroom. Others may feel that involving parents should be restricted to fund-raising, whilst other groups see it as being linked with management and decision-making within a school or other organization. It is important to recognize that there can be many ways in which this term is interpreted, each with its own philosophical and ideological basis.

Before beginning to examine the notion of parental involvement, it is important to realize that this is a concept based on the values of those who encourage or discourage participation. Involvement by parents has not always been encouraged, and there are still many examples of this today. Those who do encourage the practice usually take the view that the relationship between home and school, nursery or institution needs to be changed in a positive way to make this possible.

In Britain today the family is seen as the basic unit of society. Although we may see this as a social construction rather than a 'natural' one, it is the unit that most of us come from and identify with. Within this umbrella term a wide variety of kin relationships exist, and in all our involvement with parents we need to recognize and accept this. It is important to recognize that other family and cultural patterns may exist with which we are not familiar, and this will require us to examine our own values and attitudes.

Figure 4.1 Extended family

Children from nought to five years are largely cared for at home, after that the state has a statutory duty to provide education. However, there are a whole range of types of day care and education available for pre-school children involving parents in widely different ways according to the reason and philosophy of the care provided. This provision is patchy and variable throughout Britain and can be loosely divided amongst the private sector which will include childminding, private nurseries or workplace crèches, the voluntary sector which would cover such provision as pre-school playgroups, community nurseries, and care provided by the large voluntary organizations, and thirdly, the statutory sector which includes the social services, (local authority) health and education departments. Furthermore, provision may be divided into part time, or full time, 'care' or 'education' producing a rather confused and inconsistent picture. Unfortunately, despite recommendations from many agencies for an integrated and comprehensive service this is still far from the case in Britain. There have been attempts by individual authorities, sometimes in partnership with the voluntary sector, to rationalize existing services, and these have been successful to some extent. However, services are still lacking in most areas and although there is an argument for providing a great diversity of provision which may reflect 'market forces' in a particular area, there is still a need for rationalization of provision and adequate funding, in order to meet the needs of young families.

The degree of parental involvement in early care and education reflects the above picture: it is variable, patchy and reflects local circumstances, both social and political. The type of organization involved will greatly influence the attitude towards parents, and, of course, within institutions nominally in favour of considerable parental input, there will be individual variation. It is our intention to look at the commonalties of parental involvement within broad groupings, to look at the underlying ethos, and practical ways in which practitioners can work with parents.

The education service

Background

Traditionally, home and school were seen as separate, and parents were often physically excluded except on occasions such as special open evenings. Signs saying 'No Parents' or similar were not uncommon until the 1960s, and in some cases the underlying attitudes still exist. The exclusion of parents from the area of their young child's education reflected the prevailing attitude that teacher knew best and that parents were better kept outside. When they were invited in there was not likely to be an assumption of mutual support and understanding, but a one-sided attempt to influence parental values and behaviour.

The exception to this rule could be found in the work of Margaret McMillan, who could be termed the founder of modern nursery education. In the early years of this century her voice was heard arguing for the right of mothers to participate in their child's education and in the management of the nursery schools they attended. Some of her ideas emerged in the 1960s and 1970s, particularly the notion that mothers should be able to enter the school when they wished and that their views were to be respected.

Figure 4.2 Child and parent going to school

Scenario 1	Some years ago this would not have been an usual set of circumstances and in places these attitudes persist.

Some years ago this would not have been an usual set of circumstances and in places these attitudes persist.

A family in a rural community are isolated and have very limited neighbourhood networks. The middle child Jane is aged four years; she has a sister of seven and a brother of two. The mother has great difficulty in getting Jane and her sister to school on time as the children are often uncooperative, and she is frequently late collecting them.

The school's policy is to keep parents outside as far as possible. There is no opportunity for the mother to explain her practical difficulties to the teacher, or to discuss the children's difficult behaviour. The mother finds great difficulty in communicating through the school secretary and headteacher. She is becoming increasingly alienated from the school as getting the children there is such a burden and she feels they would not be sympathetic to her problems. If the toddler is sick, or there is tension at home, or extremely bad weather, often the mother will keep the children at home.

What practical measures could this school take:

(a) For this particular mother?
(b) For this rural community?

Equality of opportunity

It was during the 1960s and 1970s in the period of greater political interest in issues of educational disadvantage and deprivation, that the importance of parental influence on a child's overall attainment at school came to the fore. In one particular study a group of children born during a week in March 1958 were studied. Amongst many variables examined over a period of years the effect of social class and disadvantage on children's educational attainments was considered. The findings, along with other research of the period, were that children from working-class homes did not succeed as well in the education system as children from the middle classes. The Plowden Report (1967) discussed the importance of parental attitudes to their child's education as being a crucial factor in the child's success or failure. As a result, greater levels of parental participation were recommended, although the notion of the school's accountability to parents was not on the agenda until many years later.

The influence of child development theory

The political interest was also fuelled by a move away from the previously held convictions concerning intelligence. These theories supported the view that educational attainment primarily depended upon innate ability. In the post-war period and beyond, theories were emerging which stressed the importance of early environment in enabling children to reach their educational potential.

Early mother/child relationships and their link with other aspects of development, cognitive as well as emotional and character development were stressed by workers such as John Bowlby (see chapter 1). Projects such as Head Start in the USA were set up with the aim of encouraging parents to work through an educational programme with their children. The short-term benefits of these seemed to be inconclusive, but longer-term studies of the children at 15 and 16 years showed that this type of intervention did have benefits (see High Scope in chapter 3).

The development of language was seen as a crucial area of importance for working-class children who were thought to be linguistically deprived at home, and therefore disadvantaged in the middle-class school culture. These attitudes are demonstrated to some extent in the Bullock Report (1975). At this time parent education concentrated on demonstrating the importance of talking and reading to children, but at the same time they were not encouraged to involve themselves in teaching their child to read which was a job for the 'professionals'. Although the stress on language persists, it is much less likely that researchers and educationalists today will see working-class children as a group linguistically deprived. The responsibility is placed firmly on the school to offer an appropriate linguistic environment not to blame 'inadequate' homes.

Parental pressure

Pressure for more involvement in schools has not come just from political groups. Parents themselves have formed consumer groups which press for more information and influence in their children's schooling. The Advisory Centre for Education (ACE) provides parents of children in State Education with free information and advice. It also acts as a national watchdog body. The National Confederation of Parent Teacher Associations which represented the various parent groups and PTAs also act as a pressure group.

Legislation

The Taylor Report on school management (Department of Education and Science, 1977) and the Warnock Report on Special Educational needs (DES, 1978) together with other legislation culminating in the 1988 Education Reform Act, have all contributed to involving parents in the management of schools and involvement in their children's learning. Following on from the Warnock Report in the field of Special Education, the Education Act 1981, an important piece of legislation stresses the sharing of experience, knowledge and skills between schools and parents. The notion of parents as partners is an important emphasis in the Act.

Reasons for involvement of parents

It is important that parents are welcome in schools and are as involved as possible in their child's education, not just at the nursery/infant stage, but beyond. They are, after all, the prime educators of their children. It is widely recognized that such involvement brings great benefits to children and parents alike. The advantages for the institution are also considerable. As well as perhaps raising money for much-needed material resources, parents are themselves invaluable human resources and their involvement in schools and increased understanding of child development and the educational process have many benefits. Children learn best when there is continuity in their experience, and parents can inform and help plan the curriculum in all areas especially regarding the child's social and cultural context. Parents themselves often report a growth in confidence and self-esteem as they work alongside professionals and feel their contribution is equal and valued. As the above legislation indicates, this is a view increasingly held by government, as well as professionals involved in education. The quality of their involvement is crucial. Although attitudes vary, it is important that parents are involved not merely on the periphery but in the central issues affecting their children. Research has shown how the use of schemes such as PACT (home and school reading) and IMPACT (home and school mathematics) in which parents are involved in the curriculum, has brought about higher levels of achievement in children. There are many examples of attempts by local schools and individual authorities throughout Britain to link school and community and to promote parent education and involvement. However, there is no coherent nationwide strategy and the current changes in education, with increasing demands on teaching staff, make it unlikely that it will be seen as a priority in the near future.

Barriers

Staff in schools, even when generally in favour of encouraging parents to come into school, may find difficulties in the management of extra adults in the classroom and may feel personally threatened. Teachers do not generally receive training for working with parents, but are often asked for their advice on a wide range of social and welfare issues, as well as child care and educational development. Clear lines of communication are needed to avoid misunderstanding and to ensure common goals. Staff are sometimes concerned that their roles as educators are being diluted as their time is taken up with issues not directly concerning the education of children. Genuine parental involvement does mean a change of emphasis for workers with young children calling for further professional development and training.

Some staff may feel that their professionalism and adequacy in the classroom are being scrutinized; they may feel that as teaching is a skilled activity which requires professional training, parents are not needed or wanted. Staff may need support from management in accepting parental help and in viewing it as a resource. It is possible that some staff will view this unpaid help as unethical and will find it difficult to accept when they feel more paid ancillary help and smaller classes would be appropriate. All these concerns, which occur with the sharing of power and professional expertise, are understandable, and policy on parental involvement needs to be understood and agreed by members of staff.

Social services

Background

Historically, the provision of welfare services had its origins in the Poor Law of 1834. The rationale was simple: people became poor largely through their own fault. The workhouse system was harsh and families were often split up. Services improved with the coming of the post-war welfare state, which aimed to eradicate poverty and ignorance, but prior to the Social Services Act 1970, care for children and parents was likely to be undertaken by different local government departments often with very little liaison between them. Today every local authority is obliged by law to provide a social services department, and within that department, services to young children are an integral part.

Local authority social services departments offer a patchy and varied child and family welfare service throughout Britain. They have a statutory responsibility to register and monitor the variety of establishments and individuals such as childminders who offer care or education to pre-school children (see Children Act 1989 in chapter 8). At the same time they have a clear responsibility for child protection, and are closely involved with families where children are deemed to be at risk. This can and often does lead to a certain tension in relationships between social services and their clients.

Traditionally, the involvement of social workers with families has led to a deficit view of those families, although staff today usually work hard to avoid this situation. This means families can be seen as in need of help and support, and implies that their parenting skills are likely to be deficient. As a result of these attitudes, decisions concerning children have often been taken out of parents' hand, and although the Children Act 1989 is designed to improve this situation it remains to be seen just how effective it is. All this has profound implications for parental involvement, and the delicate relationship that exists between client and worker demands high levels of interpersonal skill and empathy.

Figure 4.3 Father and baby

Family centres and day nurseries

Many social services departments provide family centres and/or day nurseries, although many of these cater only for children and families in particular need. In some areas (although this is rare) parents are offered places to enable them to work or study, and this provides for a more representative mix of children in the nursery. Children are now less likely to be cared for on a full-time basis, but hours offered are, where possible, tailored to the needs of the child and family within the constraints of the setting. Most social services establishments will operate a key worker system, where a designated worker will take the primary responsibility of working with an individual family.

Family centres often presuppose a greater degree of parental involvement and many day nurseries are now moving towards this model. Here parents are encouraged to be actively involved with their children, parenting skills are modelled and high quality interaction with the child is encouraged. This is an important role for family centres where a central aim is likely to be the creation of a safe and facilitating environment for children within stable homes.

Combined nursery centres

In some areas of the country there are combined nursery centres run by both social services and the local education authority. In some places all pre-school group care comes under the LEA. It is important to recognize that the providers will to a large extent determine the ethos and emphasis of the provision.

Reasons for involvement of parents

It is easy to assume that parents with involvement in social services day care will have little to give back to the institution, and will somehow or other be recipients only, but the emphasis today is away from the parent as somehow 'lacking' towards the parent as partner. Although it would be foolish to deny that this is always an easy relationship the establishment of family centres and the move towards greater parental participation does indicate a changing emphasis. The basis of this is a move towards empowering parents to take control of their own lives through encouraging decision-making and building up self-esteem. In this way it is postulated they will become better parents and more positive and whole people.

Social services generally see parental involvement as being integral to the work taking place with the family. However, parents today are less likely to be passive recipients of professional advice. They are more likely to be consulted and involved with the management of the nursery or centre and encouraged to use its facilities. General community activities may take place there, and self-help is encouraged. Parent education often takes place informally as well as in more formal ways, as parents see good child care demonstrated. Parent education can also help understanding of child development and the role of play, and helps to make expectations of their child more realistic. Parents are actively supported in their own personal growth and development with the recognition that to be effective parents they may need help and direction to meet their own needs.

Barriers

Much of the work with families involved with social services is likely to be amongst some of the most stressed, vulnerable and disadvantaged individuals in society (see scenario 2). Some parents will be at the nursery or centre as part of family rehabilitation when children are being returned home 'on trial' after being in care. They are often confused and angry, and the children can exhibit difficult and testing behaviour. Parents can often be depressed and feel unable to cope, their self-esteem will be low and they feel powerless. Work with this type of client group, although potentially very rewarding, is demanding upon staff at all levels. Parents need skilled help and parenting for themselves in some cases, before they feel able to become involved with their child or others in the institution.

Whilst recognizing this, it is also important that parents are encouraged to become involved and to begin to take control over their own lives. It is often difficult for staff to work positively with parents who perhaps have not cared for their children and who seem to have little motivation to do so.

Scenario
2

Teenage parents of a two-and-a-half-year-old child are anxious to have the child returned to them after a brief spell in care. At two years the child was found to be seriously underweight, and the health visitor had discovered he was left alone during the evenings when his parents went out. The parents are very anxious about their son and want to try again; they have been visiting him at the foster parents regularly where he was seen to be thriving.

A recent case conference has been held and, although invited, the parents arrived too late to participate. Since then a contract has been drawn up whereby the parents have to attend the local family centre with their son at a regular time each day.

The aim is to spend a major part of that time in direct interaction with their son and other times to participate in a group with other young parents. However, when the worker tries to involve them in play activities with their son they are unable to participate, seem stiff and awkward and soon get bored. They are very quiet in the group and seem overwhelmed and intimidated by the set-up.

(a) The parents really want their child back with them: how might they be feeling in this situation?

(b) How might staff in the family centre be feeling?

(c) What practical steps could be taken to encourage the parents involvement?

(d) What are the main concerns for the staff?

Legislation

The Seebohm Report of 1968 indicated a need for clients to be much more closely involved with decision-making and delivery of service. The Children Act 1989, which is dealt with in Chapter 8, is likely to be influential in forming attitudes towards parents as partners. The emphasis is changing from parental rights to parental responsibilities.

Voluntary and private sector _____

In the voluntary sector there is a proliferation of groups both large and small providing care and education for young children. There are many different types of organization in this sector with varying functions. Organizations such as Home Start provide trained volunteers to support families under stress; often these volunteers are parents themselves with a deep understanding of what their clients are experiencing. The Pre-school Playgroup Association was started by a parent, and relies heavily on parental involvement to exist. It provides for an enormous number of children and families and is typical of the move towards self-help and community initiative which has characterized the past 20 to 30 years.

Many of these initiatives have arisen out of a lack of statutory provision, and although self-help groups are often criticized as possibly preventing real social change, in general they are an invaluable additional resource. There is a considerable difference between large organizations employing staff, and small self-help groups run by parents. However, the voluntary and charitable status of large institutions such as the National Children's Homes, can assist in their relationship with parents and carers as there is less stigma associated with them than with social services. Parents are more likely to be involved in the management and day-to-day organization of voluntary groups. As such they may be clients and consumers as well as managers with varying but often substantial degrees of involvement.

In the private sector which would cover childminding, workplace crèches, and private group day care, the relationship is not always as straightforward as consumer and provider. For example, sponsored childminding through a local authority is using what was traditionally a private sector resource to care for young children, and sometimes to monitor the parenting. There are variants of this type of scheme throughout Britain, e.g. day fostering.

For social, demographic and other reasons, the numbers of women in paid work seeking day care for their children has risen in recent years and this has led to an increase in private-sector provision, for example in the provision of workplace crèches. Many of these are run as business ventures and may offer a corporate image policy. Part of this will involve a corporate philosophy which may or may not involve positive parental involvement. Involving working parents is difficult in itself as they are usually pressed for time and tired after work. They may also live some distance from the crèche.

Figure 4.4 Parent handing over children to childminder

Reasons for involvement of parents

In the voluntary sector it is expected in general that there will be a high level of parental involvement, which will, of course, vary with the purpose of the organization. Often the organization is set up for parents, by other parents who participate together in management and the day-to-day running of the service. Often parents can be more involved as they work within informal neighbourhood care networks, which are flexible in terms of hours and access. As parents work together, with help from professionals where necessary, they can gain more confidence and be empowered to move on. Small voluntary groups are more flexible to local needs and attract local people as resources.

Barriers

Barriers depend again on the purpose of the organization. Funding is often a great problem, and these difficulties can restrict the scope of the various projects and make it difficult for all but the most dedicated. Lack of training for staff and poor or non-existent salaries also affect relations with parents. Sometimes there can be difficulties in ensuring common goals, and young parents may not always have the time and support networks to be involved in voluntary organizations, even those designed specifically for them.

Scenario 3

A recently divorced mother of two pre-school children is trying to overcome the difficulties of the past year or so and make a new life for herself. The elder child has joined the local playgroup but the mother is finding great difficulty in coping with other parents and staff members who are attempting to draw her in to help. She is not working outside the home at present and although there are money problems they are not overwhelming. She has a few friends but no family locally.

(a) How might she be feeling at this point?
(b) What advice and help could the play leader offer to her, and what community resources might be available?
(c) Discuss this parent's needs and consider what advantages or disadvantages the involvement in a voluntary sector playgroup has over other forms of pre-school provision.

Working with parents _____

Parents vary in their levels of confidence and in their parenting skills, but it is important that workers recognize the central role they play in the life of the child. Below are some general principles and attitudes considered to be vital in effectively involving parents although there are many more linked with particular settings:

- Parents usually know more than anyone else about their child.
- Parents are equal partners.
- Workers and settings should contribute positively and actively to welcoming parents.
- The setting has a responsibility to involve parents.
- Workers should recognize and value the parent, parental culture, heritage and language.
- Parents can offer effective care and education to their child.
- Parents have a right to regular and relevant information.
- Parents can be learners with their child and with staff.
- Parents have useful skills and personal strengths.
- Parents have a right to be consulted on changes affecting their children.
- Parents have a role to play within the setting.
- Parents have a right either to participate in management or to be represented.
- Parents have rights as citizens and tax payers.
- Parents have a right to negotiate with staff over issues affecting their children.
- Parents should be given every opportunity to understand what is going on in the setting and the rationale behind it, e.g. different types of play activity.
- Parents should understand and participate in the formulation of aims and goals for their child.
- Parents can be effective policy-makers for the setting.
- Parents should be given opportunity to participate in observing and assessing their children.
- Parents need encouragement in their parenting and a positive relationship with staff of all disciplines.
- Parents and workers need to develop mutual trust.
- Workers should recognize the need for confidentiality in dealing with parents.
- Parents sometimes need a break from their children.
- Workers should recognize the personal and environmental stresses affecting parents.
- Some parents will not agree with the goals of the setting for a variety of reasons.

If these principles and attitudes are generally understood it is likely that parents will feel much more able to participate and that they have something valuable to contribute. However, there are parents who, for whatever reason, either do not wish to become involved in the care and education of their child outside the home, despite every encouragement, or may prefer to be visited at home. This should be respected generally, but there are some situations, such as in a social services establishment, where the setting has made a contract with the parent in order to achieve a particular goal. This may mean the parent is breaking the contract and steps will be taken to deal with the situation.

It should be acknowledged that involving parents is not always easy: it takes effort, commitment and time. Not all parents will share the goals of the institution, some will seem to sabotage efforts made to involve them. Demands on staff can seem very heavy at times, and recognition of this and adequate support systems should always be available.

Practical ways of involving parents

Ways in which parents are involved will depend largely on the setting and the ethos of the setting. Some factors to bear in mind are:

- Wherever possible, parents should be given their own room where they can sit and talk with other adults, make coffee and relax without undue pressure.
- Wherever possible, parents should have open access to staff, headteachers, and officers in charge.
- Physical access should be as straightforward as possible and the environment friendly and encouraging.
- Storage for buggies and prams should be available.
- Toilets, nappy-changing areas and so forth should be clearly marked.
- Information should be available in all community languages and readily accessible.
- At the initial interview parents should be given information on session times and so forth, and the settling-in policy should be explained together with its rationale.
- Information on community resources and persons to contact in particular situations should be readily available.
- The rules and policies of the setting, including policy on equal opportunities, should be available for all parents with details of appeals procedures and so forth.
- It should be made very clear to parents that their presence is welcomed and open discussion should take place about the type of involvement where appropriate.
- Provision of a crèche may be vitally important to some parents to enable them to participate in activities.

Parental involvement in schools or other group settings

Parents can be involved in many different ways which utilize their individual skills and where they feel confident. Where parents cannot offer a particular service, their contribution should be valued, no matter how small. The list below is not exhaustive and there are many other ways parents become involved:

- As governors and policy-makers.
- In curriculum planning.
- In fund-raising.
- In the classroom or nursery, offering general support to the staff, or more specific help such as hearing children read, or cooking with small groups.

- Playing with children or general supervisory help.
- Help with basic care and management.
- Repairing and maintaining equipment.
- Maintaining the environment.
- Running libraries for books or toys.
- Helping with outings.
- Helping to run groups or support other parents.
- Helping with parent/parent teacher association.
- Helping with swimming or sports.
- Visiting as part of their occupational role, e.g. firefighter.
- Providing specific skills and services.
- Helping with cultural events and festivals.
- Helping where there may be a language difficulty.
- Helping with social events and open days.

Figure 4.5 Parents working alongside staff

Starting school or nursery

A parent of a young child starting school or nursery usually has mixed feelings about the experience. This applies to parents of children going to a childminder or private day nursery alike. On the one hand they are glad that their child is growing and becoming more independent. On the other hand there can be a deep sense of loss mixed with guilt at leaving the child. Some parents feel guilty at the sense of relief they feel at having time to themselves. Together with this is often a concern for the child they have to relinquish to professional carers and educators who do not have an intimate knowledge of their child.

For workers involved in this family transition it can become difficult to understand fully the feelings that are being displayed. The behaviour of even the most stable and supportive parents may show them to be confused and upset. It is infinitely more beneficial to staff, parents and children if an open-door policy towards parents exists. Firstly this may lessen the pain of this transition for parent and child; secondly it can encourage parents and widen their knowledge; thirdly it can enable the child to be seen in context not as an isolated entity. It is important for all professional child care and education workers to adapt and meet this new challenge.

Assignment 1

You are working in a community nursery where a third of the families represented are from Afro-Caribbean or Asian backgrounds and several children have English as a second language. You are conscious that the nursery still presents a very 'white' mono-cultural image, and that there are racist elements in the local community.

Task   Devise an activity or theme to use with the children which includes definite possibilities for involving all the children and families. Discuss how you would use this theme/activity to involve parents from all the ethnic groups in a manner that is likely to present a positive world view and to increase awareness.

Assignment 2

You are a childminder in an inner city area, and have been asked by social services to take two children aged one and three years from a family where the mother has a history of depressive illness. She is currently receiving treatment at a local hospital and day centre which takes up about half a day three times a week. You do not feel you really know much about this condition and are concerned to find out as much as possible before the children start with you.

Task   Devise a plan of action which would help you to find out this information. Discuss the types of general information you would find helpful, as well as that specific to this problem.

Discuss strategies for ensuring clear lines of communication with the parent, designed to ensure that the parent does not feel excluded and that there is real partnership between you both.

Assignment 3

Devise and produce a leaflet designed to introduce parents to a group pre-school child care/education setting. Stress the aspects most likely to encourage parental participation.

Assignment 4

Objective To help parents feel more at home in the nursery.

Task In discussion with your supervisor, look critically at the waiting area, hall or room where parents spend time. Devise a series of alterations/improvements to the area which might make it more welcoming, wherever possible implement these and discuss the outcomes.

Discussion Evaluate the outcome of your efforts, noting comments from parents and staff.

Assignment 5

Objective To encourage parents to become more involved in a particular aspect of play or other child-centred activity.

Task In discussion with your supervisor, work with a parent or group of parents in a play area, creative activity, or other. Encourage the parents to allow the children to explore and express themselves. Where possible, demonstrate that the process is more important than the product.

Discussion Discuss with parents their feelings about the session. Briefly record what you have learned and the value of the session to parents and children.

References and further reading

Central Advisory Council for Education (England) 1967. *The Plowden Report: Children and their Primary Schools*. London: HMSO.

Craft, M. *et al.* (eds). 1980. *Linking Home and School* (3rd edn). London: Harper and Row.

Cyster, R. Clift and Battle (eds). 1990. *Parental Involvement in Primary Schools*. Windsor: NFER.

Douglas, J.W.B. 1964. *The Home and the School*. London: MacGibbon and Kee.

Department of Education and Science. 1975. *The Bullock Report: A Language for Life*. London: HMSO.

Department of Education and Science. 1978. *The Warnock Report: Committee of Enquiry into the Education of Handicapped Children and Young People with Special Educational Needs*. London: HMSO.

Lynch, J. and Pimlot, J. 1976. *Parents and Teachers*. Basingstoke: Macmillan.

Pugh, G. and De'Ath, E. 1989. *Working Towards Partnership in the Early Years*. London: National Children's Bureau.

Seebohm, F. 1968. *Local Authority and Allied Personal Social Services*. London: HMSO.

Smith, N. 'Parental perspectives', *Social Work Today*, 21: 47 [2nd August] 25.

Taylor, T. 1977. *A New Partnership for our Schools*. London: HMSO.

Tizard, B., Mortimore, J. and Burchall, B. 1981. *Involving Parents in Nursery and Infant Schools*. Oxford: Grant McIntyre/Blackwell.

Wolfendale, S. 1983. *Parental Participation in Children's Development and Education*. London: Gordon and Breach.

Wolfendale, S. (ed.). 1989. *Parental Involvement: Developing Networks Between School, Home and Community*. London: Cassell.

Chapter 5
Children with
special needs

Chapter objectives _____

Historical perspectives
The Warnock Report
Current perspective
Statement of educational needs
Education Act 1981
Provision for the under-fives
Bonding
Conductive education

Portage scheme
Children with specific learning difficulties
Self-image of children with disabilities
Advocacy and empowerment
Links with units C17, C18, C19, M6
(this chapter links with all units as
special needs are integrated throughout
the national standards)

It could be argued that at some time in their lives all children have special needs which may require extra attention from the parent or carer: however, the children referred to in this chapter are those who have conditions which may handicap or partially handicap their all-round development. When referring to children with special needs it is important to be sensitive in the language that is used. For example, it is better to refer to 'children with handicaps/disabilities' than to refer to 'handicapped/disabled children'. By using the former it makes it clear that the children come before the handicap, thus we talk about 'children with special needs', 'children with a hearing impairment', etc. Descriptive labelling is a sensitive area and where possible should be avoided, although, even the Warnock Committee realized that some form of distinction was required between the types of special need in order to ensure that needs were met.

The terminology relating to special needs has changed dramatically in recent years, mostly in response to legislation. However, not all the textbooks that you read will be written in terms which reflect these changes. In recent years, people with disabilities have been enabled to state publicly their views on these matters and this has gone a long way towards changing the attitudes of society.

The major underlying philosophy relating to good practice in special needs is one of integration. This means that, wherever possible, children with special needs should be integrated within the mainstream of society, including the education and day care systems. Integration does need to be carefully thought through so that the child benefits most from the process, for as Margaret Clark (1988) points out: 'to place some children with special needs in an ordinary unit may indeed not be to integrate but to deny their special needs.'

It is not the intention in this chapter to offer medical definitions and the causes of handicapping conditions, although conditions may be mentioned as examples of certain types of special need which may benefit from specific types of care and education. What this chapter is doing is looking at the reports and legislation that have led to present-day attitudes and examining the role of pre-school education and care for children with special needs.

Historical perspectives

During the past twenty years the attitudes of society towards its members who have handicaps or impairments has changed dramatically. The UK was once a place which generated large institutions such as workhouses, psychiatric hospitals and hospitals for the mentally handicapped; it is only since the 1970s that the philosophy has changed and moved towards community care.

As recently as the 1950s, if a child was born with an obvious handicap such as Down's Syndrome or cerebral palsy, it would have probably have spent only the first few years of its life within the family before being admitted to a large mental handicap hospital where it may have spent the rest of its life. This was not due to callousness or lack of feeling on the part of the parents but what at the time was viewed as the best possible treatment for the child. Lack of facilities in the home, such as washing machines, bathrooms, inside toilets and central heating, made it impossible for the majority of parents to care for such a child within the home. The large institution was the place where the child could live and have all the specialist care that would be required, including 24-hour nursing care. These institutions/hospitals were usually based on the outskirts of large towns and cities, making it difficult for parents and family to visit regularly. As the child grew older and lost the bond with its immediate family, so visits were likely to lessen. It could be said that many of these children were abandoned to the institution.

The Education Act 1921 recognized five categories of handicap: blindness, deafness, physical defectiveness, mental defectiveness and epilepsy. This did not necessarily mean that the state provided educational facilities for the children in all these categories, although it was not uncommon to find residential establishments for the blind or 'deaf and dumb'.

The Education Act 1944 made it the legal duty of the local education authorities (LEAs) to provide education for children with disabilities, either in special schools or via some other arrangement. This Act defined eleven categories of handicap: blind, partially sighted, deaf, partially deaf, physically handicapped, delicate, diabetic, epileptic, maladjusted, educationally subnormal and speech defective. Not all the children in these categories were educated or had special educational provision, for the Act clearly stated that the provision could be schools or other arrangements. In many cases the 'other arrangements' were within the large institutions, where schoolrooms were set up and the children sent to these for certain hours of the day. The teachers in these hospital schools were paid by the LEA (rather than by the health authority which ran the establishment), and so the authority claimed that it was carrying out its duty in accordance with the Act. The children never left the confines of the institution, and as teaching in such schools was not seen as a prestigious job, the schools did not always attract good teachers.

The Education Act 1970 made provision for those children with severe mental handicap and who prior to the Act were not provided for as they were seen as uneducable. Once again the LEAs were given the responsibility of making arrangements for the education of these children. The way most LEAs responded to this was, once again, to set up schoolrooms within the existing institutions.

The Warnock Report

A major breakthrough for children with handicaps came in 1974 when the Warnock Report was published. A committee under the Chairmanship of Mary Warnock was set up by the government to:

> review the educational provision in England, Scotland and Wales for children and young people handicapped by disabilities of body or mind.

The terms of reference were broad and this meant that the committee had a free rein to investigate most aspects relating to educational provision of children with handicaps. The Warnock Report made a number of recommendations:

- The abolition of the categorizing of children by the nature of their handicap.
- The introduction of the concept of special educational needs.
- Special educational needs were defined as mild, moderate or severe.
- The introduction of the term 'specific learning difficulties' for those children who had difficulty in just one area of the curriculum.
- The conclusion that one child in five is likely at some time to require some form of special education provision.
- A change of emphasis from where education took place to the type of education required.
- The notion of integration and the concept that where possible children should be educated with their peers.
- That there should be a partnership between parents and the school, and that parents should be kept fully informed of all facilities and support services available to them.
- Early identification of children's special needs by a five-stage model of assessment. Assessment could be undertaken at the parents' or local authority's request.
- Special emphasis on the needs of the pre-school child.

The Warnock Report provided the basis for the Education Act 1981 which totally changed the framework for special education. Following the Act the government published two circulars (8/81 and 1/83) which not only offered advice to local authorities in interpreting the Act but also made it clear that a child's special educational needs referred to its abilities as well as disabilities, and that assessment should be ongoing.

Other legislation brought in prior to and after the 1981 Act facilitated its implementation. Legislation brought in benefits for the families of children with handicaps, such as mobility allowances, attendance allowances, laundry allowances, money to carry out essential conversions on homes in order to enable access for wheelchairs, etc. Local authorities provided transport for children to and from school and facilities were available for holiday and respite care. All these things went a long way to encouraging parents of a child with special needs to care for that child within the family.

Around this time changes were also being made in the National Health Service which discouraged the continuation of large institutional hospitals for specialist care, viewing them as detrimental to the welfare of the patients and expensive to run. These hospitals were slowly being emptied and their clientele rehabilitated to live within the community. People whose only home had been the hospital were now finding that they were capable of living in sheltered hostel accommodation. Social services departments actively promoted foster care programmes for children with special needs who were unable to remain with their families or had previously been housed in one of the large hospitals.

The Education Reform Act 1988 makes scant reference to children with special needs except to state that all subjects and stages of the National Curriculum must be taught in special needs schools. This has led to a number of criticisms from educationalists who feel that time in these schools could be better spent than trying to get children of doubtful or little ability through National Curriculum tests.

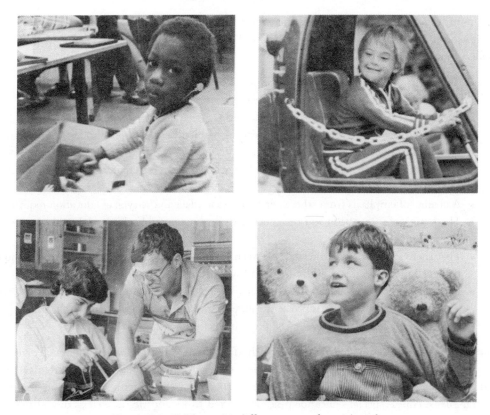

Figure 5.1 Children with different types of special need

Present perspective _____

The present situation is one whereby most children with special needs are able to be accommodated within the family, and those that are not are able, to live with foster parents. Education for these children may be in a mainstream school or in a special school which caters for their specific learning difficulties. Some mainstream schools have special units attached to them such as a partially hearing unit. The children are educated within the special unit but at all other times they join the children from the main section of the school. In this way the special needs are met but the children do not miss out on the social aspects of their education. It is not uncommon to find children with special needs attending playgroups, opportunity groups, community nurseries, nursery schools and day nurseries. However, Clark (1988) makes the following point which questions whether a day nursery could be considered as appropriate mainstream provision:

> many or indeed most children attending such units are already 'at risk' in many ways, to such an extent that it must be questioned as to how 'ordinary' such provision indeed is.

Whilst there is a major emphasis on integration, there is also an emphasis on avoiding the early labelling of children into special needs categories. Psychologists and others are loath to assess children under the age of five years, although parents do have the right to ask for an assessment. If pre-school children are allowed to integrate into mainstream provision it is far easier to ascertain what their abilities are and what they may be capable of in the future.

The Children Act 1989 makes social services departments responsible for providing for children 'in need'. One of the categories of 'in need' is:

> a child is disabled if he is blind, deaf, or dumb or suffers from mental disorder of any kind or is substantially and permanently handicapped by illness, injury or congenital deformity or such other disability as may be prescribed.
>
> *(The Children Act Guidance and Regulations.*
> *Vol. 6: Children with Disabilities*, 1991)

The local authority social services departments are bound to provide services for children with a disability, and such services should be of the appropriate range and level to 'safeguard and promote the welfare of children in need'. The Act charges local authorities to provide services which will enable children with disabilities to be cared for within the family. A requirement of the Act is that social services departments must keep a register of children with disabilities, but obtaining services is not dependent upon a child's name being on that register, and parents are not obliged to register their child. Unlike the local education department which deals only with children of statutory school age, social services facilities are available to children from birth. The Guidelines to the Act mention 'packages of services' which may be provided through statutory and voluntary agencies. The NHS and Community Care Act 1990 requires social services departments to assess the needs of those people who may need community care services; this assessment becomes part of the long-term 'care package' that is devised for each client. A contract is drawn up between the child's family and the service providers which clearly states what will be provided for the child.

The Children Act and the NHS and Community Care Acts place emphasis upon coordination of the services which are available to each family. In the past there have been numerous examples of families that have had more than twenty people going into one household to give different caring services to one child. Inevitably such uncoordinated situations are expensive, lead to unnecessary overlap and instil confusion in the parents or carers.

Statement of a child's educational needs

Part of the assessment process requires a statement to be written on the child's specific learning needs. The aims of the statement are to identify the areas of need and define the treatment/educational requirements for such needs. The statement on the child must be updated regularly in conjunction with the programme of ongoing assessment. Parents must be informed of the local authority's intention to assess their child before any action can be taken and parents have a right to respond within twenty-nine days. Most parents respond positively to the request as they realize that the assessment is for the benefit of their child. Once the assessment has taken place and the statement drafted, it is usual to send a copy to the parents; the parents have a right to appeal against the contents of the statement.

Children with special needs who attend mainstream educational establishments should have a statement which clearly lays out the extra resources they require. In the absence of such a statement the school is not able to obtain the money to fund such resources and therefore is unlikely to be able to provide them. This is particularly pertinent to children with physical disabilities who may require a full-time carer to help them with their mobility, toilet or feeding. Special facilities such as speech therapy, physiotherapy or hydrotherapy need to be clearly documented in the statement if the local authority is to provide the services.

Some children have very minor special needs, particularly those with communication difficulties. In the past such children would have had access to the peripatetic speech therapists who worked in mainstream schools, and would therefore not have needed to be 'statemented' in order to obtain this facility. In recent years, economies by local authorities have led to a cutback in the number of speech therapists employed for mainstream schools, resulting in many children not being supplied with the service. If a child has a statement which requires them to have regular speech therapy then the local authority is bound to provide this; without such a statement there is no guarantee that the child will receive the service. There is a requirement upon local authorities to review statements annually to ensure that the provision is relevant to the child's needs.

Scenario 1	Michael is three years old and has Down's Syndrome. Recently his mother Mary found that the sounds he is making are beginning to form speech patterns. Mary is keen not to let the opportunity pass if Michael is now attempting to communicate using speech.
	What would Mary need to do in order to ensure that Michael can get the speech therapy that the needs?

The Children Act 1989 lays down clearly the responsibilities of the local authority in relation to children in need. However, a child will be required to be diagnosed and labelled 'in need' before the local authority will respond. There are some obvious handicaps which leave no element of doubt that a child is in need, e.g. cerebral palsy, Down's Syndrome, deafness or blindness. There are other handicaps which are not so clear-cut and which may not be assessed until a child reaches school age, such as communication or emotional difficulties, and for which there are unlikely to be any special facilities available for children under five.

Integration

Section 2 of the Education Act 1981 sets out the requirements for integration of children with special needs into the mainstream school system. The philosophy for integration came from the Warnock Report and hinges upon the idea that teachers should be encouraged to look at the needs of all the children in their class and adapt the curriculum accordingly. In 1987 a government select committee reported on the implementation of the 1981 Act. On the question of integration the committee recommended that local authorities should have a clear policy statement taking into account the quality and appropriateness of the integrated provision. The Fish Committee stated:

> The concept of integration as a dynamic process is difficult to grasp. It is often confused with physical location and discussed in terms of specific situations rather than the whole life styles of children. Integration is about planned interaction between a child and his or her environment and is not about changing the concept of special education needs but about its context.

> *(Fish Report: Equal Opportunities for All? 1985)*

Most local authorities are developing their integration policies gradually as long-term commitments would require a significant input of resources, for example providing ramps, lifts, special toilet facilities.

Scenario 2

Molly and Jim are bringing up their grandson Jason, he is six years old and has spina bifida. He is a bright boy, who is wheelchair-bound and at present attends the local school for children with physical disabilities. All his friends are able-bodied and Jason is often sad that he cannot go to the same school as them.

Recently, Molly and Jim saw a programme on television about integrating children with handicaps into mainstream education. They feel that this would be the best thing for Jason.

(a) Using your local policy, find out how Molly and Jim would go about enabling Jason to attend the local mainstream school.

(b) Are there likely to be any reasons that this might not be possible?

When the Education Act 1981 was published many people thought that the integration policy would lead to the closure of special schools and parents flooding to local authorities to ensure that their children could be educated in a mainstream school. For a number of reasons this did not happen. Parents were sensible in their approach to integration and realized that it may not always be the best option for their child. Parents were very conscious of the good adult/child ratios and the wealth of equipment that is provided in the special schools and wanted their children to have the continued benefit of these things. For children with mobility difficulties access to some mainstream schools was a problem, and the government did not offer schools extra resources in order to undertake structural adaptations.

Some special schools have closed down, but it is difficult to determine whether this is as a result of integration or of the fall in the birth rate and therefore a decline in the number of children needing that particular service.

There is no doubt that integration does offer benefits for both the child with special needs and the other children in the class. To be treated as 'normal' is far better than to stand out as being different. Children who spend time with others that have special needs learn to understand that we are not all the same and that some people may need help at certain times. Integration also goes a long way towards removing the stigma that society attaches to those with special needs. Children who have gone to school together often develop positive relationships that can continue throughout their lives.

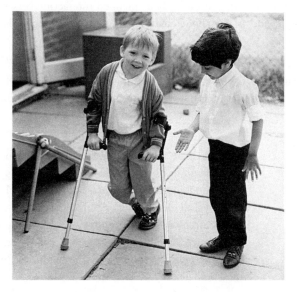

Figure 5.2 Integration in practice

Provision for the under-fives

As previously stated, local authorities are not keen 'to statement' children under the age of five unless a specific request is made by the parents. The first five years of life are an important period in a child's development and for this reason it is better not to label children at an early age. Some children are slower to develop than others but they may have caught up by the time they are five. The Children Act 1989 states:

every local authority should provide services designed –

(a) to minimize the effect on disabled children within the area of their disabilities; and

(b) to give such children the opportunity to lead lives which are as normal as possible.

(The Children Act 1989, Para. 6, Schedule 2)

Once a need has been defined, then, the local authority social services department must match that need to the available services. For pre-school children this may be a place in a day nursery, family centre, nursery school, pre-school playgroup, opportunity group, etc. It may also involve people working with the child within its own home, such as family aide worker or a Homestart visitor or Portage teacher.

Research has shown that families that have a child with a disability suffer more stress than other families. Services which enable the child to spend time outside the home not only benefit the child but offer respite for the family. Often, people going into the home to work with the child find themselves having to act as family counsellors for they may be the only people that the family feel they can talk to.

Scenario 3	Trevor and Janice have three children: Zoe who is eleven years old, Mark who is eight and Daniel who is three. Daniel is autistic and exhibits very bizarre behaviour patterns, ranging from severe temper tantrums to prolonged repetition of one movement or activity. Recently, Zoe has been getting poor school reports and Mark has started to wet the bed at night. Trevor and Janice are getting to their wits end as it seems that now all the children have developed problems.

You are Trevor and Janice's home visitor and are having little success in getting Janice to be interested in playing with Daniel: all she wants to do is talk about her problems.

(a) What can you do for Janice to help her through this difficult period?

(b) What facilities are available for Daniel?

Bonding

There are many examples of mothers rejecting their children because they have been born with a disability. In some cases such rejection is temporary; in others it may be more long-lasting, with the mother needing help in order to overcome her feelings. Everyone wants a perfect baby and it can be a great shock to a mother to find that she has given birth to a less than perfect child. Feelings of rejection are often accompanied by feelings of guilt: that it was something that the mother did wrong during her pregnancy which led to her child being disabled. In most cases such guilt feelings are irrational as the reasons for many handicaps are still unknown.

Rejection may not always happen at birth but at a later date when the child may not be responding as it should. For example, Fraiberg (1977) found that the mothers of blind babies withdrew from them because they were unresponsive and did not make eye contact. There are now special programmes to help mothers of blind babies to bond with their children.

The bonding process does not happen overnight but takes a number of months to become established. Early intervention can help the parents to bond with their disabled child and counselling can help them to overcome any feelings of guilt.

In some cases parents may bond too strongly with their child who has a disability and this may lead to other children in the family being neglected. There is an old adage that says, 'It is not just a handicapped child but a handicapped family', meaning that the whole family is affected when one of its members has a disability. Such strong bonding can also inhibit a child's development as the parents may be over-protective and unwilling to allow the child to develop its independence. In these situations it is most beneficial for the child to spend some hours of the day away from the home by attending some form of pre-school provision.

The policy of keeping children within the family helps the family to bond with the child and it is extremely rare to find a mother who never bonds with her child once she has recovered from the initial shock of finding that it has a disability.

Conductive education

The Peto Institute for Motor Disorders in Hungary is now world famous for its specially devised methods of conductive education. The clinic was founded in 1945 by Dr Andreas Peto and was loosely based on the theories of the Russian psychologists, Pavlov, Luria and Vygotsky. The aim of conductive education is to assess the child's potential in relation to the next progressive stage; it does not concentrate on the child's current abilities. Conductive education is only of use in cases of motor disorders, and in all cases the first step is an assessment to decide whether the child will benefit from this treatment. Conductive education takes an holistic approach to the child and does not concentrate only on the area of the handicap; hence it requires staff who have multidisciplinary skills. The Hungarian Peto staff have undergone a four-year multidisciplinary training which includes skills in teaching, nursing, physiotherapy, speech therapy and occupational therapy. The children's programme is intensive and requires them either to be resident at the institute or to come in daily from 8 a.m. to 5 p.m. The programme is best started when the children are very young (under two years) and continued over a number of years. The children that appear to fare best from conductive education are those that suffer from cerebral palsy, and it is with these children that the programme has had its greatest successes.

There has been criticism of conductive education, one of the main arguments being that the one-to-one intensive situation is responsible for the child's improvement rather than the education programme itself. Whatever the reason, conducive education does seem to work and is much sought after by the parents of children with cerebral palsy. There is now a centre for conductive education in Birmingham, and no doubt we shall see more of these centres opening in the UK in the future. Conductive education has the backing of the Spastics Society and other voluntary organizations and in recent years has had a high media profile.

The Portage programme

Portage is an idea that originated in America in the 1960s and consists of a home-teaching programme for pre-school children whose development is delayed due to specific handicaps. A specially trained Portage teacher visits the home regularly and shows the family how they can work with the child. An activity sheet is drawn up so that parents can register the child's progress.

Portage uses the six main child development areas: language, self-help, motor, socialization, cognitive skills and stimulation, and devises a structured learning programme for specific tasks within these areas. Each task is broken down into small steps which are arranged in a developmental sequence. Parents and carers are then able to work with the children on these small steps; once one has been mastered they move to the next step until the whole task is achieved. A record is kept of the child's progress so that each achievement can be seen. Families are given a Portage Kit which contains record sheets and small cards on which the steps towards a task are written, one card for each step. The cards are colour-coded for developmental area and difficulty of the task.

The Portage scheme has been very successful as it involves all members of the family working with the child and achievements are shared by everyone. It also offers parents and carers a positive interaction with the child, enabling them to see even the smallest progress that the child is making. Portage can be used with children who have specific handicaps or with those who may only have minor developmental problems. Many of the tasks can be incorporated into play situations making it fun for the child and carer.

Children with specific learning difficulties

Specific learning difficulties was a term used by the Warnock Report to describe children who may have a disability in just one particular area of their development. These children are likely to need a specific learning programme in order to overcome the disability.

Children with dyslexia

There is a long and hard debate surrounding the specific learning disability called dyslexia; part of this debate relates to the difficulty in diagnosing the condition and whether there is a distinct group of children with the condition. Basically, dyslexia is a condition whereby children have difficulty in acquiring literacy skills; it may also affect the acquisition of language. Stow and Selfe (1989) refer to the following 'alerting signs' which children with this specific learning difficulty may have:

- skills requiring sequential or spatial ordering of letters or numbers (for example, they may muddle months of the year, or reverse numbers or letters);
- rote or short-term memory for letters and number (for example, they may have problems remembering their tables; etc.);
- laterality (for example, knowing their right from their left, body awareness and direction);

Age Level	Card	Behaviour	Entry Behaviour	Date Achieved	Comments
0.1	1	Sucks and swallows liquid		/ /	
	2	Eats liquified foods, ie. baby cereal		/ /	
	3	Reaches for bottle		/ /	
	4	Eats strained foods fed by parent		/ /	
	5	Holds bottle without help while drinking		/ /	
	6	Directs bottle by guiding it toward mouth or by pushing it away		/ /	
	7	Eats mashed table foods fed by parent		/ /	
	8	Drinks from cup held by parent		/ /	
	9	Eats semi-solid foods fed by parent		/ /	
	10	Feeds self with fingers		/ /	
	11	Holds and drinks from cup using two hands		/ /	
	12	Takes spoon filled with food to mouth with help		/ /	
	13	Holds out arms and legs while being dressed		/ /	
1.2	14	Eats table food with spoon independently		/ /	
	15	Holds and drinks from cup with one hand		/ /	
	16	Puts hands in water and pats wet hands on face in imitation		/ /	
	17	Sits on potty or infant toilet seat for 5 minutes		/ /	
	18	Puts hand on head and takes it off		/ /	
	19	Pulls off socks		/ /	
	20	Pushes arms through sleeves, legs through pants		/ /	
	21	Takes off shoes when laces are untied and loosened		/ /	
	22	Takes off coat when unfastened		/ /	
	23	Takes off pants when unfastened		/ /	
	24	Zips and unzips large zipper without working catch		/ /	
	25	Uses words or gestures indicating need to go to bathroom		/ /	
2.3	26	Feeds self using spoon and cup with some spilling		/ /	
	27	Takes towel from parent and wipes hands and face		/ /	

Figure 5.3 Portage record chart

- sound blending;
- systematic visual scanning.

These children will undoubtedly under-achieve unless they are given a special educational input. The Warnock Committee took the heat out of the dyslexia debate when it devised the category of 'specific learning difficulties' which was intended to cover a wide spectrum of areas which could result in a child under-achieving.

High-ability children

Children who have abnormally high ability or, as they are sometimes called, 'fast learners', are often overlooked when it comes to categorizing children with special needs. The other term which is sometimes used to describe such children is 'gifted'; however, as Sylvia Wyatt points out this term is a misnomer as slow learners often have isolated 'gifts'. Children with high ability may have accelerated learning in a specific area such as mathematics or music or may be all-round fast learners. Ogilvie (1973) offered six areas in which children are likely to show high ability:

1. Physical talent
2. Mechanical ingenuity
3. Visual/performing abilities
4. Outstanding leadership/social awareness
5. Creativity
6. High intelligence

Parents are not always the best judges of whether their child is of high ability because they lack the experience of dealing with large numbers of children over long periods of time and are therefore unfamiliar with the normal ability range. High-ability children often exhibit behavioural difficulties which may be the result of boredom or frustration. At the pre-school stage these children are best helped by attending playgroups, nursery schools or nursery classes where they can be offered activities which will meet their needs. Some children with high ability may have social or personality problems and find it difficult to mix with other children. Children who have high ability in selected skills may under-achieve in other areas; this is often the case when parents have concentrated their efforts on developing the 'gift' of the child rather than on the all-round development of the child. The recent introduction of computers into nursery schools and playgroups has meant that these children are less frustrated as they can have an individual programme to work on and do not have to undertake the same activities as their classmates.

Other groups with specific learning difficulties

Other groups of children may also be designated as having specific learning difficulties, such as children with behavioural or emotional difficulties or those with communication difficulties. The latter may include children with speech impediments, those who have English as a second language or those with poor language development. Most of these children would benefit from nursery education in the pre-school years and, given the right opportunities to develop, may start school on a par with other children.

There is no doubt that children with special needs benefit from early attendance at nursery school or playgroup where they can socialize with mainstream children and participate in activities which will aid their development.

The self-image of children with disabilities

Many children with disabilities suffer from having a poor self-image and lack confidence to explore the world around them. Woolfson (1989) lists the behavioural signs likely to be exhibited by children with poor self-image:

- Find difficulty in giving love to or receiving love from other children and adults including parents.
- Do not relate well to their peers and feel socially isolated from those around them.
- Tend to make derogatory remarks about anything they do even when these achievements are of a satisfactory standard.
- Are more likely to be ashamed of themselves, to have guilt feelings and even to be depressed.
- Have a high level of anxiety and therefore find everyday experiences unusually stressful.
- Have difficulty in being honest in their relationships with other people because of lack of trust in themselves.
- Are defensive when relating to other children and adults and assume the worst of everyone.
- Take longer to settle down when they start school and have slower academic progress.

A poor self-image can be a problem for any child whether it has a disability or not. For the child with a disability though, there is a strong likelihood that it will need help to develop a positive self-image. Children develop their self-image from the way adults and other children interact with them, by comparing themselves and their performance with that of other children, and by becoming familiar with their own bodies and how these may be the same or different from those of other children. It does not take a child with disabilities long to realize that they are different from other children.

A child care worker can do a great deal to help children with disabilities to develop a positive image of themselves. In many cases the child care worker may be the first adult that the child meets outside its own home, and for this reason the carer's reactions to the child are important:

- Always treat the child as an individual and ensure that the child is considered first and the disability second.
- Never address the person pushing the wheelchair, always address the occupant even if it is a small child.
- Make an effort to ensure that the child mixes with the other children, do not leave it

isolated.

- Do not allow other children to poke fun at the child, the able-bodied children must be taught to respect the child with disabilities.
- Always praise and encourage the child even for the smallest achievement.
- Involve the child in all the activities that are going on and encourage it to explore its environment.
- Report the child's progress to the parents/carers on a regular basis and make sure they are aware of the child's achievements, however small.
- Do not make exceptions for the child's behaviour: the child must be encouraged to develop the same self-discipline as other children.
- Have realistic expectations of the child and its abilities.
- Provide activities appropriate for their ability so that they have a chance of achieving.
- Give opportunities for the child to make decisions and encourage it to make choices.

A child care worker should set an example of good practice for the other adults that come into contact with the child. It is also important to adopt a supportive attitude for the parents/carers of the child as this will encourage them in their efforts to help the child lead a lifestyle that is as normal as possible.

Advocacy and empowerment

The movement for child advocacy started in the USA in the 1960s. It was used initially to describe every type of action that was undertaken on behalf of children; however, it is a term which is becoming more frequently used in the UK to describe adults ensuring that the wishes of the child are heard and considered. This is a concept now enshrined in the Children Act 1989. Along with advocacy goes the concept of empowerment, where the child is enabled to make its wishes known to adults. Advocacy and empowerment are very strong concepts which need to be included in all work undertaken with children with special needs. These are the children who are least likely to have a spokesperson and least likely to have their wishes considered. It is an important aspect of the child's self-image that they can have a voice and it is probably no co-incidence that the National Children's Bureau uses as its motto: 'The powerful voice of the child'. Child care workers must be alert to situations and not condone a child being treated in a way that is degrading or against its wishes. If the child cannot make itself heard, then the adult carer must act as advocate for the child. The carer should also undertake activities with the child which will empower the child to make its own wishes known by helping with communication, giving the child choice and decision-making skills.

Assignment 1

You are a playgroup leader and in one week's time you will be admitting a new child, Tommy, who has spina bifida. How will you prepare the other children in the playgroup for Tommy's arrival?

Assignment 2

Your neighbour has an eighteen-month-old child who has Down's Syndrome. You think that the family might benefit from participating in a Portage programme. How do you explain Portage to the family and what advice would you give them as to how they could become involved in this scheme?

Assignment 3

Many recent policies on the care of children with special needs mention advocacy and the empowerment of children. What do you understand by these terms? How would you integrate advocacy and empowerment experiences into the daily activities of children with special needs?

Assignment 4

A new child who has been admitted to your reception class is termed as a 'statemented child'. What does this mean? What will the school need to provide for this child?

References and further reading

Children Act 1989. London: HMSO.

Clark, M. 1988. *Children Under Five: Educational Research and Evidence*. London: Gordon and Breach.

Department of Education and Science. 1978. *Warnock Report: Special Educational Needs*. London: HMSO.

Fraiberg, S. 1977. *Insights from the Blind*. New York: New American Library. Also in *The Developing Child* (5th edn), edited by H. Bee. London: Harper and Row.

Fish, J. 1985. *Equal Opportunities for All? Report of the Committee Reviewing Provision to Meet Special Educational Needs*. London: ILEA.

HMSO. 1991. *The Children Act Guidance and Regulations. Volume 6: Children with Disabilities*. London: HMSO.

Ogilvie, E. 1973. *Gifted Children in Primary Schools*. Basingstoke: Macmillan.

Stow, L. and Selfe, L. 1989. *Understanding Children with Special Needs*. London: Unwin Hyman.

Wyatt, S. (n.d.) *The Identification of Fast Learners*. Gifted Children's Information Centre, London.

Woolfson, R. 1989. *Understanding your Child*. London: Faber and Faber.

Chapter 6
Children in hospital

At some time during the early years of its life a child is likely to become sick. The type of illness they may contract can range from the common cold, an infectious disease such as chickenpox, to a serious illness which requires hospitalization. The study by Davie *et al*. (1972) found that almost half of the children in Britain were likely to have been in hospital at least once by the time they were seven years old.

This chapter concentrates on the needs of children in hospital, and assumes that the reader will already have studied common childhood illnesses. The more serious aspects associated with children in hospital, such as terminal illness and death are discussed. The chapter also looks at the roles of the multi-disciplinary care team and the support networks that are available for the child and its family.

Hospitalization _____

The fear associated with being admitted to hospital is the 'fear of the unknown'. We do not know about hospitals, they are not part of our everyday environment nor are they accessible to be explored in advance, the people inside hospitals often appear as white-coated strangers and uniforms are abundant. Hospitals are places where it is likely that you will experience physical pain, whilst at the same time they may represent a relief from pain. Many adult's deep-rooted fear of hospitals can be traced back to a hospitalization experience of their childhood which may have involved themselves or a member of their family. This is not surprising: scenario 1 describes what admission to hospital used to be like for children.

Scenario 1	In the 1960s, Monday morning on the paediatric ward was the day that children were admitted to have their tonsils removed. At a pre-arranged time approximately a dozen children aged between three and ten years would arrive on the children's ward accompanied by their relatives. In an efficient and professional manner the nursing staff would send the relatives away (making sure they understood that there would be no visiting on operation day), strip the children of their day clothes, dress them in their nightwear and put them to bed. The children would be cared for by many nurses, each involved in a different activity. None of the nurses would have time to spend with individual children, nor were they encouraged to do so by their managers.
	This was just the beginning of a four-day stay which often got worse for the children as the days went on. How do you think these children felt during their stay in hospital?

In the 1960s the nursing staff were not deliberately callous or uncaring in their treatment of the children but were following the philosophy of the time, which was based upon the physical aspects of the child's care and did not take into account the psychological aspects. Lack of understanding of child development or the importance of play, and the attitudes of that time which viewed children as 'mini-adults' led hospitals and nursing staff to take a 'clinical' approach to children.

Hospitals are large institutions which expected those entering them to take on the role of the patient: a role subordinate to that of the medical and nursing staff. The medical knowledge of the staff who knew how to treat and cure disease engendered in them power to decide what was best for the patient. Hospital wards were designed on 'Nightingale' lines: rows of beds, offering little privacy for the individual. To protect themselves from any emotional involvement with the patients, the staff donned uniforms to set themselves apart, and were actively discouraged from getting to know patients in anything other than a clinical way. Patients were identified by their illness and not their name, and it was considered that psychological factors could not be capable of interfering with the healing process.

During the 1970s and 1980s there were radical changes in attitudes towards patients, a move away from the clinical approach towards a patient-centred approach. Such changes had come about as a result of research findings relating to the sociological and psychological effects of hospitalization. In many hospitals, nurses now adopt a procedure called the 'Nursing Process' which ensures that on admission each patient is assigned a nurse who is the patient's key worker. This nurse not only elicits the medical history of the patient but also talks to them about their home circumstances and any fears they may be experiencing about their hospitalization or illness.

Parallel to the developments in the nursing and medical field there were significant research findings relating to child development. In the 1950s John Bowlby put forward major theories about the effects upon children relating to their attachment to and any subsequent loss of their carer. Bowlby developed the theory that it is necessary for children to 'bond' with an adult in order for the child to have psychological stability in its early years. Bowlby's bonding theory in conjunction with the work of James and Joyce Robertson which filmed children in brief separation situations, led to the major present-day theories regarding the attachment and loss reactions of healthy children. Bowlby's work on attachment and loss describes the three stages – protest, despair and detachment – which children go through when separated from the person that they are bonded with. (Although more recent research has challenged the notion of 'one' carer, usually the mother, being responsible for the child's psychological health through bonding, it is true to say that there is a general consensus amongst child psychologists that multiple carers are detrimental to a child's stable development.)

The Robertson's films of children being admitted to residential care and hospital reinforced Bowlby's theories and produced visual evidence of the three stages he proposed. During the first stage of separation the child will cry, become angry and demand the return of their mother or carer. This is the stage of protest and may last for several days; if a parent or carer returns during this period it is unlikely to have done the child lasting damage. If the adult does not return then the child will enter the stage of despair wherein they become quiet but are still preoccupied with the absent person and hoping for their return. If the adult does return during this stage it is likely to take the child some time to rebuild the relationship and to trust the adult. If the adult still does not return then the child enters the final stage of detachment where all hope is given up and the child appears to have forgotten the adult. If the adult returns after this stage, the child may not recognize the person and will not greet them as somebody to whom it is related.

When a child is hospitalized it will pass through the three stages of protest, despair and detachment if steps are not taken to avoid the separation of children from their carers or by the provision of a satisfactory substitute. The length of the separation will determine the number of stages the child may pass through and the amount of subsequent psychological damage that is done to the child.

The work of Bowlby and the Robertsons has done a lot to change the attitudes of the adults who deal with children in separation situations. Thanks to the work of Hugh Jolly and organizations such as Action for Sick Children (prior to October 1991 they were known as the National Association for the Welfare of Children in Hospital, NAWCH) hospitals have totally changed their attitudes towards children who become patients. Parents and relatives are now allowed to stay with children when they are admitted to hospital, children are allowed to bring their favourite toys, wear their own clothes, are not confined to bed unless it is a necessary part of their treatment and have nursery nurses and play specialists working with them to encourage and develop play activities.

Prepared hospital admission

The majority of children going into hospital are admitted from the waiting list and therefore have the benefit of prior notice of the event. Before the admission they would have attended the out-patient department and would be familiar with the building and the doctor who will be treating them. Out-patient departments are likely to have children's waiting areas with toys and play equipment, although this may depend upon the resources of the health authority. In some areas the Pre-school Playgroup Association (PPA) and Save the Children run playgroups inside hospitals. Ideally, the doctors, nurses and paramedical staff will be trained in the best ways to handle children in order to cause them the least amount of stress.

A child who is going to be admitted to hospital can be prepared for the event by parents, relatives, playgroup leaders, teachers, childminder or other carers. The first stage of preparation is to explain to the child what is wrong with them and what the hospital treatment is likely to be. For example, if a child is to have its tonsils removed, then it needs to be explained that it is the tonsils which have been the cause of their sore throats and pain. Using a mirror and a tongue depressor the child can be shown its tonsils. The child should be told that the tonsils will be removed whilst they are asleep and they will not feel it happening as they will breathe a special gas which will put them into a very deep sleep. When they wake up their throat will be very sore. It is important to be honest with children about the medical procedures and about pain, this way the child will know what to expect. Dishonesty about these matters will lead to the child mistrusting the adult and this can permeate all future relationships with the child. Many treatments and operations will hurt the child and this needs to be explained in advance. In many cases the short-term hurt will progress to long-term good health; however, in cases of children who are chronically sick the pain will not be short term and may not give them future good health but many enable them to live longer. There are many story books about children going into hospital, and these can be shared with the child. A doctor's or nurse's outfit can enable a child to play out their fears of hospital and a home corner can easily be adapted to represent a hospital to encourage imaginative play. Talking to the child about the event is important and can be done by all the child's carers. Preparing a child for hospital should be done with the cooperation of all the people who care for the child in conjunction with the child's immediate family.

Figure 6.1 Children playing in hospital corner

There has been a great deal of 'opening up' of paediatric wards, and it is now possible to arrange a pre-admission visit so that the child can meet the nursing and medical staff, the play therapists and the other children. Such a visit does much to allay a child's fears as the hospital then becomes a familiar place.

Admission

The night before admission the child should help to pack its bag and put in its favourite toys and books. On the day of admission the parents or carers should accompany the child and one of them should be prepared to stay with the child. Most hospitals have facilities to enable at least one person to stay overnight, and they do not restrict visiting on paediatric wards. Ideally a parent or relative should stay with the child throughout the hospitalization period and most families are able to organize a rota. This is not so easy if a child is being fostered or has no relatives that live nearby. These children will need more attention from the play therapist and nursing staff, particularly the key worker nurse. The constant presence of a parent or relative means that a child does not go through the trauma of loss as described by Bowlby nor does it have to overcome the problems of having multiple carers.

Emergency hospital admission

When a child is suddenly taken ill or has an accident requiring emergency admission, there is no time to prepare the child for future events. In some instances the child may be unconscious upon admission or arrive at the hospital unaccompanied by a parent or relative. The events leading up to the admission are likely to have been traumatic for the child, i.e. a sudden severe pain, a fall or a road accident: the child will be very frightened and desperately in need of the presence of parents or familiar carers. It is likely that the child would have been admitted via the accident and emergency department and the staff there would have made every effort to contact the child's relatives. The child will not be left alone but the person with them may be a stranger and they will encounter numerous other strangers such as doctors, clerks, radiographers, porters. If the parents are with the child they may be upset and shocked, perhaps they had not previously realized the extent of the child's illness, or feel guilty because the accident had happened when they were not with the child. Emergency admission can be as traumatic for the relatives as it is for the child, possibly leaving the parents unable to cope with comforting their child and needing a great deal of reassurance themselves.

It is the period following the child's admission and when it is out of immediate medical danger that the greatest help can be given to overcome the trauma and fears of past events. It is at this time that the role of the play therapist becomes crucial in helping the child to relieve pent-up emotions via a selection of play activities. These activities are designed to allow the child to explore different situations and roles through dramatic play and release tension through play with clay, dough, hammer-and-peg toys. In the clinical atmosphere of the hospital many play therapists believe that messy play has a great therapeutic value. The child may be feeling guilty, knowing that its condition has upset its parents or knowing that an injury was the result of disobedience. The child needs to be given the opportunity to talk about these things or work through its feelings using play therapy. The nursing staff or hospital social worker will be available to comfort and reassure the parents. The child needs to be told about its operation or injury, and the future treatment explained. The child can be introduced to other children on the ward, there may be another child who has had a similar operation or treatment. Once the child has mobility it needs to be shown all the facilities that it may otherwise have discovered on a pre-admission visit. Children are often very flexible to new situations once their fears are allayed and may quickly come to terms with their new environment.

Chronic or terminal illness

Children who are suffering from chronic or terminal illness have to face regular treatment and periods of hospitalization, the seriousness and extent of these depending upon the diagnosis and available treatment. For these children and their relatives there is continuous stress and anxiety which can place a strain upon family relationships. If the child's condition is due to a genetic defect, parents may feel guilty, and this may interfere with their relationship with the child. Although the individual periods of hospitalization may be short (the average length of stay for a child in Great Ormond Street Hospital is two weeks), they may occur regularly over a long period of time. During these periods in hospital a child may be subjected to numerous tests and treatments, some of which may be painful, and it is easy to envisage how a child may fear the prospect of hospital admission. Parents and staff can do a great deal to alleviate the child's fears by discussing treatment procedures and allowing the child time to come to terms with its situation using play therapy.

Although chronic or terminal illness may interfere with a child's physical development, its psychological, emotional and social development may not be impaired, and it is important that the child is given appropriate activities to enable normal development. Long-term illness may mean that a child is unable to control its own body, so it is important to give the child activities which allow it to make decisions and experience being in control of other situations. One way of doing this is to allow the child to choose its own food, clothes and toys, and to give the child games that encourage decision-making skills.

Discipline can often pose problems for the parents and carers of these children, as imposing rules upon children who may only have a short time to live or are undergoing painful treatments may appear cruel and callous. Discipline and rules are often the very things that offer stability to a child when other things around them are in a state of confusion. Provided that such discipline and rules are carried out with understanding and a certain amount of flexibility, they are unlikely to be detrimental to the child's welfare.

It is important that these children have the love and support of their families and carers during their illness. Regular hospitalizations are disruptive to family life and may cause friction in relationships. The child's siblings may become jealous of the extra attention that the sick child is receiving. It is important that siblings are encouraged to be involved in the illness of their brother or sister, and this can be done by explaining the illness and treatment, taking them on visits to the child in hospital, and involving them in any special treats or trips that the sick child may have. It is significant that organizations such as Dreams Come True or Make-A-Wish, which provide finance to chronic or terminally ill children to have holidays or once-in-a-lifetime trips, usually ensure that the money given enables at least one sibling or family member to accompany them, and sometimes there is enough money granted to enable the whole family to go.

With the advent of chemotherapy and radiotherapy treatments, children with cancer now have a greater chance of a longer life and in some cases a complete cure. However, such treatments have side-effects that are very distressing for the child, such as loss of hair, nausea and vomiting. Some of the side-effects will only last the duration of the treatment but it can take a considerable time for hair to grow back. It is important that children are told about the side-effects of the treatment before it is started so that they know what to expect. Children are offered wigs to wear whilst their hair grows, as this will be happening long after they have left hospital and when they have returned to playgroup, nursery or school. Some young children find wigs uncomfortable and refuse to wear them; they should not be forced to do so. Children will need the support of their family and carers to help them overcome any worries that they may have about returning to the world outside the hospital, and this is the time when there needs to be a good liaison system between the home, the school and the hospital.

Some children may have illnesses which require them to take steroids and the side-effects of these are likely to change the shape of the child's face into a 'moon shape' and their body may become fatter. Once again, it is important that the child knows why these changes are taking place and is told that its body will return to normal once the drug treatment ceases. Any treatments which change the child's body shape can be frightening, and the child will need a lot of preparation and follow-up support to help cope.

| Scenario 2 | Mandy is five years old and knows that she is not well as she has 'bad' cells in her blood which are fighting the 'good' cells. The doctor has told her about the treatment she must have to get rid of the 'bad' cells and how this will make her hair fall out. Today she is feeling very tired and wants to be sick. When she woke up this morning lots of her hair had fallen out and was on the pillow. The nurses have given her a wig to wear: this was fun at first but it soon made her head hot and itchy so she took it off. Yesterday she had felt very cross and cut all the hair off her favourite doll and her mother had been angry with her about this and had shouted at her.

If you were Mandy's carer/play therapist what activities would you devise for her that could help the way she is feeling? |

Coping with death _____

How do children cope with death? This may be their own forthcoming death due to a terminal illness or the death of a close relative or significant person in their lives. Research shows that under
the age of five years a child's reactions to the death of a loved one take on a similar pattern to those
of the child who is separated from its parent or carer: they go through the stages of protest, despair
and detachment. A young child's first encounter with death may be when a pet dies; such experiences enable children to develop and rehearse emotional responses. How a parent or carer answers a
child's questions about the death of a pet or death in general will be very important to the child's
conceptual development. In a misguided desire to protect the child's feelings, parents may describe
death as 'going to sleep' or 'going away', such explanations can cause anxiety and confusion for the
child. It is important that the child is told once an animal or person is dead that they will not
return or participate in future activities. Explanations given to the child may also depend upon the
cultural and religious beliefs of the family but there is a need to remember that explanations which
refer to places in an afterlife can be equally confusing for small children. Television does not help
children to develop a concept of the finality of death as characters in films and plays may die one
day and then reappear on the screen the next day. When children have talked about or encountered
death it will often feature in their imaginative and fantasy play and this should not be discouraged.

A young child with a life-threatening illness may be unaware of, or unable to conceptualize what
death means. The policy in many US hospitals is to make children aware of, their illness and treatment, and, if necessary. to help them prepare emotionally for death. In Britain, most doctors make
decisions with the parents regarding how much a child should be told about its illness. For older children (eight years and upwards), there is much to be said for the idea that a child should be made
aware of its situation, and thereby enabled to prepare for death. Adults have the opportunity to prepare for death by making wills and sealing relationships; in the same way children are likely to appreciate the opportunity to distribute their favourite toys and have last meetings with their friends.

There is little research on the reactions to death of children under five years, the extent to
which a child is able to be prepared for death being dependent upon the child's ability to understand the concepts involved. Such understanding is probably linked with the Piagetian stages of
cognitive development, the child being more equipped to deal with these concepts when they are
in the concrete operations stage, which usually begins around the age of six years. Dr Cecily
Saunders advocates that whatever the age of the dying child, it is important that the child has a
'climate of security'. This may be difficult for parents and relatives to sustain at a time when they
are feeling insecure, anxious and are probably least able to cope with the situation. The emotions
of parents and relatives are quickly picked up by the child, who may in turn become anxious and
feel guilty about causing distress to the family. Children may become confused as they may not
know what it is about them that is responsible for giving stress to their families.

Support for the child and family

There are many people and organizations offering support to a dying child and its relatives; however, it is not uncommon for adults to deny that the child is in a terminal condition. When this

happens, offers of help and support may also be rejected. Within the hospital there may be social workers, bereavement counsellors or religious figures who are able to offer help. Parents and relatives need an opportunity to talk to someone, perhaps even another parent who has been through a similar experience. Staff in hospices (there are hospices for children) and the Macmillan nurses who undertake home-visiting are trained in the best ways to offer support to the child and its family. Organizations such as the Society of Compassionate Friends are able to link relatives with somebody who has had a similar experience. If a child is very young they may miss getting support unless they are exhibiting behavioural problems and are referred to a psychologist. The play therapist and nursing staff are the people most likely to be on hand in the hospital to support the child. Parents and relatives may get comfort from being allowed to provide some of the care for the child and should be encouraged to help with feeding, washing, dressing and joining in with the child's play activities. Such involvement enables the adults to share the last moments of the child's life. By being involved in the care of the child the relatives will feel more adequate and will not be left with the feeling that there was nothing that they could do.

When the child has died it is important for the relatives to be allowed to see the body and go through the healing ritual of the funeral service. Following this there will be a period of grief and ways of expressing this will vary depending upon the cultural and religious beliefs of the family. Some cultures and religions are specific about the period of mourning e.g. Jews sit 'shiva' for a week following a death and the full mourning period lasts for one year. Such ritualized expressions of grief may be a more healthy way of expressing feelings than the quiet introverted process encountered in the British culture. Colin Murray Parkes has studied and written about the grief reactions of white British adults and suggests the stages of grief are numbness, pining and depression. When a child has died suddenly, the initial reactions of the relatives and carers are likely to be anger, aggression and guilt. Each stage of grieving has its own characteristics and differs from person to person, thus comfort for bereaved people comes via individualized, personalized counselling. For many people, talking about the dead child will be a comfort, and a major skill of bereavement counsellors is to be a good listener. It must be remembered that nothing can replace a dead child and the grief processes will be the same whether there are other children in the family or a new baby is born at a later date. Research carried out in this area with families who have lost a child through a cot death (sudden infant death syndrome) has found that even though the families have gone on to produce another child the memory of the dead child remains with them.

Role of the play therapist

The majority of paediatric wards will have a play therapist whose role is to work with the children to alleviate trauma and anxiety through play. Play therapists may be qualified nursery nurses (NNEB) or hold other child care qualifications, and they may also have the Hospital Play Specialist Board Certificate or they may be psychotherapists who have specialized in children. Play therapists design activities that will bring out any fears or misunderstandings that a child may have about its admission to hospital and its treatment. For example, when asked why he was in hospital, one child replied, 'Because I stole sweets from my friend.' In this case the child was viewing its admission to hospital as a punishment. Another child when told that they were to have their blood taken was very frightened because they thought this meant all the blood would be taken from their body. By establishing a good relationship and dialogue with the children in their care, a play therapist is able to ascertain and deal with such fears and mis-understandings.

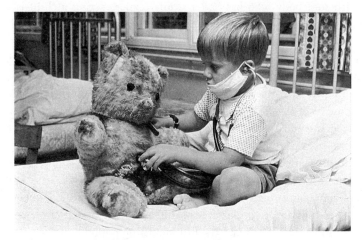

Figure 6.2 Play therapy in action

Play therapists work with individual children and groups of children, and will choose toys and activities which satisfy the needs of all these children. Toys often come into two categories: diversional and therapeutic. Diversional toys divert the child's thoughts away from its illness and enable it to develop new skills, be creative and gain enjoyment and satisfaction from the activity. Diversional toys are things such as paint, puppets, rattles, mobiles, board games, audio and video cassettes and video games. Therapeutic toys allow children to 'play out' their treatment and include medical kits, medical puppets, anatomically correct dolls, mirrors, tape recorders, clay, sand and hammer toys.

As previously mentioned, children who are hospitalized are no longer in control of their bod-ies or their environment, and a major role of the play therapist is to provide activities that will enable children to make decisions enabling them to gain some control and the ability to engage in the healthy activities of fantasy and role play. For the very young child the play therapist needs to provide activities that will encourage normal development. For example, an eighteen-month-old child will need activities to stimulate language development, motor co-ordination, fine manipulative movements, and so forth. Children in hospital are likely to regress in their develop-ment and will need a great deal of stimulation and encouragement to catch up with their peers. Older children who regress may need to be given activities that are designed for a younger child so that they can complete these and have a sense of achievement.

For the child over five years of age the paediatric wards will have a teacher on hand and may even have a classroom. These teachers are provided by the local education authority and work closely with the play therapists in designing a package of education and play for each child. Many

Figure 6.3 Pastry making

play therapists undertake an advisory and counselling role with parents and relatives, helping them cope with the child's illness and suggesting appropriate toys and activities that they can share with the child.

There are no age limits to the children that play therapists may be working with, and older children may welcome the opportunity to regress without losing self-esteem. For children who are in hospital over a long period or are admitted at frequent intervals, there is a danger that they will become institutionalized. When this happens the hospital becomes their main environment and they lose touch with the outside world. There has been a great deal of research on institutionalization undertaken with children in residential care. Children who have become institutionalized have problems in coping with the environment outside the institution and are often deficient in their decision-making skills. Many hospitals have gone a long way to prevent this happening by allowing children to make decisions about food and clothing, allowing them to go on outings or weekends home, letting them visit the hospital shop and allowing unlimited visiting by friends and relatives. Play therapists also help by enabling children to take the decision-making role in their play.

Scenario 3	The play therapist arrives on the ward with a box full of stuffed cloth dolls which have no features, clothes or hair. The children are invited to choose a 'patient' and to decide who it is, colour it with crayons and practise carrying out a 'treatment' on their patient. The children are allowed to be doctors, nurses, physiotherapists or whatever role they like. What do you think is the value of this activity for the children?

The role of the play therapist is crucial, requiring special skills as it involves the care of children who will make good recoveries and those who may die. A play therapist may be confided in by a child wishing to tell whom it will leave its treasured possessions to when it dies. Children may ask the play therapist how best to deal with their parents or relatives who may be having more difficulty than the child in coping with the diagnosis. In a lighter vein, a play therapist may have to organize a ward birthday party, cope with the whole of Form 5A visiting Mary and go shopping for presents on behalf of the child.

Assignment 1

Find out what facilities are available for children in the out-patient department of your local district general hospital. Do you think the facilities are adequate?

Assignment 2

Devise a programme of activities to occupy a five-year-old in hospital between the hours of 9 a.m. and 4 p.m. Give reasons for your choice of activities.

Assignment 3

The goldfish in your nursery has just died. Write down the explanation of death that you will give to the children and a list of associated activities that you could carry out with them.

Assignment 4

Review a children's book which tells the story of a child going to hospital.

References and further reading

Bowlby, J. 1969. *Attachment and Loss. Vol. 1: Attachment.* Harmondsworth: Penguin.

Bowlby J. 1969. *Attachment and Loss. Vol. 2: Separation, Anxiety and Anger.* Harmondsworth: Penguin.

Bowlby, J. 1979. *The Making and Breaking of Affectional Bonds.* London: Tavistock.

Davie, R., Butler, N.R. and Goldstein, H. 1972. *From Birth to Seven.* Harlow: Longman.

Hughes, J. 1981. *Questions Children Ask.* Tring: Lion.

Lansdown, R. 1980. *More Than Sympathy.* London: Tavistock.

Lindley, K. 1984. *Helping Children Cope with the Loss of a Fellow Pupil.* Clwyd: School Psychological Service.

Roberston, J. 1970. *Young Children in Hospital.* London: Tavistock.

Rutter, M. 1972. *Maternal Deprivation Reassessed.* Harmondsworth: Penguin.

Saunders, C. 1969. 'The management of fatal illness in childhood', *Proceedings of the Royal Society Medicine,* **62:** 550.

Ward, B. and Houghton, J. 1987. *Good Grief: Talking and Learning about Loss and Death.* Good Grief Associates.

Wells, R. 1988. *Helping Children Cope with Grief: Facing a Death in the Family.* London: Sheldon Press.

Chapter 7
Child protection

Whilst recognizing that accidents to children in the home and on the roads account for the highest cause of death and serious injury in the 0–4 years age range, this chapter does not deal with protecting children from accidents. The term 'child protection' as used here refers to keeping children safe from neglect and abuse. This terminology reflects the recent trends in the field which have moved away from concentrating on the signs and symptoms of neglect and abuse, towards taking a more positive attitude by exploring ways in which children can best be protected from these situations.

Historical perspectives _____

Sociologists argue that the neglect and abuse of children is a social construct. To understand this terminology we need to look at the way society has viewed and does view childhood. Historically, the period of life that we refer to as childhood has been defined in many different ways. Aries (1973) gives a full account of the way European society has, over time, viewed the status of childhood. For example, children have been treated as 'mini-adults', the property of their parents or other adults and have been handled accordingly. Most people are familiar with the Victorian adage that 'children should be seen but not heard'; this is in contrast to the present-day attitudes which encourage adults not only to hear children but to listen to them. At present there is a movement towards the view that children should be treated as individuals with their own rights within society. The way that society perceives children has great bearing on the way that society treats children; this is what sociologists mean by a 'social construct'.

Many of our classic novels offer descriptive examples of situations which today we would classify as child neglect and abuse. They were set in the times when children were treated as property. It is a reflection of those times that in 1875 the first case of child physical abuse was brought before a court in the USA under the laws relating to cruelty of animals. Even today, many child care campaigners feel that it is a reflection of the present-day attitudes that the society for protecting animals has royal patronage (Royal Society for Protection of Animals) whereas the society for protecting children does not (National Society for the Prevention of Cruelty to Children, NSPCC).

In a document entitled *Child Abuse: The Child's Viewpoint* from the Children's Legal Centre 1988 it states:

> In our view the major cause of all kinds of abuse of children in our society ... arises from the deeply rooted and negative attitudes to children.

In England the first laws to protect children from physical abuse were passed in 1889; however, it took until the 1960s for child abuse to be taken as a serious subject and for researchers to start looking for causes. Part of the reason for this was that adults did not think that events in childhood had a lasting impression or affected the way that a person behaved as an adult. It was Sigmund Freud (1856–1939), the Austrian psychiatrist, who first argued that events in childhood could lead to mental disturbances, fears and phobias which were in turn reflected in the quality of adult relationships.

In the 1960s a number of researchers put forward important theories which argued that children had feelings and were affected by events such as the loss of, or abandonment by, their parents or carers. The work of John Bowlby on attachment and loss reactions in children was backed by the visual evidence of films made by James and Joyce Robertson which showed children's reactions to brief separations from their parents when they were taken into hospital or residential care.

At around the same time in America, Harlow undertook experiments with monkeys which clearly showed that the removal of the mother had severe effects upon their emotional development. The results of these pieces of research were to have a significant effect upon the way society viewed children.

In 1968, Kempe, an American paediatrician, put forward the idea of the 'battered child syndrome', and thus brought child abuse to the front of the research arena. Kempe also looked at abusing parents and put forward the idea of the 'cycle of abuse', whereby parents who themselves had been battered in their childhood in turn battered their own children. In 1978 Kempe stated:

> Child abuse occurs in the presence of four factors:
> 1. the parents must have a background of emotional or physical deprivation and perhaps abuse as well;
> 2. a child must be seen as unlovable or disappointing;
> 3. there must be a crisis;
> 4. there are no effective sources of aid at the moment of crisis.

For many years the pattern for intervention strategies in child abuse relied heavily on the work of Kempe, thus we saw programmes to break the cycle of abuse, therapy for abused children, crisis counselling and help lines for parents.

Present situation

Is child abuse more prevalent in the 1990s than it was in the past? In the past there were poor definitions of abuse; accurate records of incidents were not kept so there are no statistics to compare; children were often not believed if they made disclosures of abuse and may have even been blamed and punished for the incidents; society in general did not welcome the subject of abuse being raised privately or publicly. More recently, many of the above positions have been reversed; statistics are now kept; children are listened to and are likely to be believed; professionals are trained to take a pro-active role in dealing with cases of abuse.

In the DHSS guide, *Working Together* (1991) it states that:

> A child's statement about an allegation of abuse, whether in confirmation or denial, should always be taken seriously. A child's testimony should not be regarded as inherently less reliable than that of an adult. However, professionals need to be aware that a false allegation may be a sign of a disturbed family environment and an indication that the child may need help.

Organizations such as ChildLine have been set up specifically to listen to children wishing to disclose incidents of abuse. Professionals working with children and their families are now very aware of child abuse in all its forms and are able to keep a protective eye on the children in their care. Because of changes in society and in the facilities for reporting abuse, cases are more likely to become statistics, thus showing what may appear to be a sharp increase in incidence. Local authority social services departments keep 'child protection' registers where the names of children/families that are considered to be at risk of abuse and therefore in need of protection are entered. Such records are also likely to become part of the national statistics even though abuse may not have taken place.

Lastly, it is necessary to look at the role of the media in publicizing the more extreme cases of abuse. The broadcasting of television documentaries and publication of sensational articles in the press have given child abuse a high profile. In turn, this may lead people to believe that there is a much higher incidence of abuse within society than there actually is.

Always look carefully at any statistics before drawing conclusions, particularly the definitions of abuse that the researchers are using. It is important that workers with young children and their families are not influenced by sensationalism in media reports. Incidence rates and statistics should never be put before believing a child. Later, this chapter examines the concept of family dysfunctioning which is a contributory factor in child abuse; such dysfunctioning can occur in *any* family.

Definitions of child abuse

There are many definitions of child abuse and it would neither be useful nor possible to reproduce them all here. Using the guidelines laid down by the Department of Health, each local authority draws up its own policy on child protection. The Department of Health makes it clear that its definition is just one of many and it does not necessarily mean that other definitions are wrong.

The Open University (1989) uses the NSPCC definitions with some enhancements to include examples which enable people to understand them more easily. These are as follows:

> *Neglect.* Where parents (or whoever else is caring for the child) fail to meet the basic essential needs of children, like adequate food, clothes, warmth and medical care. Leaving young children alone and unsupervised is another example of neglect; refusing or failing to give adequate love and affection is a case of emotional neglect.
>
> *Physical abuse.* Where a parent (or somebody else caring for the child) physically hurts, injures or kills a child. This can involve hitting, shaking, squeezing, burning and biting. It also involves giving a child poisonous substances, inappropriate drugs and alcohol, and attempted suffocation or drowning. It includes the excessive use of force when carrying out tasks like feeding or nappy changing.
>
> *Sexual abuse.* When adults seek sexual gratification by using children (boys or girls). This may be by having sexual intercourse or anal intercourse (buggery), engaging with the child in fondling, masturbation or oral sex; and includes encouraging children to watch sexually explicit behaviour or pornographic material, including videos.
>
> *Emotional abuse.* Where children are harmed by constant lack of love and affection, or threats, verbal attacks, taunting or shouting.
>
> (Open University, 1989)

In addition to the above, the Department of Health defines one more category:

> *Grave concern.* This category should not be used lightly and should be needed only in exceptional circumstances for children whose situations do not currently fit the above categories. This may be where there is an explicit and serious concern that the child is not developing as would be expected (and all medical causes have been eliminated) or there is a sudden, unexplained change in that child's normal behaviour pattern. If the cause of the child's condition is later established as fitting one of the above categories, a case conference should amend the cause of registration.
>
> (Department of Health, 1991)

It is sometimes difficult to distinguish between neglect and abuse, and those working in the field of child protection are trained to make such fine distinctions. For the majority of child care and education workers it is sufficient that they be able to recognize that something is happening to a child and that they know to whom to pass that information. All local authorities have policies and procedures for dealing with child protection and the reader is advised to make sure that they are familiar with their local policy.

Theories on the causes of child abuse

There are numerous theories offering explanations as to why adults abuse children, but only a few will be mentioned in this chapter.

The medical model

In 1962 Kempe and Kempe, coined the phrase 'battered child syndrome' which led to the causes of child abuse being viewed as a disease with specific signs and symptoms (see Kempe's four factors for child abuse which appear earlier in this chapter). The medical view was heavily criticized and in 1976 Kempe and Kempe changed their terminology to 'child abuse and neglect'. Presenting child abuse as if it were a disease led people to believe that it was predictable, preventable and curable, just as any other disease: but as we know, it is not.

The sociological model

Sociological research has concentrated on the changing patterns of society and how these have affected the functioning of the family. Unemployment, poverty, poor housing, poor health care and social deprivation are given as reasons for people abusing their children (Parton, 1985). If this were true then one would expect all child abuse to occur in families who were social class 5 on the Registrar General's social scale. However, statistics show that child abuse occurs in families from all social classes.

The psychological model

Psychologists have put forward theories which relate to the way a household functions as a family and refer to the breakdown of these relationships as family dysfunctioning. This theory hinges upon the idea that family therapy can repair poor relationships and thus prevent child abuse. Alongside this theory is the idea of 'scapegoating' whereby all the aggression and frustration of poor family relationships is directed towards one member of the family (often the weakest) and that is the person who will be abused. Whilst there is no doubt that in some abusing families one particular child may be the recipient of the abuse, there are cases where all the children in a family have been abused.

The feminist model

With the advent of sex abuse being openly discussed, a number of theories have been put forward by feminists. These theories are based mainly upon sexual politics and examine power relationships between men and women. The fact that it is men who are the main perpetrators and men who are the judges of these perpetrators enables the feminists to put forward very convincing theories. Beatrix Campbell (1988), when writing about the Cleveland case, states: 'the gender factor was salient to Cleveland'. She proceeds to illustrate how the whole affair challenged society's stereotypes of doctors, abusers and victims. Whilst offering powerful arguments in relation to the causes of sex abuse, the feminists ignore the fact that some ten per cent of sexual abusers are women; and that victims can be both male and female. Although the feminists' arguments concerning power relationships are valid, they do not appear really to have tackled the questions raised about physical and emotional abuse, although Miller (1983) does attempt to do so by examining how punishment and sanctions against children are inculcated in our child-rearing practices and legitimized as being 'for the good of the child'.

In spite of the large number of theories put forward, there is no one theory which can be applied to all cases of child abuse. Each situation is different and occurs for different reasons, and therefore needs to be viewed individually. The theories that appear to be the most popular with child protection workers are those relating to family dysfunctioning. This may be because they enable child protection workers to offer intervention in the form of family therapy whereas many of the other theories would require major changes in society's attitudes or government intervention to improve the structure of society.

Variations in family functioning

In present-day society it is difficult to define the term 'family' as it is likely to mean different things to different people. Sociologists have defined three types of family that they maintain represent the normal household unit in the UK.

1. *The extended family.* Parents, children, grandparents, aunts, uncles, cousins, etc. all living in close proximity.
2. *The nuclear family.* Parents and children living together.
3. *The one-parent family.* A mother or father living singly with their children.

Scenario 1

Mr Brown is unemployed and Mrs Brown has a full-time job as a cashier at the local supermarket. Although Mr Brown is at home all day it is Mrs Brown's responsibility to organize all the child care for their two children and run the household. Mr Brown is not the sort of man that participates in these activities, in fact he feels that to be seen hoovering or looking after the children would make people think he was not a 'real man'. The Browns do not have any family or relatives living nearby who could help out with the children. There are frequent quarrels between the parents, and Mrs Brown is often depressed because she is unable to meet the demands placed upon her. Often the children are blamed for being so demanding and Mr Brown has little patience with them. This is a potentially explosive situation.

Write a sequel to this scenario that either offers the Browns help with their predicament or leads to a crisis.

There are many other combinations of relationships that may go to form a household and which describe themselves as a family unit. The high divorce rate in the UK means that many children live in a family where one of the parents is not their natural parent. (It is probably significant that the Children Act 1989 enables step-parents to apply for parental responsibility – see chapter 8.) The people that make up a family unit and the roles that they undertake within it are not important provided that the family is able both to operate as a cohesive group and to meet the needs of all its members, particularly those of the children. It is when needs within the family are not met, or when adults' needs are met at the expense of the children's, that problems will arise.

In other situations, such as an extended family, where the senior male may take on the role of decision-maker for all the family but does not take into account the feelings and opinions of individual members, there can be considerable family conflict. In a one-parent family where the adult has no help from relatives or friends, there may be difficulties coping with all the responsibilities. Our society exerts a great deal of pressure upon the family unit and it is easy to use one particular member as a scapegoat for the family's stresses.

Scenario 2	Mr Smith has a poorly paid job and Mrs Smith tries to subsidize the family income by doing early morning office cleaning. The have three children aged between 8 years and 3 years; the eldest two attend the local primary school and the youngest has a part-time place at the local nursery school. The family receive income support and it is a daily nightmare for the parents trying to manage their financial affairs.
	Recently, the eldest child demanded his parents buy him a computer so that he could play games like his friends. The parents conceded and are paying for it under a hire purchase scheme. Yesterday the middle child, aged 6 years, demanded a pair of designer label training shoes which cost £70, refusing to go to school until he got them. Mrs Smith bought these using an in-store charge card. The family are seriously in debt and each day seems to bring more financial problems.
	Mr Smith, jealous of the fact that a lot of his hard earned money is being spent on the children, has taken to nightly visits to the pub. Mrs Smith, tired from her daily work rents videos to watch while her husband is out. There have been numerous quarrels about money and Mrs Smith feels that her husband is taking it out on the children, particularly the youngest child.
	Write a continuation of this scenario which either helps the Smiths to solve their problems or leads to a situation which requires intervention by the social services department.

Housing is a problem in some areas, and families with children may find themselves in unsuitable high-rise blocks, temporary short-life accommodation or living in bed-and-breakfast hotels or hostels. None of these is conducive to bringing up children and places considerable strain upon family relationships. These situations do not make it easy for parents to answer the needs of their children.

Scenario 3

Gillian and her two children aged 3 years and 7 years are living in bed-and-breakfast accommodation in a shoddy hotel in a poor district of the city centre. Her husband Bill is not allowed to stay there and is sleeping on the floor at a friend's house. They had been living in a nice three bedroom flat which they were buying from the local council. Bill was made redundant from his job and they were unable to meet the mortgage repayments so the building society had repossessed the flat. Since that time Gillian and the children had been living in bed-and-breakfast accommodation.

Gillian is suffering from depression and spends most of her days in the small hotel room with the children. The only cooking facility is a gas ring in the room where she can boil water or soup. The eldest child has not attended school since they moved into the hotel as they now live too far from the school to walk and Gillian cannot afford bus fares.

There have been complaints from the hotel management about the noise the children make running up and down the corridors. Gillian has lost her patience with the children and frequently hits and shouts at them in order to get them to be quiet. Gillian is also worried about Bill as he is visiting less and less frequently and she is afraid that he may have found another woman.

Write a sequel to this scenario which either shows how Gillian can be helped or depicts what the next steps may be in the way Gillian handles the children.

In addition to the social problems that people might face there are some families who have inadequate or undeveloped parenting skills (Winnicott, 1964, coined the term 'good enough parenting'). Parenting skills are not a subject that is on the secondary school curriculum although some schools do have child development as a curriculum subject. In the past, if people found that they were unable to cope as parents they could hire a nanny or rely on members of the extended family to show them how things should be done and to offer care and support. Today, many families have nobody to ask advice from if their child gets three month colic or has temper tantrums, so parenting can become a 'hit and miss' affair. In many cases parents rely on treating the child as they themselves were treated by their own parents. This is all right unless their parents were abusers, in which case the 'cycle of abuse' which Kempe was referring to comes into play.

The concept of 'good enough parenting' _____

Pugh and De'Ath (1984) maintain that parents need certain skills if they are going to care adequately for their children. These skills fall into the following categories:

> The ability to love and undertake relationships, to care, to support and nurture other people, to be sensitive to their needs.
>
> Flexibility of mind and thinking, the ability to respond and adapt to changing needs and demands.
>
> Consistency of attitudes and behaviour, a reliable and dependable behaviour that provides a stable and secure environment where responses can be anticipated and rules are clear.
>
> The ability to communicate, through active listening, giving appropriate non-verbal and verbal messages, reflecting on feelings, and negotiating.
>
> The ability to make decisions and to accept responsibility for them.
>
> The ability to cope with stress and deal with conflict.
>
> The ability to apply knowledge and information, for a theory on how to cope with temper tantrums is no use unless it can be put into action.

It is unlikely that the average family would have acquired all these skills and abilities by the time the first child arrives; however, it is possible for them to increase their knowledge by talking to relatives, friends, professionals, and by reading books and magazines on child-rearing.

Research has shown that there are a number of features associated with adults who are likely to be poor parents and/or neglect and abuse their children. These are looked at next.

Parents who themselves have been abused as children

These are the people who Kempe (1978) referred to as being caught in a cycle of abuse. There had probably been a close association between love and violence during their childhood. For example, a parent may have hit a child too hard and was then immediately sorry; hugging and cuddling followed to appease the parent's conscience, and the child establishes an association between the two emotions: the receiving of violence goes hand in hand with the receiving of love. These people need a lot of help to disassociate the love and violence factors in their lives.

Another aspect of this is those parents who as children were severely chastised/abused and who take the attitude, 'It didn't hurt me so it won't hurt them'. This is more difficult to deal with as the severe chastisement in childhood has harmed them but they are unable to recognize the damage.

Parents who have had poor parenting

Some mothers or fathers are cold, unemotional people, unable to show love, inconsistent in their dealings with the child, making demands upon the child, seeking attention for themselves and denying the child's needs. All of these things affect the child and are likely to be reflected later in the way they treat their own children. Many people have only their own parents as role models, thus poor parenting practices are passed on. When their own parents have been lacking so this is perpetuated by them becoming poor parents.

Very young parents or newly-wed young parents

Some teenagers who become parents have great difficulty in coping as they themselves are still growing up. Often they find themselves in a conflict situation, wanting the freedom of their teenage years but having the responsibility for a small child. They are unable to meet the needs of the child because they are unaware of what those needs are. When people marry young and a child is born very early in the marriage, there can be problems. In this situation the couple have probably not yet come to terms with marriage and their relationship with each other when suddenly they find that there is now the responsibility of a child to rear. These situations are likely to cause fewer problems if the couple are part of an extended family which is able to offer advice and support.

Parents who have unrealistic views of their child's behaviour

Some people have the idea that children will behave impeccably as long as they are well fed and kept clean. These people have no idea about stages of child development and are likely to place unrealistic demands upon their children. When the children are unable to come up to these expectations they are punished; in some cases this punishment may be severe. In these situations love may be conditional upon the behaviour of the child.

Parents who are poor

People caught in the poverty trap can be faced with immense problems trying to manage a family budget. Making decisions about paying rent, buying the right sort of food or spending money on videos, cigarettes and alcohol do not come easily to some people. Being unable to make reasoned decisions which may mean going without certain items can lead to the family amassing large debts with no hope of ever paying them off. Whilst this process is going on, food may not be bought, clothes may not be bought, heating and lighting bills may not be paid and the child may suffer. One member of the family may be selfish and object to going without and this can lead to added stress for the rest of the family. Sometimes this situation can lead to a child being treated as a scapegoat and neglected or abused by the parents who may feel that is it the extra expense of the child that is responsible for their poor financial state.

Parents who demand affection from their children but who are unable to show affection to the child

Some people are very demanding of affection from all the people around them but they themselves are unable to give affection to others. This may lead to them using emotional blackmail with their children in order to get their own needs answered. They are likely to tell the child that if they behave in a certain way it must mean that they do not love their mother/father. This type of behaviour by adults totally confuses children emotionally.

Parents who have low self-esteem

Many things in life can lead to a person having low self-esteem. It may come about as the result of things that happened in their childhood, e.g. not being able to live up to parental expectations, or it may be due to things that have happened in adult life, e.g. a husband/wife deserting their spouse to live with someone else. In some families it can be associated with gender, e.g. the males behaving in a superior fashion and perpetually 'putting down' the female family members. Redundancy from a job can lead to a loss of self-esteem. When low self-esteem leads to the adults blaming the children for their situation or adults trying to raise their self-esteem by insisting on unrealistic behaviour from their children, it can lead to the child being neglected or abused. Adults who sexually abuse children often have low self-esteem and are probably unable to make adult sexual relationships.

Parents who are addicted to alcohol or drugs

The behaviour of people that have a problem with alcohol and drug abuse will affect the whole family. Many cases of family violence are associated with alcohol abuse, one member of the family getting so drunk that they are unable to control their reactions to normal family situations. Drug abuse can also lead to violence, but in many instances it is more commonly associated with neglect. Children are often neglected because the parent is spending all the income on drugs or alcohol rather than buying food and clothes. The effects of drugs often lead to the addict spending much time in a state of inertia and neglecting the basic needs of themselves and their children.

Parents with mental illness

If a family member has a mental illness this will place stress upon the whole family. Adults exhibiting bizarre behaviour patterns and severe mood swings can be very distressing for children. In some cases the moods may be violent and this may lead to the child being abused. If the parent is suffering from depression they may be totally unable to cope with the responsibilities of child-rearing and may neglect the child. Following the birth of a child a woman may suffer post-natal depression which can lead to her being disinterested in the baby.

None of these categories is clear-cut nor applicable to all adults that neglect or abuse their children, but they are worth considering when explanations are being sought.

Features of child neglect and abuse

Statistics show that the highest incidence of child abuse occurs in the age range 1–4 years. It occurs in all social classes and the people most likely to be perpetrators are parents, cohabitees who are not the child's natural parent, siblings and strangers. Research has identified features which may be associated with children who are likely to be at risk of neglect and abuse:

- Children born prematurely.
- Children separated from their mother for some period following their birth.
- Children with disabilities.
- Children who cry a lot.
- Children who are difficult to feed.
- Step-children.
- Children who are not the sex wished for by the parents.

General indicators of child neglect and abuse

There are a number of indicators that have been put forward by professionals in the field of child protection in order to raise awareness in those who are working on a daily basis with children and their families. The following lists have indicators which apply to children and their parents. It is most likely that your local authority policy and practice documents state the local guidelines, the following are generalized indicators.

Parents who may neglect or abuse their children may exhibit the following:

- Rejection of the child.
- Rough handling of the child.
- Failure to keep appointments with child care staff.
- Frequent visits to the medical services with trivial complaints about the child or themselves.

Children who may be suffering from neglect or abuse may exhibit the following:

- Unexplained failure to thrive.
- Injuries that are inconsistent with the accident as described by the parents.
- Frequent bruising, cuts, burns, etc.
- Frozen awareness, when the child carefully watches adult's expressions and movements.
- Reluctance to be alone with their parent/s.
- Sudden unexplained changes in their reactions towards their carers.

Not all children who have been neglected or abused will show all of these indicators, and one indicator alone may not denote that a child is being neglected or abused. A number of children may exhibit 'failure to thrive' and doctors may not be able to find any reasonable explanation for this but this does not necessarily indicate that they have been a victim of abuse. A child with a combination of indicators who has a parent who is also exhibiting one or more of the adult indicators could lead a carer to suspect that they may be dealing with a case of abuse or neglect.

In the area of child sexual abuse there is a different set of indicators, most of these are related to the behaviour of the child:

- Sudden changes in personality, such as wanting constant attention and reassurance.
- Lack of trust of a familiar adult.
- Aggressive or compliant behaviour.
- Withdrawal, listlessness, sadness.
- Regression in toilet training.
- Sleep disturbances and nightmares.
- Fear of being alone.
- Showing affection in a sexual way inappropriate to their age.
- Exhibiting sexual promiscuousness in their imaginative play.
- Frequent urinary tract infections and other ailments related to the genital area.
- Eating problems, loss of appetite, problems swallowing, excessive eating.

Specific indicators of various forms of child neglect and abuse _____

Neglect

Physical indicators

- Poor hygiene.
- Inadequately clothed, dirty, torn or inappropriate clothing.
- Untreated medical problems.
- Poor nourishment/failure to thrive.
- Emaciation.

Behavioural indicators

- Tired or listless.
- Low self-esteem.
- Always hungry.
- States that there is no one at home to look after them or indicates that they spend a lot of time at home alone.

Physical abuse

Physical indicators

- Unexplained bruising in places where an injury cannot easily be sustained or explained.
- Facial bruising.
- Hand or finger marks or pressure bruising.
- Bite marks.
- Burns (particularly cigarette burns), scalds.
- Unexplained fractures.
- Lacerations or abrasions.

Behavioural indicators

- Shying away from physical contact.
- Withdrawn or aggressive behaviour.
- Sudden changes in behaviour, e.g. from extrovert to introvert.

Sexual abuse

Physical indicators

- Bruises or scratches inconsistent with accidental injury.
- Difficulty in walking or sitting.
- Pain or itching in the genital area.

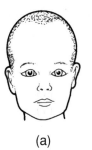

(a)

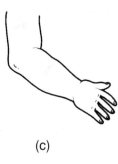

(c)

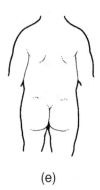

(e)

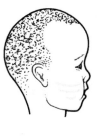

(b)

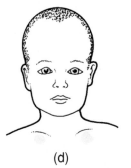

(d)

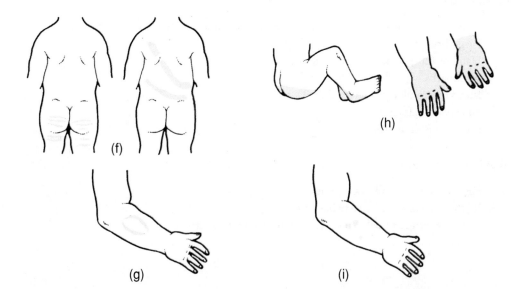

(f)

(h)

(g)

(i)

Figure 7.1 Signs of physical abuse: (a) Facial squeezing; (b) diffuse facial bruising; (c) pinch marks; (d) grip marks; (e) body bruising; (f) identifiable lesions; (g) bite marks; (h) burns or scalds; and (i) cigarette burns.

- Torn, stained or bloody underclothes.
- Bedwetting, sleep disturbances.
- Loss of appetite.

Behavioural indicators

- Hints of sexual activity through words, play, drawings, etc.
- Sexually precocious, uses seductive behaviour towards adults.
- Uses sexually explicit language.
- Excessive preoccupation with sexual matters.
- Informed knowledge of adult sexual behaviour.
- Poor self-esteem.
- Withdrawn or isolated from other children.

Emotional abuse

Behavioural indicators

- Attention-seeking.
- Withdrawn.
- Telling lies.
- Inability to have fun.
- Low self-esteem.
- Tantrums past the age when they are part of normal development.
- Speech disorders, e.g. stammering.
- Inability to play.
- Indiscriminately affectionate.

Good practice for dealing with child neglect and abuse_____

What to do if you are caring for a child who exhibits indicators of neglect or abuse

1. Be sure of your facts. One way of ensuring that you know exactly what indicators the child is showing is to undertake systematic observation of the child's behaviour over the period of a day.
2. Report your suspicions to a senior member of staff who will know the local authority's procedures for child protection.
3. Continue to observe the child and build up a picture of the indicators in preparation for writing a report.
4. Make a special point of trying to involve the child in play activities, particularly those that will enable the child to let out its aggression or will help to raise the child's self-esteem.

What to do if a child tells you that they have been abused

(In some textbooks this is referred to as 'disclosure', however, the Cleveland Report (1987) pointed out 'The undesirability of calling them "disclosure" interviews, which precluded the notion that sexual abuse might not have occurred'. The word 'disclosure' has been phased out of child protection terminology.)

1. Reassure the child, saying that you are glad to have been told.
2. Tell the child that you believe them and that you will do your best to protect them.
3. Let the child know that it is the adult who is to blame not the child.
4. Be ready to listen to what the child has to say but *do not* ask questions.
5. Report the matter to a senior member of staff so that the local authority's policy on child protection can be put into practice.

The case conference

When there is reason or suspicion to think that a child has been neglected or abused and the matter has been reported to the relevant senior staff member, it is likely that a case conference will be called. The Department of Health document *Working Together* (1991) defines a case conference as:

> a forum for the exchange of information between professionals involved with the child and family...that allows for...multi-disciplinary discussions of allegations or suspicions of abuse; the outcome of investigations, assessment for planning; an action plan for protecting the child and helping the family and reviews of the plan.

Those people invited to attend a case conference are the 'key workers' with the child and family: for example, health visitor, social worker, head teacher, teacher, nursery nurse, nursery officer, playgroup leader, general practitioner, paediatrician. Sometimes case conferences involve the police, particularly if they have had past dealings with the family. Case conferences focus upon the child whose interests and safety are paramount to all other considerations. The proceedings at case conferences come under strict rules of confidentiality. Parents/carers of the child are informed about the case conference in advance and their views sought on the issues to be raised. Whether they are invited to attend the case conference is decided by the case conference chairperson, and this decision is based upon what is in the best interests of the child. The outcome of the case conference will be an action plan which may range from placing the child's name on the Child Protection Register to seeking court protection for the child. The parents/carers must be informed of the outcome of the case conference.

At the case conference each person is given the opportunity to report on the particular area they are dealing with; there is then likely to be a discussion about the best way to proceed to ensure that the child receives maximum protection. The action plan is then drawn up. Childcarers attending case conferences should take with them any observations or notes that they have made on the child's behaviour or meetings with the child's parents. The members of the case conference will want valid evidence relating to the child or their family, and it is on this that they will base their action plan. Case conferences are formal proceedings but are often run on informal lines in order to gain the maximum information about the child without making the participants feel intimidated.

The law relating to child protection

The Children Act 1989 not only brought together a number of previous Acts but also rewrote the laws relating to child protection to ensure that there are proper safeguards for children and reasonable opportunities for the parents/carers of the child to challenge any action that the courts may take. The term 'significant harm' is used in the Act and this is defined as:

> Harm is defined as 'ill treatment or the impairment of health or development'.
> Development as meaning physical, intellectual, emotional, social or behavioural development.
> Health as meaning physical or mental health.
> Ill treatment as including sexual abuse and forms of ill treatment which are not physical.
>
> (Department of Health, 1991)

Child Assessment Order

The local authority or the NSPCC may apply for a Child Assessment Order which enables the applicant to assess the state of the child's health or development. To obtain an Assessment Order the applicant must satisfy the court that there is reason to suspect that a child is suffering or is likely to suffer significant harm and that an assessment needs to be carried out in order to determine such harm. Once the order has been granted the applicant has up to seven days to carry out the assessment. A Child Assessment Order is likely to be used when a child's parents or carers are uncooperative and there is reason to believe that a child's needs are not being met but that the situation is not serious enough to require an Emergency Protection Order.

Emergency Protection Order (EPO)

This has replaced the 'Place of Safety Order'. It is applied for and issued by a court or an individual magistrate in cases where there is reasonable cause to believe that a child will suffer significant harm if it is not removed from its place of residence. Anyone can apply for an EPO and although most applications are likely to come from social services departments it is possible for a concerned relative, teacher or neighbour to make an application.

The person applying for the EPO will need to satisfy the court or issuing magistrate that there is evidence to necessitate such a drastic step. Once an EPO has been granted the person applying for the order is given rights of parental responsibility and is able to move the child to a safe environment. The EPO has effect for a period of eight days and a court may extend this by a further period of seven days. An application may be made to the court for a discharge of the EPO but this can only be done after seventy-two hours have elapsed from the beginning of the order.

Police powers of protection

Under Part V of the Children Act, police have been given special powers for dealing with child protection cases. These allow the police to remove a child whom they consider is in a position of significant harm or to ensure that a child stays in a place where it is safe. Such orders last for a period of seventy-two hours and the police must inform the parents/carers and the local authority of the steps they have taken.

Once a child is the subject of an EPO or under police protection it is the duty of the local authority (this includes social services, education, health or the NSPCC) to investigate the situation of the child to determine what, if any, action should be taken. One such action that may be taken is for the local authority to apply for a care or supervision order.

Care Order

This order places the child in the care of the local authority or the NSPCC and only these bodies can apply for such an order. A Care Order gives the applicant rights of parental responsibility for the child and can last until the child is eighteen years of age. Care Orders are granted when it has been proven to the court that the child is likely to suffer significant harm or that there is a likelihood of the child suffering significant harm if it is left in its present environment.

Supervision Order

A Supervision Order puts the child under the supervision of the local authority or a probation officer. The person undertaking the supervision on behalf of the local authority or probation service is charged with specific duties, the main one being to assist and befriend the child. The person who has parental responsibility for the child must take reasonable steps to ensure that the child complies with the Supervision Order. A Supervision Order is given for a period of twelve months but it can be extended up to a maximum period of three years and it can be converted to a Care Order.

Voluntary organizations involved in child protection

There are many voluntary organizations that carry out child protection work in addition to their main areas of work; unfortunately there is not space to mention them all. It is a good idea to become familiar with the organizations which operate in your particular area. The following section is about three national organizations that deal specifically with child protection.

National Society for the Prevention of Cruelty to Children

The NSPCC is probably the best known and the oldest voluntary organization that is involved in child protection in England, Wales and Northern Ireland (Scotland has its own organization, the Royal Scottish Society for the Prevention of Cruelty to Children, RSSPCC). The Society was founded in 1884 by the Reverend Benjamin Waugh; Lord Shaftesbury was its President. By 1889 there were thirty-one branch offices and in 1895 the Society was granted a Royal Charter. The Royal Charter placed upon the organization, 'a duty to ensure an appropriate and speedy response in all cases where children are alleged to be at risk of abuse or neglect in any form'. As a consequence of this, the NSPCC (along with local authorities) has for many years had statutory powers which enable the organization to apply to the court for relevant protection orders for children. Under the Children Act 1989 the NSPCC is allowed to apply for Child Assessment Orders, Emergency Protection Orders, Care Orders and Supervision Orders.

The NSPCC operates on a regional basis with a Regional Social Work Manager as the leading professional officer. Social workers operate in teams and undertake therapeutic work with children and their families as well as carrying out a preventative role. Local NSPCC social workers liaise closely with the local social services departments and other child protection agencies.

The NSPCC has a national research unit which holds comprehensive statistics and undertakes studies based on reported cases. The NSPCC has its own Child Protection Register from which it is able to transfer and interpret data in order to prepare national statistics.

The most recent innovation from the NSPCC is a free telephone helpline which children who need protection or adults who need advice can contact.

ChildLine

ChildLine is a national charity started in 1986 by the television personality Esther Rantzen. It offers a free, twenty-four hour telephone advice service to children. It is staffed by trained volunteers and social workers who are able to offer counselling to the caller. It is claimed that ChildLine averages over seven hundred calls a day, but this number is said to increase to thousands if the number of attempted calls are added to the figure.

There are two main factors that make telephone helplines attractive to callers: (1) the assurance of anonymity, and (2) the assurance of confidentiality. Callers do not have to give their name, address, location where they are calling from or any other details which could identify them. The counsellors who answer the telephones do not pressurize the caller into revealing their identity unless it would appear that the person is in imminent danger. A major criticism of telephone helpline schemes has been the small number of cases which actually get followed up in comparison with the large number of calls received. The number of prosecutions resulting from information that originated from a telephone helpline call is very small. However, the main justification for this type of service is that it enables access to advice and counselling to a very large number of children. The children are offered advice on the best way to tackle the problem and this may empower the child to say 'no' to an abusing adult and seek help from sympathetic adults in the immediate locality.

Kidscape

Kidscape is an organization which originated in the USA and Canada and was brought to the UK by Michelle Elliott. It has now been established as a charity and works with schools and youth clubs offering children strategies for keeping themselves safe. The philosophy of the organization is that children should be given the tools to be able to keep themselves safe from danger and abuse. By using interactive teaching methods children are encouraged to become more assertive and not to be frightened to say 'no' to adults or other children who may be causing them distress. It also teaches children that for their own safety they are allowed to do things that they normally would not be allowed to do, e.g. kicking, biting, screaming, breaking windows. One area where Kidscape has had a great deal of success is teaching children how to protect themselves against bullying, a not uncommon form of child abuse inflicted upon children by other children.

Kidscape has produced a number of videos and books for children on how to stay safe and is able to send teams of teachers to schools and youth clubs to carry out its programme with the children.

Help for children who have been neglected or abused

Wherever possible, children who have been the subject of neglect or abuse are kept within their families. The Cleveland Report (1987) made reference to children being doubly punished, once by being the subject of abuse and then by being taken away from their families and placed in the care of the local authority. Support is given to the family by involving a number of agencies such as health visitors, social workers, educational welfare officers and psychologists. The child is likely to be given an immediate place in a day nursery, family centre or one of the specialist therapeutic nurseries run by the health service which are available in some parts of the country. Within these establishments the staff work with the child, and in some cases the whole family, to help them work through their relationships and problems.

The key worker

Family centres and day nurseries often operate a system whereby a member of staff is assigned to work with specific children and their families. This has the advantage of the key worker becoming a familiar figure for the child, somebody that can be trusted and related to. The key worker is able to build up meaningful relationships with the child and offer the type of play experiences which will help the child to come to terms with its experiences. The key worker is also able to build relationships with the parents and advise them on the best ways to deal with their child. A key worker will monitor the children they are assigned to and will be able to spot changes in a child's behaviour which may indicate that there is deterioration in the home situation.

Play therapists

Some local authorities employ play therapists who visit the nursery or family centre to undertake one-to-one work with children who have been neglected or abused. Unfortunately there are very few play therapists and the children referred to them are often those who exhibit the most disturbed behaviour. The therapist's role is to encourage children to play and through their play to express their feelings.

Therapeutic nurseries

In some authorities there are specialist therapeutic nurseries designed to deal with children and families where neglect or abuse has taken place. They are often joint ventures between the local social services and the health authority. Children are referred to them by social workers or through the local hospital or GP services. Staff in these nurseries make up an interdisciplinary team of, say, child care workers, psychologists, play therapists and social workers.

In general, children who have been the victims of neglect and abuse are likely to be mistrustful of adults. Staff who care for them need to spend a lot of time rebuilding the bonds between adult and child. This is best done by ensuring that the child has to deal with as few adults as possible. The child will need to be encouraged to play and mix with other children and this is likely to take time. Children who exhibit very disturbed behaviour patterns will need a great deal of help to channel their aggression into play activities. The child will need a lot of praise and affection and this will need to be reinforced regularly in order to build up their self-esteem. The child care worker will also need to be alert to any changes in the child's behaviour or physical condition which may indicate that the neglect or abuse has restarted. It is important to talk to children about normal, everyday occurrences and listen carefully to what they have to tell you.

Assignment 1

Miriam is aged three years and attends your playgroup five mornings a week. She is normally a quiet, timid child who has difficulty relating to other children. Recently she seems to have become more withdrawn and the playgroup leader is concerned about her. They have talked to her mother who insists that nothing has changed at home. Whilst helping Miriam to undress for gymnastics, Pat, the playgroup leader notices finger-mark bruising on Miriam's buttocks.

    If you were Pat, what action would you take next?

Assignment 2

Sharon is a precocious four year old, outgoing, chatty and inclined to be bossy with the other children. She has a full-time place at your nursery because she is on the Child Protection Register. You are carrying out child observations for a college project and spend some time observing Sharon in the hospital corner. Sharon lies on the bed and begins to behave in a sexually promiscuous manner, inviting the boys to come and examine her. You complete your observations but are worried about Sharon's behaviour.

    Explain why you might be concerned about Sharon's behaviour and describe what action should be taken.

Assignment 3

Philip who is three years old has a full-time place at your family centre because he is on the Child Protection Register. The centre staff have been trying to work with his mother who has a difficult relationship with her boyfriend who is not Philip's father. Philip's mother arrives to collect him and is very drunk, and not in a fit state to be in charge of a three year old.

    If you were the child care worker in charge of Philip, how would you handle this situation?

Assignment 4

You are a worker at the local 'One O'Clock' club situated in an inner city park. Recently Paula and her three children have been attending regularly. You are rather concerned as two of Paula's children are over the age of five years and should be at school. Paula seems depressed and you have been trying to make a relationship with her but have not mentioned your concern about the older children. Today, in conversation with Paula you find out that she is living in bed-and-breakfast accommodation.

(a) Does this information help you to understand why Paula brings all her children to the club?

(b) Is there any advice that you can give Paula which may help her and her children?

Assignment 5

Mary is 23 years old, she has two children, Robin aged three years and Katy aged 18 months. Mary's partner left her when she was pregnant with Katy. Mary rarely goes out, but recently she has met up with some of her old schoolfriends and they have invited her to go to the disco with them. Mary cannot afford a babysitter and she knows that both children usually sleep through the night from 8 p.m. to 6 a.m. Mary decides to go out with her friends and leave the children on their own as she is sure that they will not wake up whilst she is out. While she is out Katy wakes up and starts to scream, this wakes up Robin who also starts to cry and call for his mother. The neighbours hear the children and knock on Mary's door. When they get no reply they call the police.

(a)   What can the police do?
(b)   Is Mary's action considered as child abuse?

References and further reading

Allen, A. and Morton, A. 1961. *This is your Child: The Story of the National Society for Prevention of Cruelty to Children*. London: Routledge and Kegan Paul.

Aries, P. 1973. *Centuries of Childhood*. Harmondsworth: Penguin.

Campbell, B. 1988. *Unofficial Secrets. Child Sexual Abuse: The Cleveland Case*. London: Virago.

Children's Legal Centre. 1988. *Child Abuse Procedures: The Children's Viewpoint*. London: Children's Legal Centre.

Department of Health. 1991. *Working Together: Consultation Paper No. 22*. London: HMSO.

Butler-Sloss, E. 1973. *Report of the Inquiry into Child Abuse in Cleveland*. London: HMSO.

Kempe, R. and H. 1978. *Child Abuse*. London: Fontana.

Miller, A. 1983. *For Your Own Good*. London: Virago.

Open University 1989. *Unit P554: Child Abuse and Neglect*, course materials.

Parton, N. 1985. *The Politics of Child Abuse*. Basingstoke: Macmillan.

Pugh, G. and De'Ath, E. 1984. *The Needs of Parents*. London: National Children's Bureau.

Rogers, W.S., Hevey, D. and Ash, E. 1989. *Child Abuse and Neglect: Facing the Challenge*. Milton Keynes: Open University Press.

Winnicott, D. 1964. *The Family, The Child and the Outside World*. Harmondsworth: Penguin.

Chapter 8
Child care workers and the law

Chapter objectives _____

Race Relations Act 1976
Racism
Children Act 1989
Education Reform Act 1988

Sex Discrimination Act 1975
Links with units (this chapter links
across all units as equal opportunities
are integrated into the standards)

Anyone who is responsible for other people's children needs to be aware of the laws which may relate to the delivery of that care. During the past twenty years there have been a number of such pieces of legislation, including what is probably the most important legislation to have been enacted this century, the Children Act 1989.

The laws referred to in this chapter relate to the UK but it needs to be noted that there is other legislation that relates to children, namely the European Social Charter, the European Convention on Human Rights and the United Nations Convention on the Rights of the Child, and specific references may be made to these.

Whilst legislation can make people aware of situations and the legal requirements placed upon them, it is not able to change people's attitudes, and this is most significant when dealing with the areas of sex discrimination and racial discrimination. When working with children and their families it is important for the child carer to be committed to the concepts which underpin the legislation rather than acting in a certain way in order not to break the law. The laws discussed in this chapter require the reader to think beyond 'the letter of the law' and to be aware of their own attitudes and values relating to the subject. Child care is a public service and it is the responsibility of all child care workers to offer a high quality service to children and their parents. This will require them to incorporate the legislation and positive attitudes into their practice.

The Race Relations Act 1976

Racial inequality is one of the areas that UK society has not successfully combatted. Whilst we do have legislation that prevents people discriminating against others on the grounds of racial origin, we cannot have laws which prevent people holding negative and discriminatory attitudes towards those from different racial and ethnic groups. We live in a pluralistic society and all children within that society should have the right to grow up to hold good positive images of themselves.

Section 1(1) of the Race Relations Act defines discrimination as:

> (a) on racial grounds he treats that other [person] less favourably than he treats or would treat other persons...

The Act defines 'racial grounds' as colour, race, nationality or ethnic or national origins. It does not include culture or religion; however, both of these are mentioned in the Children Act 1989.

The above definition refers to direct discrimination which is exactly what it implies: treating or telling someone that they cannot do something or have something on the grounds that they are of another race, colour, nationality, etc. For example, a child care worker telling a child that it cannot go on a nursery outing because the child is black* or Irish would be direct discrimination, and therefore illegal. The converse also applies: if the worker said that the only children who could go on the outing were those that were black or Irish, then again the worker would be breaking the law.

Indirect discrimination is dealt with under Section 1(1)(b) of the Race Relations Act and occurs when rules or regulations are put into practice which are impossible for members of a particular group to conform to. The following example of this is one which was quoted by Sir Peter Newsom when he was the Chairman of the Commission for Racial Equality. A US state fire brigade required all applicants to be at least 5'11" to 6' tall and this prevented people applying for jobs if they came from races which had small stature (Asians, Chinese, Filipinos). If a child care establishment imposes rules that mitigate against certain people in the community then it would be breaking the law. For example, if a nursery school had a rule that no hats were to be worn inside the building then this would prevent Sikh, Rastafarian, Muslim and Jewish children gaining a place in that nursery as it would be impossible for them to conform to this rule. The rule would be unlawful under Section 28 of the Act which refers to discriminatory practices. Indirect discrimination is not always deliberate and may arise because people have not thought about the implications of the rules they are making. Whether it is intended or not, it is still unlawful and ignorance is not an acceptable defence in law.

Section 1(2) of the Act states:

> segregating a person from other persons on racial grounds is treating him less favourably than [others] are treated.

This means that a child care worker who sat children at tables according to their colour or racial

---

* The term black is used in this chapter as a shorthand for describing those people who are seen by white society as being black in colour and who are discriminated against on the grounds of colour even though not all of these people would describe themselves as black. This term predominantly covers those people from Afro-Caribbean, African and Asian origins.

origin would be breaking the law by treating one group of children less favourably than another. Although most child care workers would not dream of doing this it is not unknown for parents to request that their child should not be sat next to a black or Asian child. The parents, by making the request would be in breach of Sections 30 and 31 of the Act which states that it is unlawful to instruct or pressurize a person to discriminate against others. The child care worker, by carrying out the request, would be in breach of Section 1(2) of the Act by segregating the children.

When advertising a pre-school facility, care must be taken to ensure that the wording of the advert is such that it does not discriminate against certain groups. Section 29 of the Act deals with this area and the word 'advertisement' is widely defined and covers the display of notices, signs, labels, etc. whether public or not. An example of this is given by CRE (1989):

It would be unlawful to publish a list of child minders known to be prepared only to mind children from a particular racial group.

Scenario 1

The Rainbow Nursery/Playgroup is in a multicultural inner city area and the manager is very aware that they do not have any black members of staff. They now have a staff vacancy and the manager places the following advertisement in the local newspaper:

Rainbow Nursery/Playgroup requires a black Bengali-speaking worker for 36 hours per week. Please send CV to Mrs Bloggs, Manager, . . .

(a) Is this advertisement legal? If you think it is illegal then say why and which sections of the Race Relations Act you think it may be contravening.

(b) If you think that the manager could have approached this situation in a different way in order to encourage applications from members of ethnic minority groups, then suggest what could have been done.

Child care workers, except foster parents who are not covered by the Race Relations Act, are under a legal obligation to provide the same goods, facilities or services to all members of society (Section 20 of the Act). This applies to all pre-school provision whether it is statutory, voluntary or private. However, it would be lawful for a parent to ask for a childminder with particular characteristics if the parent was able to show a special need. An example of this would be a foster parent or childminder who speaks the same language as the child and its family.

Other sections of the Act deal with employment, education and local authorities. The body responsible for implementing the Act is the Commission for Racial Equality (CRE) which has the power to investigate alleged discrimination.

The Act makes it clear when it is lawful to discriminate in order to redress the balance within a particular section of society. If an employer wishes to encourage black people to apply for specific posts then they can only do so legally if they can show that particular ethnic backgrounds are under-represented in the post. Most employers do not use positive discrimination advertisements but show their intent to employ a black person by placing their advertisements in ethnic minority newspapers.

Figure 8.1 Multicultural child care

An employer requiring a worker who is fluent in a particular language may advertise for a person with that skill. This may encourage members of ethnic minorities to apply but it does not prevent a white person who is fluent in that language from applying.

Section 22(5)(c) of the Children Act 1989 states that local authorities have to give due consideration to the religious persuasion, racial origin and cultural and linguistic background of any child that comes within their care. This means that during discussions on what might be the most suitable placement for a child they must take all the above factors into consideration. It is worth noting that this Act goes beyond the Race Relations Act as it refers to culture, linguistic background and religion. The Children Act also makes it clear that a person's registration to care for children can be cancelled if a care provider has not answered the needs of a child. In its definition of 'needs', the Act includes the categories mentioned above. This means that when registering people who are deemed under the Children Act to be 'fit' to care for children, local authorities will need to take into account those persons':

> knowledge of and attitude to multicultural issues and people of different racial origins.
> (*Guidance and Regulations to the Children Act, Vol. 2*)

Children and racism

Underpinning the Race Relations Act and the above sections of the Children Act is the knowledge that racism has detrimental effects upon children and their families. Milner (1983) points out that from the age of two years children begin to notice the differences in skin colour, and as they get older begin to internalize the differences in treatment that they may receive because of their skin colour. Children are not racist by nature, but many children are open to learning racism from adults and other children. Children may ask questions about skin colour arising from their natural curiosity, and they should be given honest answers to these questions. Unfortunately, parents can transfer their own feelings and attitudes about colour and race to their children, and sometimes children will repeat these in the school or nursery. It is important for the self-esteem of the black children in the establishment that racist or cruel remarks made by children should not be ignored but dealt with by the staff in a sensitive manner. To ignore such remarks is to condone them, and this would be unacceptable child care practice. Stereotyping is another dangerous practice and should not be indulged in by child care workers. Stereotyping is the ascribing of certain characteristics to certain races and then treating people accordingly. For example, there was a myth that Afro-Caribbean children were exceptionally good at sports and this resulted in large numbers of children being encouraged into sporting activities at school and not being directed towards the academic subjects. Research does not show that black people are any better than white people at sports, music or other areas that they have been stereotyped to fit into. In the past, young black children were categorized as being hyperactive and difficult to control, and as Coard (1971) reported, this resulted in many of them being labelled as educationally subnormal (ESN). Fortunately, we are now aware of the effects upon children of stereotyping and labelling and conscious efforts are made by most child care workers to ensure that black children are able to develop positive self-images.

The damage that can be done to children by racism and discrimination is clearly recognized in the United Nations Convention on the Rights of the Child which was adopted by the General Assembly in November 1989. Article 2 states:

> The Principle that all rights apply to all children without exception, and the State's obligation to protect children from any form of discrimination. The State must not violate any right and must take positive action to promote them all.

Scenario 2	Michael aged 3 years is playing in the home corner with Ranjit aged 4 years. Michael puts a plate in front of Ranjit and says, 'There you are, one smelly curry for your dinner.' Ranjit looks upset and walks out of the home corner and tells you that Michael doesn't like him because he is smelly and eats curry.
	(a) How do you deal with this situation?
	(b) What changes could you suggest to the nursery manager that might prevent this situation arising in the future?

Fair Employment (Northern Ireland) Act 1989 _____

The position of Northern Ireland in relation to Acts of Parliament is often different from the position in the rest of the UK. Not all Acts apply to Northern Ireland and there are Acts which apply only to Northern Ireland. Discrimination (predominantly in the area of employment) against some sections of the population in Northern Ireland has a long history and the Fair Employment Act 1989 was brought in as an attempt to eradicate such discrimination. The Act requires all employers with more than twenty-five employees (from 1992 this will include all private sector employers with more than ten employees) to be registered and to submit monitoring returns which show the religious composition of their workforce. If the monitoring shows that Catholics are under-represented in a particular workforce, then mandatory affirmative action must be taken to redress the balance.

Whilst the Act only covers employment and therefore does not specifically relate to children, the quality of life for some children and their families would be considerably enhanced if it were easier for their parents to find employment.

Is also applicable for child care workers who may be seeking employment in Northern Ireland. In the 1989 Annual Report of the Commission for Racial Equality, the Chairman, Michael Day, praises the Act and says:

> We have watched with much interest, and not a little envy, the introduction of fair employment legislation in Northern Ireland. We believe that the kinds of obligations placed upon employers to avoid discrimination on the ground of religion should be matched here by equivalent provisions on race...

Education for Mutual Understanding (EMU)

This is a special project which is being introduced into all Northern Ireland schools and which has the backing of the Northern Ireland Department of Education and the Education and Library Boards. The aims of EMU are the need for children and young people...

> to learn respect and value themselves and other people,
> to know about and value both their own culture and traditions and those of others with different cultures and traditions,
> to learn the importance of resolving differences and conflict by peaceful and creative means.
>
> (Education for Mutual Understanding: A Guide. 1988)

EMU is integrated into the school curriculum and offers a focus for curriculum planning. It is too early yet to know the success of this project as it is likely to have the greatest effects upon those children who have been exposed to it for the longest amount of time.

The Children Act 1989 _____

When the Lord Chancellor introduced the Act when it was at the Parliamentary Bill stage he described it as being 'the most comprehensive and far-reaching reform of child law which has come before parliament in living memory'. The Act not only brought together existing legislation but it also took into account the major reforms that were needed in the areas of child protection and family breakdown. For the first time, the Act places duties upon social services and education departments to provide for children in need.

The Act is complex and covers all areas of child care, so it is imperative that child care staff become familiar with those parts of the Act which directly relate to their establishment and their work. In order to help people through the maze of the Act the Department of Health has produced *Guidance and Regulations* in a number of separate volumes each covering a different area, e.g. family support and day care; children with disabilities; family placements. It is recommended that child care and education workers consult the *Guidance and Regulations* which deal with their area of work.

When the Children Act was written, the following principles were seen as predominant:

1. The child's welfare is paramount and as a priority this must be promoted and safeguarded.
2. There is a duty upon local authorities to ensure that services are provided for children 'in need'.
3. There must be avoidance of delay in court resolutions and in the provision of services.
4. Those providing services must work in partnership with children, parents, those with parental responsibility or other people who have a relationship with the child or children.
5. Those providing services must take into account the religious, racial, cultural and linguistic needs of the child or children.

The Act introduces new terminology which encompasses the new concepts of the Act. The following are definitions of some of the most important terminology (those which specifically relate to child protection can be found in chapter 7):

- *Children in need.* These are children who need services to secure a reasonable standard of health and development and includes children with disabilities.
- *Health and development.* Health means physical or mental health, and development means physical, intellectual, emotional, social or behavioural development.
- *Parental responsibility.* Refers to all the rights, duties, powers, responsibilities and authority which a parent has by law in relation to the child.
- *Guardian ad litem.* This is a person appointed by the court to represent a child in certain court proceedings. The guardian *ad litem* has access to all local authority records concerning the child and may be asked to advise the court in order to ensure that decisions made are in the child's best interests.
- *Family proceedings courts.* These are the new magistrates courts which have been set up to hear proceedings under the Children Act. The magistrates who sit in these courts are chosen for their expertise in children and family affairs and would have undergone a training course on the Children Act.

Parental responsibility

A person who has parental responsibility is empowered to take most of the decisions in the child's life. Parental responsibility cannot be taken away and remains until the child is eighteen years of age. The person with parental responsibility may not necessarily be the child's parent or relative as a court may give parental responsibility rights to a person unrelated to the child, for example a step-parent.

The mother automatically has parental responsibility and the father would also have this if he were married to the mother. A father who is not married to the mother of his child can obtain parental responsibility for the child by taking out a formal agreement with the mother or by applying to the court.

Other people may get parental responsibility by making an application to the court or by the court appointing them or by the enactment of a court order. A parent may legally appoint someone to undertake parental responsibility of their child, and this is often written into wills. A person who has been given parental responsibility in a will can only exercise this when the child has no other living person who has parental responsibility. Another way of gaining parental responsibility is when a court makes a residence order in favour of a person who is not the child's parent or guardian.

The family of a child is considered under the Act to be any person with parental responsibility and anyone with whom the child has been living. The Act enables people such as grandparents, uncles, aunts or other relatives with whom the child has been living to apply for parental responsibility. Prior to the Act these people would have had to apply to take on this role.

Divorce and separation of parents

When a family splits up there are a number of orders that the court can make in respect of the child; these replace the former custody and access orders. The child is considered by the court as a child of the family and all decisions are made with this in mind.

- *A Residence Order* is made to settle the question of whom the child will live with.
- *A Contact Order* requires the person who is caring for the child to allow the child to stay with or visit or have contact with the person named in the contact order.
- *A Prohibited Steps Order* is taken out by a parent who wishes to deny the child contact with a person who has a contact order.
- *A Specific Issue Order* can be taken out to resolve a particular issue when those with parental responsibility are unable to agree on, say, the child's education or medical treatment. In these cases the court would resolve the issue and give directions to those with parental responsibility to carry out the order.
- *Finance Orders* which make provision for maintenance agreements. One of the major changes that the finance order brings about is that maintenance orders may be made in respect of married and unmarried parents and against people who are not the mother or father of the child. In the case of the latter, the court will take into consideration whether the person assumed any responsibility for the child and the extent and length of time of that responsibility. For example, step-parents who had been living with and supporting a step-child for five or six years may find themselves being expected to contribute to the continued maintenance of the child.

Residence and contact orders can cover a wide range of people such as step-parents, a person the child has lived with for at least three years or any person who has a genuine concern about the child's welfare, which can include foster parents. The court is empowered to grant these orders if it is in the best interests of the child to do so. The child itself may apply for a residence or contact order providing it has sufficient understanding to make the application.

Scenario 3

Gary aged 5 years and Sharon aged 3 years spend a great deal of time living with their grandparents, Mr and Mrs Brown. They are the children of the Brown's daughter, Tracey, who works on a cruise liner as a waitress and so is often away for long spells. Tracey is divorced from the children's father Bill Bloggs. Recently Bill has read about parental rights under the Children Act and has arrived at the Brown's house demanding to see his children. The children do not like their father very much: in fact they hardly knew him as until recently he rarely visited them, and they were very young when their parents split up. The Browns have become increasingly worried about Bill's behaviour and are frightened that he will try to take the children away.

What would you advise the Browns to do and which sections of the Children Act could they use to help the children?

Local authority responsibilities

The services that the local authority must provide for children and their families are clearly stated in Part 3 of the Children Act 1989. Such services must be targeted towards children 'in need' and their families.

Local authorities have a duty to identify the children in need in their areas and they must publish information about the services they provide. They must keep a register of children with disabilities within their area, and services for the disabled must be integrated with those provided for other children 'in need'. Local authorities must also take steps to prevent children in their area suffering neglect or ill-treatment.

There are a number of orders in the Act which put children under the care of the local authority.

- *Supervision Orders* require the child to be supervised by somebody appointed by the local authority. The role of the supervisor is to befriend, advise and assist the child and to have reasonable contact with the child. The supervision order places obligations upon those who have parental responsibility to ensure that the child conforms with the order. The supervisor can give directions for the child to submit to medical or psychiatric examination or treatment. The reports on such examination or treatment are given to the supervisor. Supervision orders are most likely to be used for older children, however, they can be used for younger children particularly in cases of child protection (see chapter 7).
- *Education Supervision Orders* are similar to Supervision Orders but relate to ensuring that the

child attends educational provision. This type of order is most likely to be used for children who persistently truant from school and whose parents take no preventative action. Supervision Orders last for one year but can be extended up to three years; they can also be changed into a care order.

- *Care Orders* place the child into the care of the local authority and can last until the child is eighteen years of age. (For further details on Care and Supervision Orders see chapter 7).

Day care

Under the Children Act 1989 the local authority has a duty to provide day care for children 'in need' and those children who have disabilities. Day care consists of the provision of family centres or other day care services, and supervised activities for children out of school hours. In *Guidance and Regulations Volume 2* (1991) there are clear guidelines on the standards of services for the under-eights and educational provision for under-fives. The minimum standards for each type of establishment are clearly stated and include staff qualifications, staff/child ratios, standards of the premises and the services that each establishment should provide.

Registration of day care services and childminding

Local authorities are responsible for the registration and inspection of day care and childminding facilities in the public, voluntary and private sectors. Anyone who looks after children under the age of eight years on domestic premises for reward or on non-domestic premises, for two hours or more, must be registered with the local authority. Those who are exempt from registration are relatives looking after the child, people who have parental responsibility for the child, foster parents, a person employed by the parent to look after the child in the child's home (nanny), a person employed by two sets of parents to look after the children from both families in one of the homes (shared nanny).

One of the conditions attached to registration is that the applicant must satisfy the local authority that they are fit to be in the company of children under eight years of age. In deciding that somebody is a 'fit person' the local authority is advised to take the following into account:

- Previous experience of looking after or working with young children or people with disabilities.
- Qualification and/or training in a relevant field such as child care, early years education, health visiting, nursing or other caring activity.
- Ability to provide warm and consistent care.
- Knowledge of and attitude to multicultural issues and people of different racial origins.
- Physical health.
- Mental stability, integrity and flexibility.
- Known involvement in criminal cases involving abuse to children.

(*Guidance and Regulations Vol. 2*, 1991)

With persons living or working on the premises the points are:

- Previous records.
- Known involvement in criminal cases involving abuse to children.

Local authorities are also required to inspect the premises where the child care will take place, including mobile facilities such as playbuses. Registration must be reviewed annually, with inspections taking place prior to re-registration. The local authority also has a right of entry to carry out an inspection at times other than the annual review. Childminders and day care establishments are registered to take a certain number of children, and it is the duty of the registered person to inform the local authority of any changes in staffing or numbers of children being cared for. A local authority may impose mandatory or discretionary requirements on a person or establishment as part of the registration procedure.

Registration can be refused or removed but the reasons for the decision must be clear and supported by evidence that would stand up in court. The local authority must give fourteen days' notice of the refusal to register or the cancellation of registration. There is a right of appeal and this can be made to a court or to the local authority.

Once registration has been agreed, the person concerned is issued with a certificate of registration and their details entered into the local authority register which must be available to the general public.

Scenario 4

Mrs Green is a childminder and has applied to the local authority for registration under the Children Act. She has her 25 year old son Matthew living with her and he helps her with the children. When Mrs Green received the forms to fill in for registration there was a question about declaring any criminal record of anyone resident on the premises. When Matthew was 19 years old he had been found guilty on a charge of possession of dangerous drugs and had served a short prison sentence. Mrs Green is in a dilemma as she is basically an honest woman but is worried that if she mentions Matthew's previous conviction she will not get her registration. She seeks the help of her Health Visitor.

What advice do you think the Health Visitor gave her and is it likely that Matthew's previous offence will prevent Mrs Green from being registered?

Foster care

When a Care Order is made on a child it is the duty of the local authority to provide accommodation for that child. One option is to place the child with local-authority approved foster parents. Foster parenting is a skilled task and to this end local authorities provide what is termed a fostering service which includes recruitment, preparation, training and support for foster parents. Local authorities must also set up procedures for assessing and approving foster parents. Only when a foster parent has gained approval and entered into a foster placement agreement with the local authority will children be placed with them. When placing children with foster parents it is expected that factors such as race, culture, religion and linguistic background will be taken into consideration. The number of children being fostered is usually limited to three but may be more if the children are all from the same family, and when deciding upon the number and ages of the children that will be placed with particular foster parents, the needs of the foster family's own children are also taken into account.

When children are taken into the care of the local authority they must be allowed reasonable contact with their parents or other significant adults. Foster parents play a major role in promoting good relationships between children and their parents.

When considering the suitability of people for fostering, similar criteria to those relating to the 'fit person' are used. In addition, the following are also taken into consideration: marital status, religious persuasion and the degree of religious observance, racial origin and cultural and linguistic background, past and present employment, leisure activities and interests.

It is the duty of the local authority to review regularly the situation of all the children in their care, and this includes children who are fostered. In cases where a child is not visited by its parents or where the relationship between the parents and child has broken down, the local authority may decide that it is in the child's best interests to appoint an *independent visitor* for the child. This person will befriend the child and visit it regularly and in some circumstances undertake an advocacy role on behalf of the child.

General points about the Children Act 1989

As previously stated, the Children Act is a complex document that has brought together twenty or more pieces of previous legislation to form a cohesive statute. It will be some time before people become familiar with its workings or understand its implications. Critics of the Act say that it does not go far enough by laying down minimum standards for child care or stating minimum qualifications or training needed for those looking after children. The Act and the accompanying Guidelines have gone much further than any previous legislation in working towards a better standard of care for children. The underlying principles of the Act should also ensure that the child's welfare and interests are put first, thus avoiding situations in which children become pawns in family disputes. All child care and education workers need to have a commitment to work as closely as possible to the Guidelines when implementing the Act as this will ensure that children will get the best out of the Act. It is inevitable that lawyers and others will find loopholes which could be to the detriment of the child; however, only time will tell us whether these are the exception rather than the rule.

Education Reform Act 1988

The Education Reform Act 1988 was responsible for significant changes throughout the field of education: the National Curriculum, new responsibilities for school governors, new methods of financing schools, schools opting out of local authority control, the reorganization of the Inner London Education Authority (ILEA), to name but a few.

For children of infant school age the most significant sections of the Act have been those relating to the National Curriculum and the local management of schools.

The National Curriculum

Part 1 of the Education Reform Act 1988 deals with the school curriculum and the arrangements for assessment and examinations. The Act states:

the curriculum should be balanced and broadly based and should:

(a) promote the spiritual, moral, cultural, mental, and physical development of pupils at the school and of society; and

(b) prepare such pupils for the opportunities, responsibilities and experiences of adult life.

(Education Reform Act 1988, Chapt. 40 Section 1(2))

There are three core subjects: mathematics, English and science; and a number of foundation subjects: history, geography, technology, music, art and physical education. For older pupils a foreign language is also required. There are attainment targets for each subject, and pupils are tested and assessed at the end of each key stage. There are four such stages:

Key stage 1 at the age of 7 years.
Key stage 2 at the age of 11 years.
Key stage 3 at the age of 14 years.
Key stage 4 at the age of 16 years.

The ages relating to the key stages are those of the majority of pupils in a class. A child who is under or over the age of that stated for the key stage test would be tested with the majority of the pupils in the class.

The Act established the National Curriculum Council (NCC) which was responsible for setting up working groups to determine the attainment targets and assessment tasks for each subject at each key stage. Key stage testing was phased in, stage 4 being the last to be implemented. Since 1989 there has been a requirement on the amount of time that pupils must spend on core subjects in all key stages; however, it is expected that in the future this will also be applied to foundation subjects.

The National Curriculum was introduced on the basis that there was a general concern to raise the standard of education; however, the National Curriculum has been the subject of a great deal of controversy, particularly relating to testing at age 7 years. Only children in nursery and reception classes are exempt from activities and lessons which must give time to core curriculum subjects. Parents who are keen for their children to succeed in the tests at the age of seven have placed pressure upon schools to introduce National Curriculum subjects into the nursery and reception classes. Some schools have responded to these demands. Early years educationalists have expressed concern that some children will be tested before they reach their seventh birthday whilst others may be older than seven years at the time of the test, and this may prove disadvantageous to those in the younger age group. There has also been concern about the pressure that the system places upon children and how this may be detrimental to them learning.

There has been a great deal of research on the positive effects of pre-school education and how those children who have been fortunate enough to have had this fare better when they start school. A major criticism of the National Curriculum is that it does not take into account a child's pre-school experience when carrying out the assessment tests at age seven. Thus, the results of one school may be far better than those of another because the majority of the children at the school with the better results had had pre-school education.

The Act places a responsibility upon schools to publish the National Curriculum test results in the school prospectus in the form of statistics (not by individual pupil name). This inevitably results in competition between schools.

Local Management of Schools (LMS)

Under Section 33 of the Act each local education authority had to present schemes whereby the management of schools was devolved to the governing body and headteacher for all secondary schools and primary schools with more than two hundred pupils. Although nursery schools are exempt, nursery classes attached to primary schools are not. Hand-in-hand with local management goes a number of delegated powers which were given to governing bodies in order to carry out the management role. Although this section of the Act is referring to budgeting and accounting procedures, it does have implications for staffing, resources and the maintenance of school buildings. Schools were also given the choice to opt out of local authority control and to obtain their budget directly from the government. At the outset, this option looked attractive as the government budget was far in excess of that being given to schools by local authorities. However, in the fullness of time, there have been a number of problems encountered by schools that have opted out, particularly in cases where there is a clash between governors and the headteacher.

School governors were often ill-equipped to deal with their new delegated duties and powers, and in spite of numerous training courses some are still finding the situation difficult. More recently there have been large numbers of school governors resigning because they are unable to cope with the very large workload that is now part of a governor's role: it must be remembered that being a school governor is a voluntary activity.

Where resources have been limited there have been cuts in the nursery class sectors in favour of providing for the older children. In some cases, cost-cutting has meant the appointment of an unqualified classroom assistant to work in the nursery rather than a qualified nursery nurse. Some schools which are on very tight budgets have had to cut back on the provision of consumables such as books, paper and pencils. Whilst there is much to be said for a school holding its own budget, if that budget is calculated in such a way as to be insufficient for the smooth running of the school, the governors then find themselves in the unenviable position of having to make decisions which may weight one group of pupils against another. Maintenance of school buildings has also been a bone of contention under LMS, particularly when local authorities have calculated budgets on the basis of minor building works rather than offering larger sums for major building. Many school buildings are old and have reached the time when major investment is needed to bring them up to standard.

As the LMS system settles we find more families agreeing to pay voluntary contributions for school outings, books, computers and other equipment to aid their children's learning. In schools in areas where unemployment and poverty are high and parents unable to provide voluntary contributions, the children are likely to have to go without some of the things that children in more affluent areas may have. The Act clearly states that parents cannot be charged for their children to go on outings or for other educational services; however, many schools would have to forgo such activities if they were unable to rely on the voluntary contributions made by parents.

Sex Discrimination Act 1975

The Sex Discrimination Act prohibits people discriminating against a person on the grounds of sex in the areas of employment, housing, education and in the provision of goods and services. The body responsible for administering the Act is the Equal Opportunities Commission which has the power to investigate alleged discrimination. The Act applies to both men and women.

There is also an Equal Pay Act 1972 which relates to equal pay being given for like work, irrespective of the sex of the worker. There is often confusion between the two Acts and even lawyers have difficulty in distinguishing them. The two Acts cannot be read together as they do not represent a cohesive body of legislation.

Both of these Acts are relevant to those who provide services e.g. child care. As the field of child care and education is dominated by females, extra efforts need to be made to ensure that the relatively few males working in the field do not get treated differently. Differences in treatment may not always be negative: for example, expecting female child care workers to change nappies but exempting male child care workers would be unlawful under the Sex Discrimination Act. Men entering the field of child care should undertake the same tasks as women and have exactly the same job descriptions. Conversely, always asking the men to move furniture or undertake the heavier tasks in the nursery or playgroup would also be unlawful.

Figure 8.2 Men running a crèche

Gender issues in child care

Gender stereotyping begins at an early age and research has shown that it is detrimental to both sexes. Girls are affected by their relatively poor development of mathematical and spatial concepts, whilst boys suffer in their emotional development by being expected to react in an emotionally different way from girls. Childcare workers must make concerted efforts to ensure that gender stereotyping does not take place in their establishments and this may require them to take affirmative action to overcome the problem. Such action will involve changing their language and attitudes, providing resources and activities for children that are not gender-specific and encouraging all children to participate in all the activities provided. A more detailed account of gender issues in the early years can be found in chapter 3.

Figure 8.3 Girls must be given the chance to use all available equipment

Assignment 1A

(For those working in inner city areas.)
Find out which ethnic groups reside in the locality of your work place. Write a list of the ways in which your establishment provides positive experiences for children from those ethnic groups. Suggest ways in which the provision could be enhanced.

Assignment 1B

(For those in rural areas.)
It is probable that there are few if any children from ethnic minority groups in your establishment: however, it is important that the children in your care gain positive attitudes towards people from different races. Write down how best you could achieve this and then discuss with your manager how this could be incorporated into your day-to-day practice.

Assignment 2

Obtain a copy of your local authority guidelines for implementing the Children Act 1989. Study this thoroughly, write down the points that you do not understand and discuss these with your line manager.

Assignment 3A

(For those working with under-fives.)
The National Curriculum does not apply to the children in your care, however, many of the activities that you undertake with the children are teaching them concepts in preparation for the National Curriculum subjects. Analyse one week's activities and link these with the National Curriculum subjects. Devise a leaflet for parents explaining how these activities are preparing their children for the subjects that they will be taking in the National Curriculum.

Assignment 3B

(For those working within the National Curriculum.)
The children in your care will be preparing or working towards their key stage 1 assessments in the National Curriculum. Find out about the attainment targets for key stage 1 and describe how these link with the weekly timetable of activities in your classroom.

Assignment 4

Good child care practice does not discriminate between 'girls' activities' and 'boys' activities'. However, research has shown that when boys and girls play together in the home corner they fall into stereotypical societal roles, the girl cooking and the boy waiting for his dinner. Carry out a series of observations of children playing in the home corner and record your findings.

(a) Do you think, as Browne and France (1986; and see chapter 3 of this book) advocate, that home corners perpetuate stereotypical roles?

    (b) If your observations show that Browne and France are correct, how can you change the situation?

Assignment 5

(For those working in Northern Ireland.)

This chapter has drawn attention to the EMU Project. At present the project is only taking place in schools. Find out about the project and investigate whether parts of it could be adapted to fit into early years provision. Draft a plan of activities that you could carry out with your children which could incorporate parts of the EMU Project.

References and further reading

Race relations

Ahmed, S., Cheetham, J. and Small, J. 1986. *Social Work with Black Children and their Families.* London: Batsford.

Brown, B. 1990. *All our Children.* London: BBC Education.

Coard, B. 1971. *How the West Indian Child is made Educationally Subnormal in the British School System.* London: New Beacon Books.

Celestin, N. 1986. *A Guide to Anti-Racist Childcare Practice.* London: VOLCUF.

Commission for Racial Equality. 1989. *From Cradle to School: A Practical Guide to Race Equality and Childcare.* London: CRE.

Derman-Sparks and the ABC Task Force. 1989. *Anti-bias Curriculum: Tools for Empowering Young Children.* Washington DC: National Association for the Education of Young Children/London: VOLCUF.

Hazareesingh, S., Simms, K. and Henderson, P. 1989. *Educating the Whole Child.* London: Building Blocks.

Maxime, J. E. 1987. *Black Like Me: Black Identity.* Emani Publications.

Milner, D. 1983. *Children and Race Ten Years On.* London: Ward Lock Educational.

Race Relations Act 1976. London: HMSO.

Children Act 1989

Allen, N, 1991. *Making Sense of the Children Act 1989.* Harlow: Longman.

Children Act 1989. London: HMSO.

An Introduction to the Children Act 1989. London: HMSO.

National Children's Bureau. *Working with the Children Act 1989.* London: NCB.

Smith, F. and Lyon, T. 1991. *Personal Guide to the Children Act 1989.* Children Act Enterprises.

Department of Health. 1991. *The Children Act Guidance and Regulations Volume 2: Family Support, Day Care and Educational Provision for Young Children.*
Volume 3: Family Placements.
Volume 6: Children with Disabilities.
London: HMSO
Working Together: Under the Children Act 1989. London: HMSO

Northern Ireland

Department of Economic Development. 1989. *Fair Employment in Northern Ireland: Key Details of the Act.* Department of Economic Development.
Fair Employment (Northern Ireland) Act 1989. London: HMSO.
Northern Ireland Council for Educational Development. 1988. *Education for Mutual Understanding.* Belfast: NICED.

Education Reform Act 1988

Davies, B. and Braund, C. 1989. *Local Management of Schools.* Plymouth: Northcote House.
Department of Education and Science. 1987. *The National Curriculum 5–16. A Consultation Document.* London: DES.
Department of Education and Science. 1988. *Education Reform Act: Local Management of Schools.* London: DES.
Education Reform Act 1988. London: HMSO.

Sex Discrimination

Adams, C. and Laurikietis, R. 1980. *The Gender Trap. Book 3: Messages and Images.* London: Virago.
Aspinwall, K. 1984. *What are Little Girls Made of? What are Little Boys Made of?* London: National Nursery Examination Board.
Belotti, G. 1975. *Little Girls.* Aylesbury: Writers and Readers Publishing Co-Operative.
Browne, N. and France, P. 1986. *Untying the Apron Strings: Anti-sexist Provision for the Under Fives.* Milton Keynes: Open University Press.
Equal Pay Act 1972. London: HMSO.
First Reflections. Equal Opportunities in the Early Years. London: ILEA.
Further Education Unit. 1989. *Implementing Equal Opportunities: Language and Images Guidelines.* London: Further Education Unit.
Grabrucker, M. 1988. *There's a Good Girl: Gender Stereotyping in the First Three Years of Life.* London: Women's Press.
Mullin, B., Morgan, V. and Dunn, S. 1986. *Gender Differentiation in Infant Classes.* Coleraine: Equal Opportunities Commission N. Ireland.
Sex Discrimination Act 1975. London: HMSO.
Sharpe, S. 1987. *'Just Like a Girl'.* Harmondsworth: Pelican.

Spender, D. 1982. *Invisible Women: The Schooling Scandal*. London: Writers and Readers Publishing.
Walkerdine, V. 1989. *Counting Girls Out: Girls and Mathematics Unit Insitute of Education*. London: Virago.
Whyte, J. 1983. *Beyond the Wendy House: Sex Role Stereotyping in Primary Schools*. Harlow: Longman.

General

Newell, P. 1991. *The UN Convention and Children's Rights in the UK*. London: National Children's Bureau.

Chapter 9
Aspects of children's behaviour

Chapter objectives_____

Positive behaviour   Techniques for problem behaviour
Negative behaviour   Specific behaviour problems
Factors linked to problem behaviour   Comfort habits
Discipline and boundary-setting   **Links with units C6, C7**

The *Concise Oxford Dictionary* defines behaviour as 'manners, moral conduct, treatment shown to or towards others'. This implies that there is an element of judgement which we use when talking of a person's behaviour, based on our own standards, attitudes and values as well as our training and experience. When dealing with children this is particularly so, and workers continually make judgements regarding children based on the child's observable behaviour. Everyone who works with children has to learn to cope with all sorts of difficult and damaging behaviour which can range from children who are tired or having an 'off' day to very serious self-destructive behaviour with a variety of potentially worrying root causes.

'Behaviour' covers everything children do and is one of the principal means by which we can recognize what they are thinking, feeling and experiencing. Behaviour is linked to their stage of development, personality and capacity to cope. Generally we have to be tolerant of many different types of behaviour and usually only become concerned when we see extremes. Children who are happy, loved, healthy and well adjusted will sometimes display difficult behaviour temporarily in response to specific situations but more often they will relate well to others and behave in a positive manner. Other children with a different life experience or who may have particular problems, such as learning difficulties or food sensitivity, can sometimes behave in very negative ways and where this is the predominant behaviour over time, workers are alerted and concerned.

Although some behaviour in the newborn is innate, for example searching for the nipple and sucking, the vast majority of human behaviour is learned in the same way as any other activity. Children learn through their senses and through exploring and experimenting with their world. They also learn through modelling (copying) the behaviour of adults and others who are important to them (see chapter 1). Children learn that certain types of behaviour are usually rewarded in some way, for example with a smile or hug. Conversely, they learn that other forms of behaviour receive a frown or result in cross words or in some cases a smack. Children usually want to please those who care for them, especially if they have a good relationship, and over a period of time they learn how to behave in ways which adults will reward. If adults are inconsistent and change from day to day, children become confused and uncertain of how to behave and what will be acceptable.

Adults' expectations of children's behaviour have to be realistic and linked to the child's stage of development and particular needs. For instance, it is rare that toddlers willingly share their toys as they are more concerned with what they themselves want and are naturally 'self-centred' at this age. Expecting toddlers to share is unrealistic, but adults should model sharing behaviour and encourage young children when they begin to behave in this way. Adults sometimes worry that they are spoiling their baby when they attend promptly to its needs even though it is unlikely that a baby under one year can be spoilt in the usual sense of the word. Young babies should not be punished as if they have been deliberately naughty when at this age intense curiosity and attention-seeking behaviour are reasonable and normal. Judgements concerning behavioural issues must always be based on a sound knowledge and understanding of child development, on careful observations and assessments of the child, and in consultation with parents and other professionals.

Positive behaviour

Deciding what is positive behaviour for a child can be very subjective. In general, our society values independent, individualistic and self-assertive people who are able to exercise personal autonomy and decision-making. However, there are cultural groups within society who are more likely to stress co-operation and interdependence. It is important, therefore, that workers consider the social and cultural background of the children in their care and no not impose a set of behavioural expectations and values which may be inappropriate and out of context for today's pluralist society. This means that all workers should be aware of their own values and attitudes. There are, however, many universally accepted positive aspects of behaviour and these should be encouraged. For example, sharing, turn-taking, considering others and showing caring and empathetic behaviour. It is important that children should be able to negotiate and see other points of view. Another goal for our children is that they should learn to handle their emotions and cope with difficulties and stresses. This can be encouraged by adults modelling such behaviour in day-to-day activity and rewarding children through praise and encouragement when they follow suit. Some nurseries play games designed to encourage co-operation and pro-social behaviour and provide toys and equipment which are not likely to encourage aggressive play.

Negative behaviour

Workers have to decide whether or not they find a particular behaviour unacceptable as tolerance levels vary. They also have to accept that their personal values may be at odds with those of the parents. A good guide is to consider whether behaviour affects others negatively or is personally unconstructive for the child concerned. Some behaviour, such as temper tantrums, may be problematic but are common and workers expect the child to grow out of it. Treating all children equally is a mistake as children vary and should be treated differently according to their individual needs. This is not the same as preferential treatment.

This chapter looks at some common aspects of behaviour which can be worrying and the techniques that are sometimes used to deal with them. It does not consider deep-seated and intransigent behavioural disorders which require specialized help. It is sometimes very difficult to know when particular behaviour has gone beyond the point to which staff can cope with it and when specialized help is needed. With all the forms of behaviour discussed below it is possible they may become so extreme and so bizarre that outside help is need.

Figure 9.1 Child showing strong emotion

Outside agencies

There are a variety of statutory or voluntary agencies that can be involved in helping the child and family. These will vary according to local availability, the age of the child and the severity and nature of the problem. They may include the following:

- Child and family guidance.
- Family therapy clinics.
- Educational psychologists.

- Social services.
- Health visitors.
- Hospital psychiatric departments.
- Speech therapists.
- Child and family assessment centres.

Factors linked to problem behaviour

Behavioural problems are not usually related to one factor only but to several, of which the following constitute only a sample.

Physical

- Reactions to additives and foods which may lead to hyperactive and aggressive behaviour.
- Poor diet.
- Tiredness or hunger exacerbate difficult behaviour.
- Physical illness may be linked to regressive behaviour where the child behaves as if at an earlier stage of development than previously.
- Lack of exercise and fresh air.
- Sensory impairment may contribute to frustration and lead to problem behaviour.
- Problems and frustrations associated with poor physical skills.

Socio-emotional

- Children who lack love, care and acceptance.
- Children under stress of all kinds may regress and/or show behavioural symptoms such as withdrawing or becoming aggressive.
- Family difficulties such as parents' separation or arrival of a new sibling.
- Poor self-esteem or lack of confidence.
- Excessive fears, phobias or anxieties.
- Poverty and deprivation may exacerbate existing behavioural problems but are unlikely to be the sole cause.
- Poor social skills.

Cognitive and language

- Poor language skills to express feelings and anger.
- Restricted vocabulary.
- Learning difficulties.
- Lack of concentration.
- Boredom.
- Over-stimulation.
- Constant failures.

Environmental

- Lack of play opportunities.
- Lack of space.
- Noise and no opportunity for quiet play.
- No privacy.

Discipline and boundary-setting

Discipline and boundary-setting are necessary to provide children with a secure framework of rules which they can understand and which are necessary to ensure that they learn consideration for others and how to behave in a constructive manner for themselves. A child learns rules and is most likely to accept them if they are applied fairly and consistently and in a caring context where the child is loved and accepted for itself not just for good behaviour. The goal for children is to learn self-discipline without the need to have external discipline imposed upon them. How long this takes varies from child to child according to their level of maturity and life experiences. In a few tragic cases, children never seem to learn and become disturbed, anti-social adults.

Most children learn right from wrong very early and around the age of three years may experience guilt when they disobey the rules. For the majority of children, by the time they are in school their conscience is well and truly in place. They may not always understand why rules are there but they feel bad when they break them. Some children who have particular problems, either developmental or environmental, take longer to reach this stage, especially if they have poor attachments to adults. Some children are used as scapegoats because they always seem to feel guilty and take the blame even when they are not in the wrong. This can derive from the home or other setting when adults tend to blame one child constantly for the family ills until that child actually believes it is always in the wrong. This is very damaging, and children who are scapegoats will suffer until the situation is dealt with.

Forms of discipline

The form that discipline should take depends on the stage of development of the child, its personality and level of maturity. Adults may have a variety of styles of discipline and different tolerance levels but should not be extreme. Adults who are warm and caring towards a child may be either permissive or authoritarian in their style of discipline, but usually the child is responsive and wanting to please. Where adults are negative and uncaring towards children, the child will be confused and often aggressive and uncontrolled. If children are too strictly disciplined in a home where there is little warmth they may repress their anger and frustration and become withdrawn and uncooperative.

All discipline should be consistently applied and directly related to the unwanted behaviour and should be applied at the time of the behaviour, not much later when the child cannot remember the incident. The discipline should focus on the unwanted behaviour not on the child. For example, it is better to say 'I don't like what you have done', rather than 'you're a very naughty girl'.

Physical

Physical discipline can take many forms and varies in severity from a beating with a strap or other instrument to a light tap on the hand. There is no legislation in this country to stop parents punishing their children in this way as there is elsewhere, but in care and education settings it is no longer considered appropriate. Indeed many workers feel that to punish a child physically is a violation of human rights and no better than common assault. As a result of this, other form of non-physical discipline and boundary-setting are more widely used and are very effective when applied consistently, fairly and with the child's full understanding, taking into account stage of development.

Children who are consistently smacked for various reasons are often driven to worse forms of behaviour and can become very skilled at hiding their behaviour. For example, if they are smacked for stealing they learn quickly how not to get caught. Children are also thought to learn how to be physically violent and aggressive by watching adults who act in this way.

Non-physical

Children are all different and there are no hard and fast rules regarding discipline. For most children being deprived of a favourite television programme, toys or foods, or being sent to bed early can work, and sometimes these are useful. They are more effective if the child concerned is clear concerning the rules and used to being praised and rewarded for good behaviour. Children who are secure and loved will generally accept these forms of discipline as being fair although they will grumble at the time.

General principles

If children are well treated, loved and cared for and have all their basic needs met it is unlikely they will exhibit serious problem behaviour except on a temporary basis. There are, of course, exceptions. The following general principles underpin much work with children and are guidelines for good practice. They are often common sense and used in many therapeutic approaches and different situations:

- Praising and rewarding positive behaviour.
- Minimizing negative behaviour within a framework of safety and consideration for others.
- Adults providing safe and consistently applied boundaries.
- Adults modelling positive ways of behaving back to the child or within the group.
- Discussing issues with older children.
- Distracting, not confronting, young children.
- Giving children the language to use to express themselves.
- Providing a caring and safe environment where a child is accepted for itself.

- Providing a stimulating and developmentally appropriate curriculum.
- Providing equipment and materials through which children can 'play out' their strong feelings.
- Giving attention on a one-to-one basis wherever possible.
- Meeting basic needs for love, care and personal attention.

Specific techniques for problem behaviour

Children's hours/special times

Children's hours are special times given to individual children, usually on a one-to-one basis. They are based on the writings of Dr Rachel Pinney and have been further developed by Madge Bray (1989) and others. They are now used in the management of difficult behaviour, sometimes with abused children, and take the view that *all* children need attention and if they do not have their emotional needs met they will devise other strategies for gaining adult attention.

The original Children's hours took place with one adult, one child. During that time the child was allowed to do whatever it wished and make its own decisions and choices in order to prevent the adult imposing limits.

The 'hour' can be a shorter or longer period according to circumstances but children should know in advance how much time they will be getting. During this time the adult focuses on the child and comments on their activity without judging or interpreting. Within this framework the adult decides on what is unacceptable behaviour usually on the basis of safety and what individual adults can tolerate. The process is therapeutic and enriching for the child a it is allowed to be itself with an adult's full attention. There is no need, therefore, for attention-seeking strategies.

Figure 9.2 Child in therapeutic situation

Workers using this technique have found that children work through aspects of their difficulties in these sessions and become more secure. As a result, the difficult and demanding behaviour often improves.

Behaviour modification

Behaviour modification technique can be very effective and varies from carefully worked out regimes of rewards organized by psychologists and other specialists, to simple techniques such as rewarding good behaviour and ignoring or punishing that which is unwanted by ordinary staff working with very young children in various settings. This technique is based on the work of Skinner and other behaviourists who state that punishments become unnecessary if rewards are carefully and appropriately applied. This is not the same as bribing a child with sweets or outings, and concentrates on reinforcing only those aspects of behaviour which are wanted. Behaviourists such as Skinner suggest that the unwanted behaviour, if not rewarded, will diminish and eventually disappear. Rewards can, of course, consist of praise, a hug or expression of pleasure from the parent or worker (see chapter 1).

Play tutoring

Play tutoring is where adults become involved with children's play (see chapter 2). The aim is to extend and enrich the play in order that the child should develop healthy and socially acceptable ways of dealing with feelings. Play tutoring can take several forms. Sometimes it is useful to assist in the development and extension of imaginative play: here adults can take on a role in the play scenario or can provide ideas, props and so forth without taking on a role in the dramatic sequence.

Adults may accompany a child at play or through a period of time when they may be involved in non-play activity. During this time the adult comments on the activity and acts as the child's externalized conscience. Using simple comment and offering insights to the child as well as praise and reward can have a positive effect even on deeply disturbed children. Play tutoring gives the child a good deal of personal attention as the member of staff usually works with the child on a one-to-one basis.

Play therapy

There are many forms of play therapy. It is a form of therapy widely used in hospital and other therapeutic settings and is based on the idea that children can 'play out' their hidden fears, anxieties and aggressions. Play therapists in these settings often have post-basic training and a deep knowledge and understanding of child development and behaviour. They usually work as part of a multidisciplinary team and have their own area of expertise.

Play therapy can drawn on many of the techniques mentioned in this chapter and will modify them appropriately. It relies, as its name suggests, primarily on play, and therapists will supply a wide range of play experience for children. For example, a child in hospital may be given 'medical' props such as masks, gowns, stethoscopes, syringes and dolls to help their imaginative play and the play therapist might act as a play tutor in this case.

Empowering children

Empowering children is an important part of the therapeutic process as well as being a positive goal for all children. Children should be given a sense of control over their lives and ownership of their environment. This can be done by allowing them freedom and choice within firm boundaries of safety and consideration for others.

Empowering children through positive action programmes is also an effective technique. This is useful for many children but can be used to help victims of discrimination or abuse to become more assertive through raising their self-esteem and self-confidence. It also helps perpetrators understand the effect they have on others. Examples of this technique are valuing cultural diversity and countering children's racial and gender stereotypes through activities which show positive acceptance of difference, and encouraging activities which allow girls to be seen as strong and active and boys to be serious and reflective.

Teaching children basic social skills and ways of dealing with their feelings which are socially acceptable is very important. This means modelling a variety of different approaches to conflict resolution based on non-physical discipline. It also involves giving children the words and language to use to defend themselves and techniques of assertiveness, not aggression. It should include other forms of representation such as drama. The provision of playthings which can facilitate the release of tension and aggression is also helpful.

Encouraging children to talk through difficulties and to express themselves through play and creative activities is useful. Adults should create an environment where children can be themselves and know they are loved and accepted even when their behaviour is less than perfect. Children are then more able to take risks and experiment by breaking old habits and learning new forms of relating to others; this will build their self-esteem and help to reduce self-destructive behaviour.

Specific behaviour problems

Spoilt children

The term 'spoilt children' is very emotive and frequently leads to judgmental attitudes concerning the child. The usual meaning of the term is a child who is used to having its own way in the home and to having toys and playthings on demand. Often these children cannot tolerate any delay in having their demands attended to, and will behave in an anti-social manner if they do have to wait. In general it is better to avoid labelling a child using this destructive term and to concentrate on any specific problems they may have. For example, such children often have to learn how to share and to take their turn; this can be a painful experience for them, and their behaviour often makes them unpopular with others. Spoilt children are often fearful of the power they appear to wield over the parents and insecure as a result. Some 'spoilt' children are 'hurried' children who are encouraged to grow up too quickly and pressured to succeed. These children are fearful of failure and may develop problems in coping with the adult world.

Coping with spoilt children

Staff should avoid punitive attitudes towards children they consider spoilt. They should explain why the answer has to be 'no' on occasions and attempt to get the child to understand the effect that self-centred behaviour has on others. As well as being firm, consistent and fair, staff should concentrate on positive features and praise the child when it shows consideration for others or is willing to share and so forth. These children should be encouraged to make small decisions for themselves to increase their feelings of autonomy. In attempting to teach them to share, adults should not be extreme but should allow the children some (not all!) of what they ask for.

Scenario 1	You are a student nursery nurse on placement in a reception class in a school in a middle-class suburb. At the beginning of term, twelve new children started school all aged four years. Alice is an only child of very caring, rather over protective parents who have very high expectations for her. Alice is not used to coping with the rough and tumble of large groups of children and is becoming increasingly upset and angry at having to share and wait her turn. She insists on being at the head of the line for playtime and pushes the other children out of the way.

> (a) What would be the best method of dealing with Alice?
> (b) What immediate practical steps could you take?

Disruptive/attention-seeking behaviour

Some children are disruptive in school or nursery, constantly seek attention and cause difficulty with other children using many different strategies. Many disruptive children cannot concentrate even for short periods and their attention is easily diverted.

Coping with disruptive/attention-seeking behaviour

Early years workers have to make sure that such children are not give undue attention at the expense of other children, but at the same time their basic needs for care and adult attention are met. Sometimes the children are simply bored and under-stimulated and find their daily routine and curriculum are not relevant to them or do not offer any challenge. Simple organizational changes within the setting might help such as allowing more free play or encouraging more use of the outdoor areas. Staff should be aware of changes at home which might affect behaviour and work with parents to improve things for the child, wherever possible. If children are anxious, providing play activities which allow them to express themselves in a safe environment is very helpful. For example, a child who has a new sibling can find domestic play helpful especially as they can get angry with dolls in a way they could not with their sibling. Some staff use the technique of time out or 'children's hours' very effectively. Others find simple behaviour modification techniques are useful. At other times if staff are available 'play tutoring' techniques have been used successfully.

Children whose disruptive behaviour continues with no apparent external cause which can be dealt with and who respond neither to the use of common-sense approaches nor to the techniques mentioned in the chapter, should be monitored carefully and assessments should be made to decide whether the children need specialist help.

Withdrawn/shy children

Young children are often shy and seem overwhelmed by new situations or when attention is drawn to them. A baby of around nine months onwards who has become attached to significant adults will become shy with strangers. However, most children overcome their early shyness and learn to interact in a positive and social manner with others. There are certain situations which may arise through which children learn to be shy, for example if parents are pressurizing them to measure up to their peers or siblings. They may also respond in this way after being labelled 'stupid' or 'slow', or in response to external pressures or abuse.

Coping with withdrawn/shy children

It is important that all children are allowed their privacy but this is not the same as persistent and painful shyness. The very shy or isolated child may not develop the necessary social skills or choose not to use them and prefer to remain alone. Although this natural shyness which is part of personality should be respected, it is also important that the child should interact successfully and make good relationships with other children and with adults when they wish to do so.

It is of particular concern when a previously outgoing and sociable child suddenly becomes shy and/or withdrawn. This can be linked to a significant change in the child's life which may put them under stress or pressure. See 'Helping the shy/unpopular child' below.

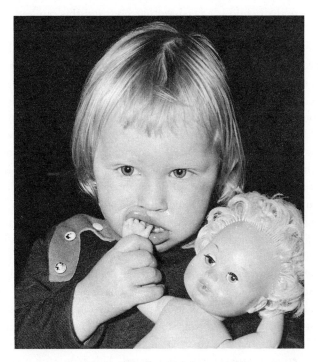

Figure 9.3 Shy, withdrawn child

Unpopular children

Relationships amongst pre-schoolers are often tenuous and fleeting. it is an everyday occurrence to see a child upset because 'X won't be my friend'. This rough and tumble and establishing a pecking order is normal amongst groups of children but it is important that adults do note the child who may be persistently unpopular and have few or no friends. It is possible to detect these children through looking at patterns of interaction and friendship, perhaps using tools such as the sociogram where friendships can be mapped out. If you ask children with whom they like best to play and check this over the next few days it is usually possible to see a pattern emerging with some children at the hub of the interactions and others marginalized and on the fringe.

Children may be unpopular for many reasons. Some are unpopular because they behave in an inappropriate way with their peers. They may be bossy and demanding or aggressive and rude, they may cry, whine or beg which other children ignore. In these cases it is possible to work with them and their families to try and enable them to see life from others' points of view. Positive reinforcement of their efforts should be given.

In some cases children are unpopular because of reasons over which they have little or no control. Children with disabilities or those from different cultural or ethnic groups may fall into this category because they do not conform to the norm. Other children may be unpopular and teased because they are fat or wear glasses or their families are poor and cannot afford to dress them fashionably. It is important that these situations are addressed and not ignored. Children must not be allowed to create a rejecting or discriminatory atmosphere for other children. Discussing with the perpetrators and making sure that standards are consistently maintained is vital. Parents often have to be involved where their child is a persistent offender and this can lead to a clash of values which makes life very difficult for the children concerned.

Unpopular children will often be sad and withdrawn but they can also be hostile and aggressive. When you suspect that children have no friends and may be targets for discrimination or teasing you must step in and deal with the situation.

Helping the shy/unpopular child

Shy or unpopular children need encouragement to mix and adults should allow the child to stay alongside them in new or strange situations until their confidence grows. The organization of the nursery can have significant effects on children's attitudes to one another. Their individual security should be encouraged and popular, confident children should be allowed to do the more public jobs such as giving out drinks and taking responsibility for small tasks. This encourages shy or unpopular children to model this behaviour and take small steps forward in confidence and makes for a more tolerant and accepting attitude in the group of children. Sometimes it is useful to pair shy or unpopular children with popular children at certain times of day or to encourage their interaction with younger children who are less of a threat. Allowing the children to stay within any loose friendship groups they may have can also be very positive.

In group situations it is possible to work using positive action programmes and anti-discriminatory practice which can assist in removing stereotypes and encouraging children to be more reflective and caring. It is important to ensure that the nursery presents positive images for all children and the caring ethos ensures no child is isolated. This requires a non-judgemental attitude from staff as children will soon tune in wherever wrong attitudes exist.

Many unpopular children have poor social skills and seem to be their own worst enemies. They can be helped with social skills not only in everyday situations but in structured programmes which are designed to encourage communication, participation, co-operation and skills for supporting other people.

Scenario 2	Darren is a four year old boy in a workplace crèche. He is part of the pre-school group which is beginning to take on more formal activities to prepare them for school. As Darren's key worker you have noticed that although he has always been a quiet, shy boy he now appears withdrawn and unhappy. Furthermore, none of his peer group wants to sit with him and work with him during these more formal activities. He is due to start school in three months' time and you are concerned about his behaviour.

    (a) What immediate steps could you take to help Darren?
    (b) How could you involve his parents?
    (c) How could you assess his state of mind and behaviour?
    (d) If necessary what agencies could you call upon?

Temper tantrums

Many children around the age of two years are prone to temper tantrums. Children of this age can become very frustrated when they do not get their own way and will express their rage violently, sometimes in self-destructive ways. This is an attempt to assert themselves in a world which is full of interesting and exciting opportunities of which they would like to take part regardless of safety or consideration for others. This phase is commonly called the 'terrible two's'. Children in the throes of a tantrum are often very frightened and feel out of control. Most tantrums follow broadly the same pattern. Some children will throw themselves to the ground often in a public place and scream loudly and furiously. Others are less noisy and will include a breath-holding session until they are blue in the face. However they manifest themselves tempter tantrums are often embarrassing for parents and carers and leave behind feelings of inadequacy and inability to cope.

Most children grow out of this phase quite soon, but some children are still having tantrums at the age of five or six years. When this happens the physical size of the child is in itself a problem.

Coping with temper tantrums

There is no right way of coping with temper tantrums as situation vary. It is always better to try to avoid creating circumstances when they are likely to occur. With very young children it is important to avoid confrontations especially in public places or when children are tired. As well as this it is important to encourage young children's sense of ownership of their environment by allowing as many choices and as much freedom as possible. For instance, homes for toddlers and young children should be geared to their needs and made safe for them to play without damaging themselves or precious possessions. They should be given opportunity for vigorous physical activity which helps them to cope with frustration. A variety of play materials are also useful such as pummelling clay or dough or acting out worrying situations through dramatic play. Children at this developmental stage and older children still prone to tantrums should be given appropriate play and learning materials with which they can succeed and not given tasks or playthings which cause them to fail and ultimately create powerful feelings based on loss of confidence and self-esteem.

No matter how careful you are, young children will still have occasional tantrums. Some people find that ignoring the situation works but this is often very difficult. Others will touch the child and talk soothingly to help them feel safe and in control again. As children get older the development of language and understanding gives them another vehicle to express their strong feelings and this should be encouraged. They will also become aware of their feelings building up and may regret the incident afterwards. Talking about angry feelings is often a good way of diffusing situations which are getting out of control.

Relaxation techniques can be useful. Madders (1978) has developed a range of relaxation techniques useful for children between four and seven years who are easily frustrated and prone to temper tantrums.

Figure 9.4 Temper tantrums

Scenario 3

You are working in a family centre with a group of parents and children aged six months to two-and-a-half years. One mother with a baby of one year and a toddler of two years three months is under a good deal of stress as the baby is very active and 'into everything' and the toddler has frequent temper tantrums, sometimes several in one day. These leave the young mother exhausted and tearful. You have noticed that the mother sometimes smacks the baby's hand when the baby explores and tells her not to be naughty. She often stops her partner picking the baby up when she cries for fear of spoiling her. The mother is very dependent on her own mother and sister for help and advice.

(a) What is the best way to help this mother to understand:
  (i) Her baby's needs.
  (ii) The toddler's behaviour.
(b) What strategies would you suggest to her concerning the temper tantrums?

Angry and aggressive outbursts

Angry and aggressive outbursts are common at around age two years and involve wild, undirected activity closely linked to temper tantrums. After around age three, children may become aggressive concerning playthings, privileges or territory. Older children who cannot control their angry feelings may exhibit anti-social behaviour which is more likely to be directed against other children or adults such as hair-pulling, hitting or biting. Older children may also use verbal abuse very effectively either to adults or other children. Such children do not seem able to tolerate being thwarted or have any of the usual range of strategies or social skills available to deal with difficult situations. This has to be dealt with and the child has to learn other ways of controlling the rage.

Angry outburst may take the form of destructiveness when a child deliberately breaks objects and destroys other children's toys, constructions and so forth. Often their rage will lead them to throw things around in a furious and potentially dangerous manner. In other circumstances anger and frustration may be much more hidden, for example a child who plays with matches and sets things ablaze or bites and pinches when not being observed by an adult.

Coping with angry and aggressive outbursts

Dealing with angry and aggressive outbursts might be done through encouraging talk and discussion if the child is old enough and enabling them to ask adults to help in disputes. This is far more effective if it takes place after they calm down.

Staff should attempt to distract and avoid confrontation in similar ways to those used to deal with temper tantrums. Occasionally, when workers see a child who is about to behave aggressively a sharp 'no' is necessary and physical removal of them or any weapon they are about to use. It is important that children understand that their behaviour is unacceptable, so making eye contact and a short reprimand may be effective. Giving too much time and disrupting a whole group of children to deal with the issue may become a reinforcement for the behaviour as the child will have gained a good deal of attention. For some children in this category, negative attention is better than no attention. It is also worthwhile noting what toys and playthings are around which are basically hostile in purpose and attempting to remove these. Children may also model hostile behaviour they see in adults or in the media, and care should be taken that they are not exposed to this.

Persuading children to apologize to those they have wronged has limited effect. Many children are very good at saying 'sorry' and then proceeding as if nothing has changed. However, they should see this being modelled amongst adults and should be encouraged to apologize if they seem genuinely repentant.

Jealousy

Children can be jealous and resentful of those who they perceive as taking what is rightfully theirs or who have things they themselves want. Many children feel strong feelings of jealousy when new siblings arrive in the family: they quite accurately perceive that their own relationship with their parents will be changed. Children usually have very strong bonds with their primary carers and can resent any change in their special relationships. They may also fear that they will no longer be loved and cared for. Changing family patterns may mean that children have to cope with step-parents and their children moving in together. This can cause intense jealousies and insecurity.

Children today are bombarded with messages from a consumer society concerned with selling to them and their families. Toys and 'educational' products are a multi-million pound industry, and advertising and marketing strategies are aimed at children. Parents are pressured to feel that they are letting their child down if they do not have all these latest toys and 'educational' items. Such pressures on children and their families can lead to conflicts and jealousies which can be difficult to deal with.

Coping with jealous feelings

Specific ways of coping with jealousy depend on the source. If a child is intensely jealous of a new sibling it will take time and patience to work with them and their parents to overcome this. Some situations are very difficult to deal with and require careful analysis of the problem and individualized strategies. Children experiencing jealous feelings may be insecure and lacking in self-esteem and need to build up their confidence and self-worth.

It is important that children are not made to feel guilty because they are experiencing jealous feelings. Jealousy is a universal emotion and children can understand that everyone feels this way sometimes. It is also true that some children are less able to cope than others, and adults should be sensitive to this.

When the jealousy concerns objects, attempt to explain at the child's level that there are benefits in sharing and that many children have less than they have.

Bed-wetting (nocturnal enuresis)

Most children develop night-time   ough it is
common for the occasional accider   ren, especially boys, go through difficultie   ssment to
them and feelings of guilt in thei   s through
the extra washing, fear of staying a

It is difficult for families to   ey receive
unhelpful advice such as 'he'll soon   dismissive
attitudes such as 'what do you exp   iously and
given adequate support. A visit to t   cal causes.

There are some simple measur   tween five
and seven years, can take before ref

- Avoid fizzy drinks, tea and   e.
- Make sure the child is fully   recognize
  the sensation of a full bladc
- Keeping records of dry or w
- Praise and encouragement f
- Avoid nappies or pads for o
- Have a potty nearby if the t
- Keep the light on in the to
- Make sure the child can ge
- Reassure the child that oth

Persistent bed-wetting

The reasons for bed-wetting are many and varied and range from simple urinary infections to
severe cases of sexual or other forms of abuse. When physical causes have been excluded (which
happens in most cases) the most likely cause is some form of stress affecting the child. For example, a child who has been dry for some time may regress and become wet after a stay in hospital or
if there is tension in the family. If there are obvious stresses and the child is showing other signs of
distress, this can form part of an overall picture of a child with serious problems and who needs
specialist help. Sometimes there is apparently nothing to cause this problem and it clears up in
time of its own accord.

Masturbation and sexual behaviour

Most young children can be found at some time or other handling their genitals. Adults who care
for them sometimes find this very natural act embarrassing and tell the child not to be 'dirty'. By
doing this they draw attention to something which is not important and gives the child comfort
not sexual relief. As a result many children will associating touching their genitals with guilty
feelings which can lead to problems for them in the future.

In some situations it is not appropriate for young children to masturbate in this way and rather than drawing attention to the behaviour it is always better to distract them. As they become able to understand, explain in a simple manner that some people do not like seeing this sort of behaviour and that those people have a right to their viewpoint.

Children who masturbate excessively and over a long period may have some underlying anxiety or fear and may do this to obtain emotional comfort and security. Where this happens specialist help may be required.

Young children are intensely interested in their bodies and those of adults and other children. They can often be found exploring their own bodies and those of other children and commenting on the differences. This is perfectly healthy, normal curiosity and should not be punished. However, children should realize that privacy is important, and this can often lead on to talking about 'good' or 'bad' touching. It is sometimes necessary to stop children playing together who persistently engage in sexual behaviour and the reasons for this should be given at the child's level. Overt sexual behaviour which mimics adult sexuality should be taken very seriously, and the policies and procedures of the work setting for suspected sexual abuse may need to be used.

Stealing

Children often take things which do not belong to them, and this has to be dealt with as part of their social development. For most young children these are isolated occurrences and they soon learn that it is unacceptable, anti-social behaviour. Young children tend to judge stealing in terms of the amount or value of what is stolen rather than the motive behind it. It is important that the child returns the stolen object, and, if it refuses, the parent or worker can model the behaviour, verbalizing the reasons that the object is being returned.

Children who steal over a period of time are often insecure and feel deprived. They are usually looking for emotional comfort and love or can be seeking attention for a variety of reasons. Adults should not condone this behaviour but should try to look at possible reasons and underlying causes. Change and stress in the family can often be a key, and with extra love and attention the problem goes away. As with all forms of difficult behaviour, persistent stealing may need specialist help.

Bullying

Bullying can occur at any age, and it is only in recent years that serious attention has been paid to the problem. There is now a special helpline for children to use who are being bullied as this has been a very common reason that children have sought help from ChildLine, a charity which runs a free helpline for children in danger or trouble.

Bullying can take many forms and it is sometimes difficult to distinguish between children who are rough and unthinking and those who are calculating and malicious. It can consist of verbal abuse such as name-calling, teasing or racial and other insults, physical abuse which can be punching, kicking, jostling, pinching, or extortion and threats.

Bullying varies in severity and in the response that it evokes. There is very little recorded evidence in pre-school children, but workers with young children have usually come across children who are beginning to bully and others who seem potential victims. Tattum and Herbert (1990) note that some children as young as three or four have already learned that being aggressive helps them to get what they want, and that making other children frightened of them is a rewarding experience.

Coping with bullying

Workers with young children have to deal with both the bully and the victim and will be looking for a pattern of behaviour which may be emerging. Bullies may be frustrated children who themselves are bullied at home and who need attention and help. Children who are victims need to have their security, self-esteem and self-worth increased. Children who are easily bullied can be helped to be assertive (Penn Green Family Centre, 1990), and in many cases this can be done by careful handling in the nursery and at home. In some instance, though, children will be referred for specialist help.

Figure 9.5 Child bullying

Swearing

There are various degrees of bad language and different levels of tolerance. Children may have been brought up in a home where swearing is commonplace and not considered shocking or unusual. Most children in those circumstances will swear at an appropriate juncture without realizing that they are using bad language. Children may have learned to swear as a form of aggression or a part of name-calling, and it is very confusing for them when they are told not to say particular words. Children who regularly use bad language may be ostracized by other children or their parents and we do them no favours by allowing the swearing to continue unchecked. These children do not get asked to birthday parties!

Coping with swearing

It is important that workers explain to children just what is acceptable in the nursery and the effects on other people of using bad language. It is also important that children are not punished in the nursery or school for swearing until they have fully understood and had time to adjust. Sometimes continuous swearing is simple attention-seeking or may be due to the child's limited vocabulary. The child may be helped to find more appropriate words as part of a general programme to develop language skills.

Workers use a variety of means to encourage the child to stop swearing. A favourite ploy is to use a nonsense word or phrase yourself in circumstances where a child may have been used to hearing swearing. So if you drop something or bang your head you would use this phrase and model something less offensive. Also encourage children to express their frustration in a less self-destructive manner such as vigorous physical play or pounding clay and dough.

Scenario 4	You are working in a day care setting in an inner city environment. Most of the children are between eighteen months and four years of age an come from a variety of cultures and backgrounds. Not all speak English as a first language. Two of the four-year-old boys in a small group of mixed ages can behave in a very disruptive manner and occasionally use racist and sexist insults, swearing and other verbal abuse towards staff and other children. The younger children admire the boys and are beginning to mimic their behaviour.

One member of the staff seems not to see this as a problem and laughs when it occurs. Her attitudes is that 'boys must be boys' and children have to learn to take the rough with the smooth. You find yourself becoming increasingly upset and angry both with her and the children after a recent spate of insults.

(a) What should you do concerning your own angry feelings?
(b) How could you deal with your colleague's attitude?
(c) How should the racist and sexist language be dealt with?
(d) What immediate steps could you take to improve the situation in the group?

Comfort habits

Comfort habits such as thumb/finger-sucking or nail-biting are usually temporary and may be in response to stress or appear to have no particular underlying cause. They seem to be a form of emotional comfort to the child, and sucking may be a regression in behaviour to pre-weaning.

Children do sometimes find it difficult to break these habits and may need help. They are usually only of concern when persistent and excessive, and in these cases it is worth attempting to discover any underlying cause.

Children who rock themselves to and fro or head bang for long periods may be suffering from emotional or sensory deprivation. These sorts of behaviour have been observed amongst babies and children of normal intelligence who are isolated and receive little love, individual attention or sensory and cognitive stimulation. Such comfort habits are more commonly noticed amongst children with learning difficulties or other special needs. Meeting a child's basic needs will go some way to helping with these problems but specialized therapy is usually required.

Figure 9.6 Toddler sucking thumb

Assignment 1

Task   Observe a child having a temper tantrum or other angry outburst. Either:

1. Undertake an event sample, In this case, over a period of days record every incident involving temper tantrums or angry outbursts for your target child, or
2. Observe one such occasion in depth. Record accurately what happened.

Discussion

(a)   What were the antecedents of the behaviour?
(b)   How was it dealt with?

(c) Does it link with past behaviour?

(d) Are there any predisposing factors that you are aware of?

(e) How were other children/staff/parents affected?

(f) What lessons can be learned?

Assignment 2

(a) Plan/implement/evaluate a programme for a child who is continually biting and lashing out at other children.

(b) Provide a brief history.

(c) Record accurately what happened and the rationale for your actions.

Assignment 3

Task   Choose a child you know who is either very withdrawn or is attention-seeking and disruptive. Plan a structured programme of work with the child:

1. To involve parents or carers.
2. To include use of structured and planned play and/or free play.

Discussion   How would you evaluate this programme?

Assignment 4

Prepare a brief set of guidelines for parents and other carers concerning the possible effects on a two-year-old of a new baby in the family.

References and further reading

Axline, V. 1971. *'Dibs' In Search of Self*. Harmondsworth: Pelican.

Bray, M. 1989. *Children's Hour: A Special Listen*. Nightingale Books.

Hennessy, E. 1992. *Children and Day Care*. Paul Chapman.

Herbert, M. 1988. *Working with Children and their Families*. London: Routledge/ BPS Books.

Laishley, J. (Lindon). 1987. *Working with Young Children*. London: Arnold.

Madders, J. 1987. *Relax and be Happy*. London: Unwin.

Penn Green Family Centre. 1990. *Learning to be Strong: Developing Assertiveness in Young Children*. Changing Perspectives.

Tattum, D. and Herbert, G. 1990. *Bullying: A Positive Response. Advice for Parents, Governors and Staff in Schools*. Cardiff: South Glamorgan Institute of Higher Education.

Stevensen, H. 1990. Tom! Using play tutoring to integrate a difficult child in a nursery school. In *TOPIC: Practical Applications of Research in Education* (Resource pack) Spring 1990. Windsor: NFER/Nelson.

Woolfson, R. 1989. *Understanding Your Child: A Parent's Guide to Child Psychology*. London: Faber and Faber.

Chapter 10
Management skills

Child care workers will require some knowledge of management when they are employed and working in the field. Most people employed in care and education work in small-scale situations and do not have on-site secretarial help. Many playgroups and community nurseries have a management committee and the workers need to understand the role of such committees and their relationship with them. In some situations child care workers will be expected to collect and bank money, order equipment, devise budgets, supervise learners, liaise with auxiliary staff and deal with difficult parents. These are areas which many college-based courses fail to include in their training packages. Now, though, there are units within the new National Vocational Qualifications (NVQs) which deal with basic management skills. This chapter outlines some of the skills which are especially relevant to child care workers.

Working as a member of a team

Membership of the team

The majority of child care and education settings require people to work as members of a team. Teams can be multidisciplinary, for example they may include managers, volunteers, students, qualified staff, unqualified helpers and parents. All people working with children should work as a team to ensure that there is an overall child care policy for the establishment and an atmosphere of consistency for the children. The overarching principle of all teams must be the welfare of the children and families in their care. Decisions made by teams must be made in the light of the team's knowledge of the children.

Good teams do not just arise but are the result of hard work on the part of members. The people that are required to work within a team cannot always be specially chosen, therefore they have to learn to work together. It is important to know one's own strengths and weaknesses and the skills that one is able to bring to a team. Joining an existing team which has developed strong working relationships is difficult and it may take a while to fit in.

Young (1987) lists three requirements for a successful team:

1. Shared aims.
2. A common working language.
3. The ability to manage relationships as well as tasks.

Teams may be set up as part of the normal work situation, e.g. all staff working in the same room in a nursery; or they may be set up for a specific purpose, e.g. to organize the summer fair. When choosing teams for a specific purpose it is useful to weigh up the skills that may be required to undertake the task and then look for participants. This may require you to look at the weaknesses and strengths of those who have volunteered their services. People with domineering personalities do not always make good team members as they are likely to prevent the weaker members participating.

Teams may be formal or informal: for example, they may be a staff group which meets regularly to discuss the children in their care and the plans for the forthcoming week, or they may be an ad hoc group which meets for mutual support. Whatever the purpose, they will need to adopt a consistent approach to dealing with problems, allow time for all members to participate and have a system for evaluating their progress in dealing with the tasks.

Aims and objectives of teamwork

The first task for any team is to clarify its aims. This can be done by answering questions such as, 'What is our objective?' 'How best can we meet that objective?' The answer to the second question should form the basis of a plan which points the team towards the way forward. When working as a member of a team, it is important to remember that there is a collective responsibility for the decisions that the team makes; you cannot be a member of a team and then abdicate responsibility if a wrong decision is made.

The case conference is a special multidisciplinary team meeting called to discuss a specific child or family. More details regarding case conferences can be found in chapter 7.

Confidentiality

Team members must share their information whilst at the same time maintaining the establishment's policy on confidentiality. This is not always easy, and it is best only to divulge information on a 'need to know basis', i.e. where a person's effectiveness in caring for a child would be aided by knowledge of the information. This is particularly pertinent where children or members of their family may have a stigmatizing situation such as being HIV positive, have AIDS or be a carrier for hepatitis B. In most cases there is no need for all the workers to know the medical status of a child as protective hygiene should be part of the normal routine and carried out by the staff when they are dealing with all children.

Individual contributions to the team

Teams cannot operate if their members do not contribute to the proceedings. This means bringing information, sharing expertise and volunteering an opinion or relevant information. It also entails undertaking some of the administrative duties, such as taking a turn at writing the agenda, being the minute/note-taker or the chairperson. Once a decision has been made at a team meeting, all members should work towards implementing it, whatever their personal feelings are about the decision. Sometimes teams are unable to make a decision without the assistance of outside expertise; it is important for team members to acknowledge this rather than trying to struggle along alone.

Team leadership styles

There are two major leadership styles: the autocratic and the democratic. The autocratic leader will issue orders and have little time for the contributions of others; these people do not make good team leaders. The democratic leadership style is one whereby the contributions of team members are taken into consideration and decisions are made on a collective basis. For example, the team is given a task and then works together to devise a strategy for dealing with it. This style of leadership is conducive to effective teamwork.

A good team leader will have the ability to:

- Respond to the team members.
- Promote a team spirit.
- Motivate the team members to carry out tasks.
- Allow team members to express their ideas.
- Enable the team to devise action plans and strategies.
- Direct the team towards making decisions.
- Use the skills of all team members effectively.
- Be supportive to fellow team members.
- Give positive feedback to team members.

Scenario 1

Jill is a new senior nursery officer who has just joined your establishment. She is in charge of the Blue Room and is your immediate line manager. The staff in the Blue Room have always been a cohesive team and the previous senior nursery officer, Mary, was respected by them all.

At Jill's first team meeting she says very little but makes a lot of notes. Two days before the next team meeting Jill issues everyone with an agenda for the meeting. At the meeting the staff are resentful, telling Jill that they worked very well with Mary and never needed an agenda. The meeting progresses, working to Jill's agenda but there is much suppressed mumbling and a general feeling of discontent. At the third team meeting Jill tells the group that she has decided to change the staff shift working pattern and proceeds to tell them the new roster. Two members of the team leave the meeting in protest. None of the team attends Jill's fourth team meeting.

(a) What has Jill done wrong?
(b) What did the team do wrong?

Figure 10.1 A team meeting

The team meeting

Team meetings are usually held regularly and can be informal or formal. They should always have an agenda to act as the discussion basis for the meeting. Participants should listen to what fellow members have to say, consider other people's ideas and offer ideas of their own. All proposals should be carefully considered before making a final decision. Participants should be objective, concentrate on the business at hand and not allow the personal attributes of a proposer to sway a decision. Decisions should be taken on the basis that they are of benefit to the child and its family, the establishment as a whole or the smooth-running of the establishment. Ideas should be pooled, participants' particular skills or expertise should be called upon, and clear lines for action drawn up. Team meetings should be opportunities to air difficulties in a healthy, open climate. Once the team has made a decision, all members must work towards the implementation of that decision.

Working under the direction of others

Most people work under the direction of others, whether this be working to a management committee or to a direct line manager. A major part of working in this way is to be able to carry out tasks which you have been requested to undertake by a colleague or a superior. Even the smallest organizations distribute and delegate work in this way. Staff need to be clear about their own role and that of their colleagues, as well as how these fit together within the management structure.

In most instances instructions are given verbally. It is important to listen carefully to what is being asked of you (write notes if the task is complex) and to be certain as to what is required of you. Clarification should be sought when anything is unclear or ambiguous.

Most people report directly to their line manager, but in some establishments certain people may have responsibility for policy areas such as child protection, equal opportunities, or health and safety. In these circumstances it may be necessary to take instructions and report back to these people and not the direct line manager.

Delegated tasks

When a number of different people give instructions to the same person, that person may need to draw up a list of priorities in order to carry out the tasks methodically. If a person is delegated too many tasks to be able to cope, then the advice of the line manager should be sought.

Some tasks may require the delegate to report back to the originator; this may be a verbal report on how well a task has progressed or a written report on information that has been requested. In other cases, the report may be required by someone other than the originator. For example, if a line manager asks for a safety check on outdoor equipment, then any faults or other dangers that are found may need to be reported to the person responsible for health and safety.

When dealing with children there are a number of tasks which may require the results to be filled in on a record sheet or written up in a report book. All such reports should be done clearly, concisely and give an objective, accurate account of the situation. A child is not helped by a report that states, 'Tommy is now able to go to the toilet unaided' if in fact Tommy still requires adult help in carrying out this task.

The confidentiality policy of the establishment must always be maintained: information must be passed only to the senior person making the request. All information in a child's records must be treated as confidential even if it does not appear to be significant.

Carrying out a task will need planning and may require decisions to be made and ideas to be modified. Standards of good practice must be maintained when carrying out tasks and if extra help is needed to ensure this, then it is important to make this need known.

Working to a management committee

Most playgroups and community nurseries have management committees which have an overall responsibility for the way that the establishment is run. Management committees determine the policy of an establishment and delegate the responsibility for the implementation of that policy to the workers. It is likely that the chairperson of the management committee will act as the direct line manager to the head of the nursery or playgroup.

Management committee meetings are likely to be fairly formal, with a chairperson, secretary, treasurer and other officials. The actual committee members may be representatives from the local Under-Fives/Under-Eights Forum, local councillors, representatives from funding bodies, parent representatives, and so on.

The agenda

An agenda states the business to be dealt with at a meeting; the secretary is responsible for taking the minutes. A typical agenda is as follows:

Rainbow Nursery/Playgroup Management Committee Meeting

AGENDA

1. Minutes of the meeting held on 15/12/99
2. Matters arising
3. Playgroup/nursery leader/manager's report
4. Treasurer's report
5. Discussion document on admissions criteria
6. Plans for the spring fair
7. Any other business
8. Date of next meeting

The preparation of the discussion document (item 5) may have been the responsibility of the nursery/playgroup leader/manager. It is likely that the management committee will decide upon the admissions policy for the establishment on the strength of the proposals put forward in the document. The document may have taken some time to prepare and compiled in conjunction with all the staff working in the establishment. The financial aspects of running the nursery/playgroup will be discussed under the treasurer's report, and policy decisions may be made about spending levels and fund-raising.

Sub-committees

Management committees may have a second tier or sub-committees to deal with specific matters such as equal opportunities, fund-raising, building maintenance, Parents Association, etc. Each sub-committee has a slot on the agenda when it can report its progress to the management committee. The agenda for the committee is usually set by the secretary in conjunction with the chairperson. The secretary also sets the deadline for items to be included in the agenda.

Organizing the budget and managing money

The budget is a fixed amount of money that is allocated to an establishment to finance its day-to-day running. The nursery manager/playgroup leader is given a budget allocation by the treasurer, sometimes as a lump sum or sometimes as specific sums under distinct headings. This latter is called a virement system. For example:

Rainbow Nursery/Playgroup Budget for the period 1/4/98–31/3/99

Consumable	£1000
Furniture	£ 250
Visits	£ 400
Computer	£ 500
Toys	£2000

It is not always possible to move money between the different categories of a vired budget. A non-vired budget is one where the manager/leader is given £4150 to spend but the ratios are unspecified: the only proviso is that the needs of the establishment are met. Some budgets are tied to virement headings to enable the management committee to decide on the priority areas for spending or because certain amounts of money have been donated or raised for specific items or budget headings.

Part of the responsibility for the budget covers the way that money is received and dispersed, and keeping accurate records of these transactions. On a daily basis, these duties may be delegated to all the members of the working team. Most establishments keep petty cash available for incidental expenses. All monies received must be signed for by a person who will take responsibility for distributing the money and ensuring that receipts are presented for any money spent. All child care establishments are subject to their financial books being examined during the annual audit.

The basic rules for dealing with money are that no money should be issued without a receipt being obtained, and all money spent must have a receipt for the goods. All receipts must be kept and transactions recorded in a book or on a form designed for the purpose. All cheques should require two signatures and must only be signed against invoices and never in advance. Some organizations set a ceiling on the amount written on a cheque, and large cheques may need to be countersigned by the treasurer or chairperson of the management committee.

All these rules help to prevent the misappropriation of funds. Money going astray even unintentionally, is a serious matter and could lead to dismissal for the person responsible.

Conditions of employment

All employees who work for at least sixteen hours a week, unless they are self-employed or volunteers, should have a document which clearly states their terms and conditions of employment. This is a legal requirement under the Employment Protection Act 1978 and the Employment

Acts 1980 and 1982. The statement must contain the following:

- The names of the employer and employee.
- The title of the job.
- The date when the employment commenced.
- The scale of pay.
- The hours of work.
- Entitlement to holidays.
- Provision for sick pay.
- Pensions and pension schemes.
- The length of notice that is required and that the employee is entitled to receive.

The statement should also lay down the procedures for any disciplinary action and/or grievance procedures. These are all minimal requirements under the law and some conditions of employment may be written in much greater detail.

Under the Employment Acts employees have certain rights available to them but these may depend upon the length of service: for example, the higher rate of maternity pay and the right to return after maternity leave is available only to those who have completed a minimum two years of service. The rights which are available to everyone regardless of the period of service are:

- Protection from discrimination on the grounds of race or sex.
- The right to be a member of a trade union and to take part in union activities.
- Time off work for being the safety representative.
- Time off work for ante-natal care.
- The right to an itemized statement of pay.

Even in small-scale settings it is important that workers know who their line manager is and what procedures exist if they have a grievance or complaint. This is particularly important information for volunteers, learners or other people who are coming into the establishment for odd hours or days. In order for people to feel secure in the workplace they need reference points, the main ones being a knowledge of the layout of the building and who is their mentor or line manager.

Whilst this section makes clear the responsibilities of employers to employees, there is also a commitment on the part of the employee to perform to a reasonable standard and to act in a reasonable manner towards the work role.

Dealing with conflicts

Conflict can arise in what appears to be the best of situations and may be between employers and employees, employee and employee, staff and management committee, staff and parents or an establishment and the local authority. The most common form of conflict arises between employees, particularly when there is a breakdown in relationships between two or more members of a team.

Young (1987) puts forward the following signs that something is wrong within a team:

- People begin to perform poorly, miss deadlines, produce substandard work.
- People expect others to solve their problems.
- People do not take responsibility for their actions.
- People break into subgroups instead of sharing work.
- People show destructive criticism or dismissive behaviour towards others.
- People get involved in serious and unresolved conflicts.
- People show no interest in team activity.

Resolution of such conflicts requires the team leader to work with the team, but it is always better for the team to find the solution and for the leader to act as the facilitator.

Personal problems may affect a person's performance and relationships with others, and in such cases the team leader needs to talk to that person on a one-to-one basis and wherever possible offer help or suggest where help might be obtained.

Conflicts between a worker and a parent need to be resolved quickly as they affect the child. Quite often, such conflicts arise because the member of staff does not understand or make allowances for the parent's problems. In situations where a manager is maintaining confidentiality about a parent's problems, the member of staff may have no idea that the parent has problems. It is possible to warn staff that a parent is going through a stressful time and therefore needs extra sensitive handling without revealing the actual problem.

Conflict will never be resolved if it is managed with aggression, ignored, or if people are not consulted about their feelings. What is likely then to happen is that the conflict becomes even

---

Scenario 2	Janice is a playgroup worker and has always had a good relationship with Toby's mother, Mrs James. However, during the past two weeks Mrs James has been arriving late to collect Toby, and Janice is getting annoyed about this. When Janice has broached the subject with Mrs James, Mrs James has just shrugged her shoulders and not offered any reason for her lateness. One of the rules of the playgroup is that children must be collected on time, so Janice decides that she must give Mrs James an ultimatum. When Mrs James arrives to collect Toby, late again, Janice tells her that she has broken the rules of the playgroup, as she has no genuine reason for this so Toby no longer has a place at the playgroup. Mrs James bursts into tears. The playgroup leader comes into the room and takes Mrs James aside. Janice feels that Mrs James will manipulate the playgroup leader and is cross that her opinion on the matter is not being sought.
	(a) What do you think could be happening here?
	(b) How do you think Janice should have handled the situation?

more embroiled and complicated, more aggressive, or may get hidden away so that it is bubbling under the surface of all other activities that the person or the team is carrying out. Managers are responsible for the smooth running of their establishments: this means that they must deal with conflict when it arises.

Children are sensitive and quickly realize that there is a problem amongst the staff or between the staff and their parent or carer; to allow conflicts to simmer, therefore, is detrimental to the welfare of the children.

Assertiveness

Resolving a conflict may require a manager or an employee to be assertive. Assertion should not be confused with aggression: assertion is having control over the situation by ensuring that you respect people's feelings and they have respect for your feelings.

Dickson (1984) puts forward the following eleven basic human rights which are the basis for assertiveness:

1. The right to state my own needs and set my own priorities as a person independent of any roles that I may assume in my life.
2. The right to be treated with respect as an intelligent, capable and equal human being.
3. The right to express my feelings.
4. The right to express my opinions and values.
5. The right to say 'yes' or 'no' for myself.
6. The right to make mistakes.
7. The right to change my mind.
8. The right to say I do not understand.
9. The right to ask for what I want.
10. The right to decline responsibility for other people's problems.
11. The right to deal with others without being dependent upon them for approval.

The field of child care is one where the majority of workers are female, and it is women who are poor at asserting themselves and ensuring that they are listened to when exerting their rights. In being assertive, a person needs to speak out firmly and clearly and 'stick to their guns' in the face of opposition. However, this does not require shouting, aggression or the use of indirect aggression such as sarcasm. There are many assertiveness training courses available and they are particularly useful for child care workers.

Being assertive does not mean always winning in a conflict situation. It means being able to put forward personal feelings on the matter in such a way that people listen. Having gained a fair hearing, people are more inclined to abide by the final decision.

Supervising learners

Most child care and education establishments have learners visiting for different periods of time in order to gain practical experience. Some establishments may be involved in YT (Youth Training) and ET (Employment Training) or have trainees who are on other Employment Department schemes and who are based in the nursery/playgroup for a large part of the week. With the advent of NVQs (National Vocational Qualifications) employees may become learners and put themselves forward for assessment.

It is important that learners are made to feel confident in the new situation. This can be achieved by assigning each learner a mentor who is a member of the full-time staff. The role of the mentor is to guide learners through the pre-assessment work to ensure that they are adhering to good practices, to help learners evaluate their own work, to advise on compiling portfolios of evidence, child observations, children's records, etc. The mentor may also need to direct learners towards suitable textbooks, journals and other resources.

The person assigned as the mentor may not necessarily be the person who is supervising or assessing the learner. In some establishments the student supervisor post carries extra responsibility and may be paid accordingly. Much good practice in child care and education is achieved by working alongside experienced practitioners, and these are often the people who are best suited to the important role of mentor.

Not all people find the learning process easy, and often tasks need to be broken down into small units in order for the learner to understand the whole. It must be remembered that individuals learn at different speeds, and it takes some people longer than others to reach the point of understanding. It is useful if the learner is given a programme with the learning aims and objectives clearly stated. Now that there are the National Standards in Child Care and Education it is possible to devise programmes which reflect those standards of competence.

Scenario 3	Sunita is the student supervisor in a family centre. She has four students from the local college and has assigned each of them a mentor. One of the students, Cathy, does not seem to be committed to the work and her mentor, Mavis, has given Sunita a long list of complaints. Sunita decides the time has come to have a serious chat with Cathy and she goes to fetch her. On entering the playroom she finds Mavis in tears, the children looking terrified and Cathy throwing Lego pieces at Mavis.
	How does Sunita handle this situation?

Assessment processes

Learners who are registered to be assessed for NVQs will have copies of the Standards for the qualifications which they are working towards. Once they feel confident that they are able to perform to the National Standards and are in possession of the relevant knowledge, they will be able to request an assessment. The assessment may be carried out by a member of the establishment staff who is a trained assessor and attached to the local assessment centre, or the assessment centre may send a peripatetic assessor to the candidate. The candidate will know who has been assigned as assessor and will have contacted them at an earlier date to discuss the types of evidence that will be required for the assessment.

Learners who are on college-based courses may have different assessment requirements and the staff they are working with should be aware of exactly how much and what level of work they need to produce. Colleges and awarding bodies may have a variety of assessment forms which need to be filled in and the supervisory staff need to have contact with the college tutors to clarify the requirements.

Induction of learners

All learners who are not employees should spend their first visits getting to know the setting, the people, the children and familiarizing themselves with the layout of the building. They need to be introduced to the relevant procedures and policies relating to the establishment, and to know who their line manager is and the regular time that has been set aside for their supervision feedback session.

Learners should be counted as team members and should attend team meetings that are involved with planning matters. They should be encouraged to make a contribution at these meetings, and it is useful if they are given a specific topic to report on. In that respect, learners should be encouraged to keep a notebook in which they can record child observations and make notes of the tasks that they have been asked to carry out.

Giving feedback

It is important that learners receive feedback on their performance: nobody should be unaware that they are doing well or failing. Confidence is built on praise, so learners should be given recognition for the good work that they have done.

Nobody likes criticism, but even more destructive to the fragile confidence that most learners have, is negative criticism. Learners are bound to make mistakes: after all even experienced people make mistakes. How these mistakes are dealt with will be important to the learner. Unless it is a safety matter which requires immediate attention, it is better to take the learner aside to a quiet place and discuss their actions. This will help the supervisor to ascertain their level of learning and find the reasons why they acted or failed to act as instructed. It is always a good idea to draw up an action plan with the learner so that they have a constructive conclusion to the criticism.

When supervising learners it is important to be impartial, objective and implement the good practices of equal opportunities. It is everyone's right to have access to a fair assessment of their capabilities. Supervisors and assessors are there to make judgements upon the product not upon the personal attributes of the producer. All learners should be judged using the same standards, and special allowances must not be made for some groups. For example, there are few males in child care and education work but those that are there must undertake the same tasks as the females and perform to the same standards. When a learner asks for help, it should be given either directly by the worker or by referring the learner to someone with the appropriate expertise.

Staff appraisal

Many posts now have inbuilt systems for a regular review of staff performance. In some areas of industry, payment incentives are linked to performance appraisal. An appraisal system enables workers to assess their progress and to identify their areas of strength and weakness. Where there are formal appraisal systems it is usual for appraisal to be carried out annually. Many child care establishments, though, have informal appraisal systems, and appraisal interviews take place more regularly. The following guidelines are useful when implementing an appraisal system:

- The system must be equitable, meaning that all employees must be appraised in the same way.
- Methods of appraisal must be the same for all employees with the same job descriptions. Results of appraisals can only be made by comparing like with like.
- The method used should be simple and understood by everyone.
- The appraisal must be objective and the personality of the appraisee should only be considered if it is affecting performance.
- Appraisal should be a continuous process with regular feedback, whether it be praise or criticism.

It is preferable to carry out an appraisal interview rather than just hand a person a form to fill in. Much more detail can be gleaned from an interview and it offers the opportunity for some immediate feedback. Who carries out the appraisal may be a moot point in a small organization. In large industries it is usually undertaken by the personnel department. Appraisal can be done from the 'top down', when the officer-in-charge interviews the deputy officer-in-charge, who in turn interviews the senior nursery officer, or it can be 'bottom up' when the unqualified assistant interviews the nursery nurse, who in turn interviews the nursery officer. Alternatively, a member of the management committee may undertake all the appraisal interviews. Whatever method is decided upon it is important that staff view appraisal as a positive action which increases the smooth running of the establishment, aids efficiency and promotes good practice. The main aim of performance appraisal is to improve performance not to punish employees; however, poor performance must be dealt with.

Dealing with unsatisfactory performance

An appraisal system will direct the management to those employees who are consistently performing poorly. It is also a useful tool for recognizing when a person's performance may be slipping. There are three ways of dealing with poor or unsatisfactory performance: prevention, corrective action or drastic action. Prevention can be used when it is realized early that a person's performance is slipping but has not yet reached the stage of being unsatisfactory. There are a number of things that can be done to prevent further deterioration, such as delegating some of their work, giving them more time to complete their work, assigning them a mentor to help them organize their workload better.

Corrective action needs to be taken when an employee is first deemed as performing in an unsatisfactory manner. This more often than not results in the employee being sent on a training course to improve their particular areas of weakness.

Drastic action is usually only taken after corrective action has not resulted in any improvement in performance. Drastic action may also be taken because there has not been regular appraisal, and although the situation has only just come to light, it has still gone too far for corrective action to be of use. Drastic action may be early retirement, sacking, redundancy, taking out disciplinary action, and so on. Needless to say, which option is used needs to be carefully thought out. With legal job security under the Employment Act (1989) any employee who has been with the establishment for two years or more will have the right to appeal to an industrial tribunal.

Before drastic action is taken it is only fair to give the employee a chance to improve their performance. It is, therefore, useful, and often necessary under employment law, to give a number of warnings. Most local authorities have a disciplinary procedure which must be adhered to.

Assignment 1

You have just taken over the local playgroup and have been asked by the chairperson of the management committee to draw up an agenda for the next committee meeting. How do you go about this and what is the agenda likely to contain?

Assignment 2

You are a nursery nurse in an infant school. A parent has made a complaint to you about the teacher that you work with. You feel that the parent is justified in her complaint. How do you handle the situation?

Assignment 3

You are in charge of a community nursery and your management committee has decided to bring in a system of appraisal. How will you explain this to your fellow workers? Draw up a plan for implementing an appraisal system.

Assignment 4

You are in charge of the local playgroup and the management committee has asked you to draw up conditions of employment for the other two workers. Draw up a model set of conditions of employment for two part-time sessional playgroup workers.

Assignment 5

You have been asked by your head of the family centre to prepare an estimate for a student supervision room. List the furniture and resources that you would need with appropriate costings.

References and further reading

Cooper, C. 1981. *Psychology and Management*. London: British Psychological Society.

Dickson, A. 1984. *A Woman in Your Own Right: Assertiveness and You*. London: Quartet.

Handy, C. 1976. *Understanding Organizations*. Harmondsworth: Penguin.

Jenks, J. and Kelly, J. 1988. *Don't Do. Delegate! The Secret Power of Succesful Management*. London: Kogan Page.

Randell, G., Shaw, R. Packard, P. and Slater, J. 1979. *Staff Appraisal*. London: Institute of Personnel Management.

Young, A. 1987. *The Manager's Handbook*. London: Sphere.

Appendix 1
Addresses

Action for the Sick Child [6]*
Argyle House Euston Road London NW1
Formerly called National Association for the Welfare of Children in Hospital (NAWCH), the organization produces pamphlets, has a reference library, publishes a quarterly magazine, sends speakers to colleges and conferences, and acts as an advocacy for children in hospital and their families.

Active Birth Centre (ABC)
55 Dartmouth Park Road London NW5 1SL
Tel: 071-267 3006

Advisory Centre for Education (ACE) [3,4]
18 Victoria Park Square London E2 9PB

AFFOR Community Resources Agency [8]
173 Lozelle Road Birmingham B19 1RN
The Agency provides a number of multicultural books and resources for use with children.

Afro-Caribbean Education Resource (ACER) [8]
Wyvil School Wyvil Road London SW5 2TJ

AIMER (Computer listing of all multi-cultural education resources) [8]
Bulmershe College Woodlands Avenue Reading RG6 1HY
Tel: 0734 663387

Anti-Racist Response and Action Group (AARAG)
c/o 112a The Green Southall Middlx UB2 4BQ
Tel: 081-574 6019

---

* Figures in square brackets denote the relevant chapters.

Arthritis and Rheumatism Council (ARC)
41 Eagle Street London WC1R 4AR

Association for All Speech-Impaired Children (AFASIC) [5]
347 Central Markets Smithfield London EC1A 9NH
Tel: 071-236 3632

Association for Brain Damaged Children (ABDC) [5]
Clifton House 3 St Paul's Road Foleshill Coventry CV6 5DE

Association for Improvements in the Maternity Services (AIMS)
40 Kingswood Avenue London NW6 6LS

Association for Post-Natal Illness
7 Gowan Avenue London SW6 6RH

Association for Spina Bifida and Hydrocephalus [5]
ASBAH House 42 Park Road Peterborough PE1 2UQ
Tel: 0733 555988

Association of Advisers for the Under fives (AAUF) [1]
Cherrystone House Church Road Worth Crawley Sussex RH10 4RT

Association of Breast Feeding Mothers
Order Department Sydenham Green Health Centre Holmshaw Close London SE26 4TH
Tel: 081-774 4769

Association of British Paediatric Nurses (ABPN)
c/o Central Nursing Office The Hospital for Sick Children Great Ormond Street London WC1
Tel: 071-405 9200

Association of Community Health Councils for England and Wales
22 Columbo Street London SE1 8DP
Tel: 071-609 8405

Association of Parents of Vaccine-Damaged Children [5]
2 Church Street Shipston-on-Stour Warwickshire CV36 4AP
Tel: 0608 61595

Association of Professions for Mentally Handicapped People (APMH)
Greytree Lodge Second Avenue Ross-on-Wye Herefordshire HR9 7HT
Tel: 0989 62630

BACUP [6]
121–123 Charterhouse Street London EC1 6AA
BACUP offers literature, newsheets and a support network for the families of children with cancer.

Barnados [7]
Tanners Lane Barkingside Ilford Essex IG6 1QG

Black Child care Campaign [8]
Wesley House 4 Wild Court London WC2B 5AO
(No known telephone number)

British Agencies for Adoption and Fostering
11 Southwark Street London SE1 1RQ
Tel: 071-407 8800

British Association for Counselling
37a Sheep Street
Rugby Warwickshire CV21 3BX
Tel: 0788 78328/9

British Association for Early Childhood Education (BAECE) [3]
111 City View House   463 Bethnal Green Road   London   E2 9QH

British Council of Organisations of Disabled People (BCODP)
St Mary's Church Greenlaw Street London SE18 5AR
Tel: 081-316 4184

British Deaf Association [5]
38 Victoria Place Carlisle CA1 1HU
Tel: 0228 48844

British Diabetic Association [5]
10 Queen Anne Street London W1M 0BD
Tel: 071-3231531

British Epilepsy Association [5]
Anstey House 40 Hanover Sq Leeds LS3 1BE
Tel: 0532 439393

British Holistic Medical Association
179 Gloucester Place London NW1 6DX
Tel: 071-262 5299

British Homeopathic Association (BHA)
27a Devonshire Street London W1N 1RJ
Tel: 071-935 2163

British Medical Association (BMA)
BMA House Tavistock Square London WC1H 9JP
Tel: 071-383 6101

British Paediatric Association (BPA) [1]
5 St Andrew's Place Regents Park London NW1 4LB
Tel: 071-486 6151

British Pregnancy Advisory Service (BPAS)
Austry Manor Wootton Wawen Solihull West Midlands B95 6DA
Tel: 0564 23225

British Red Cross Society (BRCS)
9 Grosvenor Crescent London SW1X 7EJ
Tel: 071-235 5454

Brittle Bone Society [5]
112 City Road Dundee DD2 2PW
Tel: 0382 817771

Brook Advisory Centres
153a East Street London SE17 2SD
Tel: 071-708 1390

Carers National Association
29 Chilworth Mews London W2 3RG
Tel: 071-724 7776

Cancer Relief Macmillan Fund [6]
Anchor House 15–19 Britten Street London SW3 3TZ
Tel: 071-351 7811

Child Development Research Unit [1]
University of Nottingham Psychology Department University Park Nottingham NG7 2RD
Tel: 071-239 1000

ChildLine [7]
Addle Hill Entrance Faraday Building Queen Victoria Street London EC4V 4BU

Children's Society [7]
Edward Rudolf House Margery Street London WC1X 0JL

City and Guilds of London Institute
46 Britannia Street London WC1X 9RG
Tel: 071-278 2468

Cleft Lip and Palate Association (CLAPA)
1 Eastwood Gardens Kenton Newcastle-upon-Tyne NE3 3DQ
Tel: 091-285 9396

Coeliac Society of the United Kingdom
PO Box 220 High Wycombe Bucks HP11 2HY
Tel: 0494 437278

Commission for Racial Equality [3]
Elliott House 10–12 Allington House London SW1E 5EH
Tel: 071-828 7022

Committee Against Drug Abuse (CADA)
359 Old Kent Road London SE1 5JH
Tel: 071-231 1528

Committee on Safety of Medicines
Market Towers 1 Nine Elms Lane London SW8 5NQ
Tel: 071-720 2188

The Compassionate Friends [6]
10 Woodways Watford Hertfordshire
An organization that is able to put people in touch with others who have had similar experiences, such as the death of a child.

Council for Early Years Awards (C.E.Y.A.)
26 Binney Street London W1Y 1YN
Tel: 071-629 0516

CRUSE [6]
The Charter House 26 Sheen Road Richmond Surrey TW9 1UR
Tel: 081-940 4818
CRUSE is a bereavement counselling organization with a network of local branches.

Cystic Fibrosis Research Trust [6]
Alexandra House 5 Blythe Road Bromley Kent BR1 3RS
Tel: 081-464 7211/2
The Trust supplies information on cystic fibrosis and awards research grants.

Department for Education
Sanctuary Bldgs Gt Smith Street London SW1

Department of Health
Richmond House 79 Whitehall London SW1A 2NS
Tel: 071-210 3000

Welsh office
Crown Buildings Cathays Park Cardiff CF1 3NQ
Tel: 0222 825111

Scottish Office
Dover House, Whitehall London SW1A 2AU
Tel: 071-270 3000

Scottish Home and Health Department
St Andrew's House Regent Road Edinburgh EH1 3DE
Tel: 031-566 8400

Department of Health and Social Services, Northern Ireland
Dundonald House Upper Newtownards Road Belfast BT4 2SB
Tel: 0232 650111

Department of Social Security
Richmond House 79 Whitehall London SW1A 2NS
Tel: 071-210 3000

Distance Learning Centre
Room ID35 South Bank Technopark 90 London Road London SE1 6LN
Tel: 071-928 8989

Down's Syndrome Association [5]
153–155Mitcham Road London SW17 9PG
Tel: 081-682 4001

Early Years Trainers Anti-Racist Network (EYTARN) [8]
1 The Lyndens 51 Granville Road London N12 0JH
Tel: 081-446 7056

English National Board for Nursing, Midwifery and Health Visiting (ENB)
Victory House 170 Tottenham Court Road London W1P 0HA
Tel: 071-388 3131

Epilepsy Association of Scotland
48 Gowan Road Glasgow G51 1JL

Equal Opportunities Commission [3,8]
Overseas House Quay Street Manchester M3 3HN
Tel: 061-833 9244

Exploring Parenthood [4]
41 North Road London N7 9DP

Families Anonymous (FA)
310 Finchley Road London NW3 7AG
Tel: 071-731 8060

Family Planning Association (FPA)
Margaret Pyke House 27–35 Mortimer Street London W1N 7RJ
Tel: 071-636 7866

Family Welfare Association
501–505 Kingsland Road London E8 4AU
Tel: 071-254 6251

The Foundation for the Study of Infant Deaths (Cot Death Research and Support)
3–5 Belgrave Square London SW1X 8BQ
Tel: 071-235 1721

General Medical Council (GMC)
44 Hallam Street London W1N 6AE
Tel: 071-580 7642

Gingerbread
35 Wellington Street London WC2E 7BN
Tel: 071-240 0953

Haemophilia Society
123 Westminster Bridge Road London SE1 7HR
Tel: 071-928 2020

Handicapped Adventure Playground Association (HAPA) [5]
Fulham Palace Bishops Avenue London SW6 6EA

Health and Safety Executive
Baynards House 1–13 Chepstow Place Westbourne Grove London W2 4TF
Tel: 071-229 3456

Health Education Authority
Hamilton House Mabledon Place London WC1H 9TX
Tel: 071-631 0930

Health Visitors' Association (HVA) [1]
50 Southwark Street London SE1 1UN
Tel: 071-378 7255

Herpes Association
41 North Road London N7 9DP
Tel: 071-609 9061

Highland Voluntary Association for Children with Special Needs [5]
Cluny Cottage 4 Links Place Nairn Scotland IV12 4NH

High/Scope (UK) [3]
Research and Development Section Barnado's Tanner' Lane Barkingside Ilford Essex

Home-Start Consultancy [4]
140 New Walk Leicester LE1 7JL

Hospice Information Service [6]
St Christopher's Hospice 51–59 Lawrie Park Road Sydenham London SE26 6DZ
Tel: 081-778 9252

Hyperactive Children's Support Group [5]
71 Whyte Lane Chichester West Sussex PO19 2LD

Institute of Child Health [1]
30 Guildford Street London WC1N 1EH

Invalid Children's Aid Nationwide (ICAN) [5]
Allen Graham House 198 City Road London EC1V 2PH

Invalids at Home
17 Lapstone Gardens Kenton Harrow Middlesex HA3 0EB
Tel: 081-907 1706

Jewish Bereavement Counselling Service [6]
1 Cyprus Gardens London N3 1SP
Tel: 071-387 4300 ext 227

Jewish Care
Stuart Young House 221 Golders Green Road London NW11 9DQ
Tel: 081-458 3282

Jewish Social Services
221 Golders Green Road London NW11 9DW
Tel: 081-458 3282

KIDS [5]
80 Waynflete Square London W10 6UD

KIDSCAPE [7]
82 Brook Street London W1 1YG

Kidscape Campaign for Children's Safety
World Trade Centre Europe House London E1 9AA
Tel: 071-488 4200

King's Fund Centre (KFC)
126 Albert Street London NW1 7NF
Tel: 071-267 6111

Lady Hoare Trust for Physically Disabled Children (Associated with Arthritis Care)
37 Oakwood Bepton Road Midhurst

Letterbox Library [8]
8 Bradbury Street London N16 8JN
A book club which specializes in non-sexist, non-racist books for children.

Leukaemia Research Fund
43 Great Ormond Street London WC1N 3JT
Tel: 071-405 0101

Leukaemia Society [6]
c/o Mrs Pankhurst Hamlyn's View St Andrews Road Exerter
The Society supplies information on childhood leukaemia and support materials for families.

Malcolm Sargent Cancer Fund for Children [6]
14 Abingdon Road London W8 6AF
Tel: 071-937 4538

Maternity Alliance
15 Brittania Street London WC1X 9JP
Tel: 071-837 1265

Midwives Information and Resource Services
Institute of Child Health Royal Hospital for Sick Children St Michael's Hill Bristol BS2 8BJ
Tel: 0272 251791

MIND (National Association for Mental Health)
22 Harley Street London W1N 2ED
Tel: 071-637 0741

Minority Rights Group
379 Brixton Road London SW9 7DE
Tel: 071-978 9498

Montessori Association of Teachers and Schools Ltd [3]
London Montessori Centre 18 Balderton Street London W1Y 1TG

Multiple Births Foundation (MBFI)
Queen Charlotte's and Chelsea Hospital Goldhawk Road London W6 0XG
Tel: 081-748 4666

Muscular Dystrophy Group of Great Britain [6]
Nattrass House 35 Macauley Road London   SW4 0QP
An information and support network.

Myasthenia Gravis Association
Keynes House 77 Nottingham Road Derby DE1 3QS
Tel: 0332 290219

National Anti-Racist Movement in Education (NAME) [8]
PO box 9 Walsall WS1 3SF
Tel: 081-806 8668 (Ansaphone)

National Association for Gifted Children [5]
Park campus Boughton Green Road Northampton Northants NN2 7AL
Tel: 0604 792300

National Association for the Welfare of Children in Hospital (NAWCH) [6]
Argyle House 29–31 Euston Road London NW1 2SD
Tel: 071-833 2041

National Association of Bereavement Services (NABS) [6]
122 Whitechapel High Street London E1 7PT
Tel: 071-247 1080 (24-hour answerphone for referral requests); 071-247 0617 (admin.)

National Asthma Campaign
300 Upper Street London N1 2XX
Tel: 071-226 2260

National Autistic Association [5]
276 Willesden Lane London NW2 5RB

National Board for Nursing, Midwifery and Health Visiting for Northern Ireland
RAC House 79 Chichester Street Belfast BT1 4JE
Tel: 0232 238152

National Board for Nursing, Midwifery and Health Visiting for Scotland
22 Queen Street Edinburgh EH2 1JX
Tel: 031-226 7371

National Centre for Play [2]
Moray House College of Education Holyrood Road Edinburgh

National Childminding Association
8 Mason's Hill Bromley Kent BR2 9EY
Tel: 081 464 6164

National Children's Bureau [1,3,8]
Early Childhood Unit 8 Wakley Street London EC1V 7QE
The NCB has a large number of resources, especially in its Early Years Unit.

National Children's Home [4]
85 Highbury Park London N5 1UD

National Children's Play and Recreation Unit [2]
359–361 Euston Road London NW1 3AL

National Council for Vocational Qualifications [10]
222 Euston Road London NW1 2BZ
Tel: 071-387 9898

National Deaf-Blind and Rubella Association (SENSE) [5]
311 Grays Inn Road London WC1X 8PT

National Deaf Children's Society [5]
45 Hereford Road London W2 5AH

National Ethnic Minority Advisory Council (NEMAC)
2nd and 3rd Floors 13 Macclesfield Street London W1V 7HL

National Library for the Handicapped [5]
20 Bedford Way London WC1H 0AL

National Playbus Association [2]
Unit G Arnos Castle Estate Brislington Bristol BS4 5AJ

National Portage Association [5]
4 Clifton Road Winchester SO22 5BN

National Rubella Council
Bray Business Centre Weir Bank Monkey Island Lane Bray-on-Thames Berks SL6 2EP
Tel: 0628 770011

National Society for Epilepsy
Chalfont Centre for Epilepsy Chalfont St Peter Gerrards Cross Bucks SL9 0RJ
Tel: 02407 3991

National Society for Mentally Handicapped People in Residential Care (RESCARE)
Rayner House 23 Higher Hillgate Stockport Cheshire SK1 3ER
Tel: 061-474 7323

National Society for Phenylketonuria and Allied Disorders
Worth Cottage Lower Scholes Keighley W. Yorks BD22 0RR
Tel: 0535 44865

National Society for the Prevention of Cruelty to Children (NSPCC) [7]
67 Saffron Hill London EC1N 8RS
Tel: 071-242 1626

NFER [1,3]
The Mere Upton Park Slough Berks SL1 2DQ

Northern Ireland Pre-school Playgroups Association [2,4]
11 Wellington Park Belfast BT9 6DJ

Open College, The
St Paul's 781 Wilmslow Rd Didsbury Greater Manchester M20 8RW
Tel: 061-434 0007

Open University Department of Health and Social Welfare
Walton Hall Milton Keynes Bucks MK7 6AA
Tel: 0908 74066

Parentline -OPUS (Organisation for Parents under Stress) [7]
Westbury House 57 Hart Road Thundersley Essex SS7 3PD
Tel: 0268 757077

Parent Network [4]
44–46 Caversham Road London NW5 2DS

Partially Sighted Society
Queen's Road Doncaster South Yorks DN1 2NX
Tel: 0302 323132

Play Education [2]
80 Church Street Lancaster Lancashire LA1 1ET

Play for Life [2]
31B Ipswich Road Norwich NR2 2LN

PlayMatters/National Toy Libraries Association [2]
68 Churchway London NW1 1LT
Tel: 071-387 9592

Poisons Unit New Cross Hospital
Avonley Road London SE14
Tel: 071-955 5095

Pre-school Playgroups Association [2,3,4]
61–63 Kings Cross Road London WC1X 9LL

Psoriasis Association
7 Milton Street Northampton NN2 7JG
Tel: 0604 711129

Restricted Growth Association
103 St Thames Avenue Hayling Island Herts PO11 0EU
Tel: 0705 461813

Royal Association in Aid of Deaf People
27 Old Oak Road London W3 7HN
Tel: 081-743 6187

Royal College of Midwives (RCM)
15 Mansfield Street London W1M 0BE
Tel: 071-580 6523

Royal College of Nursing of the United Kingdom (RCN)
20 Cavendish Square London W!M 0AB
Tel: 071-409 3333

Royal Institute of Public Health and Hygiene
28 Portland Place London W1N 4DE

Royal National Institute for the Blind (RNIB) [5]
224 Great Portland Street London W1N 6AA
Tel: 071-388 1266

Royal National Institute for the Deaf (RNID)
105 Gower Street London WC1E 6AH
Tel: 071-387 8033

Royal Scottish Society of the Prevention of Cruelty to Children {RSSPCC) [7]
Melville House 41 Polwarth Terrace Edinburgh EH1 1NU

Royal Society of Health
38a St George's Drive London SW1V 4BH
Tel: 071-630 0121

Royal Society for Mentally Handicapped Children and Adults (MENCAP) [5]
117–123 Golden Lane London EC1Y 0RF

Royal Society for the Prevention of Accidents (ROSPA)
Cannon House The Priory Queensway Birmingham B4 6BS
Tel: 021-200 2461

Samaritans
17 Uxbridge Road Slough Berkshire SL1 1SN
Tel: 0753 32713

Save the Children [2]
17 Grove Lane London SE5 8RD

Scoliosis Association (UK)
380–384 Harrow Road London W9 2HU
Tel: 071-289 5652

Scottish Child and Family Alliance [4]
55 Albany Street Edinburgh EH1 3QY

Scottish Council for Single Parents
13 Gayfield Square Edinburgh EH1 3NX
Tel: 031-556 3899

Scottish Pre-school Playgroups Association [2,4]
14 Elliot Place Glasgow G3 8EP

Scottish Society for the Mentally Handicapped
13 Elmbank Street Glasgow G2 4QA
Tel: 041-266 4541

Sickle Cell Society (SCS)
54 Station Road Harlesden London NW10 4BO
Tel: 081-961 7795

Sikh Cultural Society of Great Britain
88 Mollison Way Edgeware Middlesex HA8 5QW

Spastics Society [5]
840 Brighton Road Purley Surrey CR8 2B4

Standing Committee on Sexually-Abused Children (SCOSAC)
73 St Charles Square London NW10
Tel: 081-960 6376

Tay-Sachs and Allied Diseases Association
17 Sydney Road Barkingside Ilford Essex IG6 2ED
Tel: 081-550 8989

Terence Higgins Trust
52–54 Gray's Inn Road London WC1X 8JU
Tel: 071-242 1010

Thomas Coram Research Unit [1]
40 Brunswick Square London WC1

Toy Libraries Association
Seabrooke House/Wyllyots Manor Darkes Lane Potters Bar Hertfordshire EN6 5HC

Travellers Community Social Workers
Haringey Area 6 Office Willoughby Road London N8
Tel: 081-341 1100

Travellers Rights Organization
S. Crawley 4 Toneborough Estate Abbey Road London NW6

Turkish Cypriot Cultural Association (TCCA)
14 Graham Road London E8 1BZ
Tel: 071-249 7410

Twins and Multiple Births Association (TAMBA)
51 Thicknall Drive Pdemore Stourbridge W. Midlands DY9 0YH
Tel: 0384 373642

United Kingdom Thalassaemia Society
107 Nightingale Lane London N8 7QY
Tel: 081-348 0437

Urostomy Association
'Buckland' Beaumont Park Danbury Essex CM3 4DE
Tel: 0245 414294

Vegan Society
7 Battle Road St Leonards-on-Sea East Sussex   TN37 7AA
Tel: 0424 427393

Vegetarian Society of the UK Ltd
Parkdale Dunham Road Altringham Cheshire WA14 4QE
Tel: 061-928 0793

Voluntary Council for Handicapped Children (VCHC) [5]
National Children's Bureau 8 Wakley Street London EC1V 7QE

Voluntary Organisations' Liaison Council for Under Fives
77 Holloway Road London N7 8JZ
The Council has many materials on anti-racist child care and guidelines for good practice.

Wales Pre-school Playgroups Association [2,4]
2a Chester Street Wrexham Clywd LL13 8BD

Working Group Against Racism in Children's Resources (WGARCR) [2]
460 Wandsworth Road London SW8 3LK
Tel: 071-627 4594

World Health Organization (WHO)
Geneva Switzerland

World Organisation for Early Childhood Education (OMEP) [3]
c/o Thomas Coram Foundation 40 Brunswick Square London WC1

Appendix 2
Resources

Chapters 1 and 6

Robertson, J. and J. 1969. *Young Children in Brief Separation*. Ipswich: Concorde Films. A series of films made by James and Joyce Robertson depicting the reactions of children to different separation circumstances, including hospitalization.

Chapter 6

Books for children:
Braithwaite, Althea. 1982. When Uncle Bob Died. London: Dinosaur.
Braithwaite, Althea. 1989 . I Have Cancer.London: Dinosaur.
Reuter, Elizabeth. 1989. Christopher's Story. London: Hutchinson.
Varley, Susan. 1984. Badger's Parting Gifts.London: Picture Lions.

Chapter 8

Coffee-coloured Children
A video distributed by The Albany Video Distribution, Battersea Studios, Television Centre, Thackery Road, London SW8 3TW. It features two children of mixed parentage talking about their feelings.

Educating the Whole Child
A video and book produced by Building Blocks, 40 Tabard Street, London SE1 4JU which is based on the holistic approach to child care and deals with culture, race and social identity.

Let's Play Colour: Anti-Racist Child care
A video about racism and child care produced by East Birmingham Health Education Department, 102 Blakesley Road, Yardley, Birmingham B25 8RN.

Index